Rick S...

SNAPSHOT

Hill Towns
of
Central Italy

CONTENTS

INTRODUCTION

This Snapshot guide, excerpted from my guidebook *Rick Steves' Italy*, introduces you to the hill towns of central Italy. Here in Italy's heartland, you'll enjoy an idyllic landscape, time-passed medieval hill towns, and tree-lined meandering backcountry roads. Dine on Italy's heartiest food in an atmospheric farmhouse, and taste a glass of wine poured by a proud vintner whose family's name has been on the bottle for generations.

I've included a mix of towns and cities, some undiscovered, some deservedly popular. Choose among the back-door towns of Volterra and Civita, the wine lovers' towns of Montepulciano and Montalcino, touristy towered San Gimignano, manicured Pienza, trendy Cortona, classic Orvieto, tradition-steeped Siena, and spiritual, artsy Assisi—or even better, visit them all.

To help you have the best trip possible, I've included the following topics in this book:

• **Planning Your Time,** with advice on how to make the most of your limited time

• **Orientation,** including tourist information (abbreviated as TI), tips on public transportation, local tour options, and helpful hints

• **Sights** with ratings:

    ▲▲▲—Don't miss

    ▲▲—Try hard to see

    ▲—Worthwhile if you can make it

    No rating—Worth knowing about

• **Sleeping** and **Eating,** with good-value recommendations in every price range

• **Connections,** with tips on trains, buses, and driving

Practicalities, near the end of this book, has information on money, phoning, hotel reservations, transportation, and more, plus Italian survival phrases.

   To travel smartly, read this little book in its entirety before you go. It's my hope that this guide will make your trip more meaningful and rewarding. Traveling like a temporary local, you'll get the absolute most out of every mile, minute, and dollar.

Buon viaggio!

Rick Steves

HILL TOWNS OF CENTRAL ITALY

San Gimignano • Volterra • Montepulciano • Pienza • Montalcino • Cortona • More Hill Towns and Sights

The sun-soaked hill towns of central Italy offer what to many is the quintessential Italian experience: sun-dried tomatoes, homemade pasta, wispy cypress-lined driveways following desolate ridges to fortified 16th-century farmhouses, atmospheric *enoteche* serving famously tasty wines, and dusty old-timers warming the same bench day after day while soccer balls buzz around them like innocuous flies.

Hill towns are best enjoyed by adapting to the pace of the countryside. So, slow...down...and savor the delights that this region offers. Spend the night if you can, as many hill towns are mobbed by day-trippers.

Planning Your Time

How in Dante's name does a traveler choose from Italy's hundreds of hill towns? I've listed some of my favorites in this chapter. The one(s) you visit will depend on your interests, time, and mode of transportation.

Multi-towered San Gimignano is a classic, but because it's such an easy hill town to visit (about 1.5 hours by bus from Florence), peak-season crowds can overwhelm its charms. For rustic vitality not completely trampled by tourist crowds, out-of-the-way Volterra is the clear winner. Wine aficionados head for Montalcino and Montepulciano—each a happy gauntlet of wine shops and art galleries (Montepulciano being my favorite). Fans of architecture and urban design appreciate Pienza's well-planned streets and squares. Those enamored by Frances Mayes' memoir *(Under the Tuscan Sun)* make the pilgrimage to Cortona. Urbino, well off the tourist track and quite remote, is known for

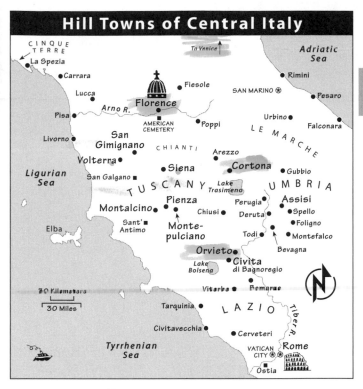

Hill Towns of Central Italy

CINQUE TERRE
La Spezia
Carrara
Lucca
Pisa
Arno R.
Livorno
San Gimignano
Volterra
San Galgano
Ligurian Sea
CHIANTI
TUSCANY
Montalcino
Sant' Antimo
Monte-pulciano
Elba
Florence
AMERICAN CEMETERY
Fiesole
Poppi
Siena
Arezzo
Lake Trasimeno
Pienza
Chiusi
Deruta
Perugia
Cortona
Gubbio
UMBRIA
Assisi
Spello
Foligno
Montefalco
Todi
Bevagna
Orvieto
Lake Bolsena
Civita di Bagnoregio
Vitorba
Bomarzo
Tarquinia
Civitavecchia
Cerveteri
Tyrrhenian Sea
VATICAN CITY
Rome
Ostia
To Venice
Adriatic Sea
Rimini
SAN MARINO
Pesaro
Urbino
Falconara
LE MARCHE
LAZIO
Tiber R.
30 Kilometers
30 Miles
N

its huge Ducal Palace. And Assisi, Siena, and Orvieto—while technically hill towns—are in a category by themselves: Bigger and with more major artistic and historic sights, they each get their own chapter. (The Orvieto chapter also includes my all-around favorite hill town, the stranded-on-a-hilltop Civita di Bagnoregio.)

For a relaxing break from big-city Italy, settle down in an *agri-turismo*—a farmhouse that rents out rooms to travelers (usually for a minimum of a week in high season). These rural B&Bs—almost by definition in the middle of nowhere—provide a good home base from which to find the magic of Italy's hill towns. I've listed several good options throughout this chapter.

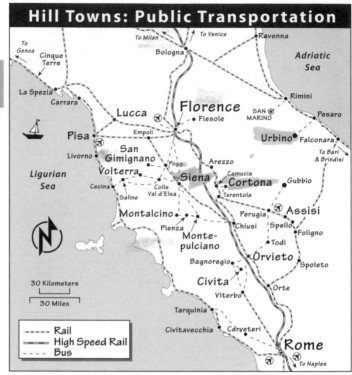

Getting Around the Hill Towns

While you can reach just about any place with public buses, taxis, and loads of patience, most hill towns are easier and more efficient to visit by car.

By Bus or Train

Traveling by public transportation is cheap and connects you with the locals. While trains link some of the towns, hill towns—being on hills—don't quite fit the railroad plan. Stations are likely to be in the valley a couple of miles from the town center, usually connected efficiently by a local bus. Buses are often the only public-transportation choice to get between small hill towns. But, as with trains, they don't always drive up into the town itself. Fortunately, bus stations are sometimes connected to the town by escalator or elevator. (For more on traveling by train and bus in Italy, see the appendix.) If you're pinched for time, it makes sense to narrow your focus to one or two hill towns, or rent a car to see more.

By Car

Exploring the hill towns by car can be a great experience. But since

Driving in Tuscany: Distance & Time

EMILIA - ROMAGNA

To Milan

To Venice

To Cinque Terre
(La Spezia)

20 Kilometers

20 Miles

LE
MARCHE

50m · 1h

50m · 1h

20m · .5h

Lucca

1.90m · 3.5h

160m · 3.5h

Pisa

Florence

50m · 1h

70m · 1.25h
(via FiPiLi)

70m · 1.5h

15m · .5h

55m · 1.5h

60m · 1.25h

40m · .75h
(via S-2)

45m · .1h
(via superstrada)

45m · 1h
(via S-222)

75m · 1.5h
(via A-1)

70m · 1.5h

Livorno

San
Gimignano

20m · .5h

30m · .75h

Volterra

T U S C A N Y

Siena

Cortona

45m · 1h

50m · 1h

20m · .75h

40m · 1h

To
Assisi

40m · 1h

25m · .75h

30m · 1h

40m · 1.5h
(via S-438)

10m · .25h

30m · .75h

San Galgano
Monastery

65m · 1.5h

15m · .5h

Chiusi

15m · .5h

Pienza

Montalcino

Monte-
pulciano

UMBRIA

To Assisi

Mediterranean
Sea

210m · 4h

60m · 1.5h

35m · 1h

60m · 1.5h

m = miles h = hours
Note: Your times may
vary based on traffic,
construction and
road conditions.

Orvieto

Bagnoregio
(Civita)

15m · .5h

75m · 1.5h

To
Rome

L A Z I O

To
Rome

a car is an expensive, worthless headache in cities like Florence and Rome, wait to pick up your car until the last sizeable town you visit (or pick it up at the nearest airport to avoid big-city traffic). Then use the car for lacing together the hill towns and exploring the countryside. For more on car rentals and driving in Italy, see the appendix.

A big, detailed regional road map (buy one at a newsstand or gas station) and a semiskilled navigator are essential. Freeways (such as the toll autostrada and the non-toll *superstrada*) provide the fastest way to connect two points, but the smaller roads, including the super-scenic S-222, which runs through the heart of the Chianti region (connecting Florence and Siena), are more rewarding.

Parking throughout this region can be challenging. Some towns don't allow visitors to park in the city center, so you'll need to leave your car outside the walls and walk into town. Signs reading *Zona Traffico Limitato (ZTL)*—often above a red circle—mark areas where no driving or parking is allowed. Parking lots, indicated by big blue *P* signs, are usually free and plentiful outside city walls (and in some cases are linked to the town center by elevators or escalators). In some towns, you can park on the street; nearby kiosks sell "pay and display" tickets. In general, white lines indicate free parking, blue lines mean you have to pay, and yellow lines are spaces reserved for local residents. To reduce the threat of theft (no guarantees, though), choose a parking lot instead of street parking when possible. Your hotelier can also recommend safe parking options.

Between Florence and Siena

Two fine hill towns—one famous, the other underrated—sit in the middle of the triangle formed by three major destinations: Florence, Siena, and Pisa. If driving between those cities, it makes sense to detour either to picturesque but touristy San Gimignano, or charming and authentic-feeling Volterra. (Or you could use one of them as a home base for reaching the bigger towns.) While they're only about a 30-minute drive apart, they're poorly connected to each other by public transit (requiring an infrequent two-hour connection); if you're relying on buses, San Gimignano is easier to reach, but Volterra rewards the additional effort.

San Gimignano

The epitome of a Tuscan hill town, with 14 medieval towers still standing (out of an original 72), San Gimignano (sahn jee-meen-

YAH-noh) is a perfectly preserved tourist trap. There are no important interiors to sightsee, and the town is packed with crass commercialism. The locals seem spoiled by the easy money of tourism, and most of the rustic is faux. The fact that this small town supports two torture museums is a comment on the caliber of the masses who choose to visit. But San Gimignano is so easy to reach and visually so beautiful that it remains a good stop. It's enchanting at night, when it's yours alone. For this reason, San Gimignano is an ideal place to go against the touristic flow—arrive late in the day, enjoy it at twilight, then take off in the morning before the deluge begins.

In the 13th century—back in the days of Romeo and Juliet— feuding noble families ran the hill towns. They'd periodically battle things out from the protection of their respective family towers. Pointy skylines like San Gimignano's were the norm in medieval Tuscany.

San Gimignano's cuisine is mostly what you might find in Siena—typical Tuscan home cooking. *Cinghiale* (cheeng-GAH-lay, boar) is served in almost every way: stews, soups, cutlets, and, my favorite, salami. Most shops will give you a sample before you commit to buying. The area is well known for producing some of the best saffron in Italy (collected from the purple flowers of *Crocus sativus*); you'll find the spice for sale in shops (it's fairly expensive) and as a flavoring in meals at finer restaurants. Although Tuscany is normally a red-wine region, the most famous Tuscan white wine comes from here: the inexpensive, light, and fruity Vernaccia di San Gimignano. Look for the green "DOCG" label around the neck for the best quality.

Orientation to San Gimignano

While the basic ▲▲▲ sight here is the town of San Gimignano itself, there are a few worthwhile stops. From the town gate, head straight up the traffic-free town's cobbled main drag to Piazza della Cisterna (with its 13th-century well). The town sights cluster around the adjoining Piazza del Duomo.

Tourist Information

The helpful TI is in the old center on Piazza del Duomo (daily March-Oct 10:00-13:00 & 15:00-19:00, Nov-Feb 10:00-13:00 & 14:00-18:00, free maps, sells bus tickets, books rooms, handles VAT refunds, tel. 0577-940-008, www.sangimignano.com).

If interested, ask if the TI is still offering a two-hour **guided walk** in English and Italian on weekends; if they are, book it the day before by 18:00 (April-Oct Sat-Sun at 11:00, €20; includes admission either to the Duomo or to the Civic Museum and Tower; pay and meet at TI). They also offer a two-hour minibus tour to a countryside winery (€20, April-Oct Tue and Thu at 17:00).

HILL TOWNS

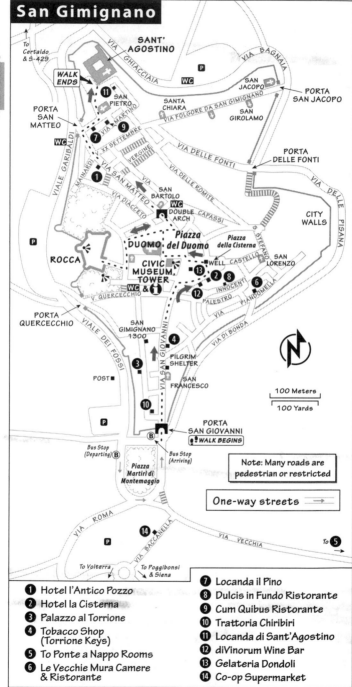

San Gimignano

To Certaldo & S-429

SANT' AGOSTINO

VIA GHIACCIAIA

VIA BAGNAIA

WALK ENDS

WC

SAN JACOPO

PORTA SAN JACOPO

SANTA CHIARA

SAN GIROLAMO

PORTA SAN MATTEO

VIA FOLGORE DA SAN GIMIGNANO

SAN PIETRO

VIA MARTINO

VIA - XX SETTEMBRE

VIA DELLE FONTI

PORTA DELLE FONTI

VIA DELLE FONTI

VERGINE

VIALE GARIBALDI

WC

VIA SAN MATTEO

MANARDI

VIA PIACCETO

VIA DELLE ROMITE

VIA DELLE PISANA

SAN BARTOLO

WC

DOUBLE ARCH

CAPASSI

CITY WALLS

ROCCA

DUOMO

Piazza del Duomo

Piazza della Cisterna

S. STEFANO

CIVIC MUSEUM TOWER & ①

WELL CASTELLO

SAN LORENZO

WC

V. QUERCECCHIO

② ⑧

INNOCENTI

⑬

⑥

PIANDORNELLA

PORTA QUERCECCHIO

VIALE DEI FOSSI

SAN GIMIGNANO 1300

④

VIA SAN GIOVANNI

PALESTRO

⑫

VIA

VIA DI BONDA

③

PILGRIM SHELTER

SAN FRANCESCO

POST

⑩

100 Meters

100 Yards

PORTA SAN GIOVANNI

WALK BEGINS

Bus Stop (Departing) Ⓑ

Ⓑ

Bus Stop (Arriving)

Note: Many roads are pedestrian or restricted

Piazza Martiri di Montemaggio

One-way streets ⟶

VIA ROMA

⑭

VIA VECCHIA

To ⑤

P

VIA BACCANELLA

To Volterra

To Poggibonsi & Siena

① Hotel l'Antico Pozzo
② Hotel la Cisterna
③ Palazzo al Torrione
④ Tobacco Shop (Torrione Keys)
⑤ To Ponte a Nappo Rooms
⑥ Le Vecchie Mura Camere & Ristorante

⑦ Locanda il Pino
⑧ Dulcis in Fundo Ristorante
⑨ Cum Quibus Ristorante
⑩ Trattoria Chiribiri
⑪ Locanda di Sant'Agostino
⑫ diVinorum Wine Bar
⑬ Gelateria Dondoli
⑭ Co-op Supermarket

Arrival in San Gimignano

The **bus** stops at the main town gate, Porta San Giovanni. There's no baggage storage anywhere in town, so you're better off leaving your bags in Siena or Florence.

You can't **drive** within the walled town. There are three pay lots a short walk outside the walls: The handiest is Parcheggio Montemaggio, just outside Porta San Giovanni (€2/hour, €20/day). The one below the roundabout and Co-op supermarket, called Parcheggio Giubileo, is least expensive (€1.50/hour, €6/day). And at the north end of town, by Porta San Jacopo, is Parcheggio Bagnaia (€2/hour, €15/day). Note that some lots—including the one directly in front of the Co-op and the one just outside Porta San Matteo—are designated for locals and have a one-hour limit for tourists.

Helpful Hints

Market Day: Thursday is market day on Piazza del Duomo (8:00-13:00), but for local merchants, every day is a sales frenzy.

Services: A public **WC** is just off Piazza della Cisterna (€0.50); others are at the Rocca fortress, just outside Porta San Matteo, and at the Parcheggio Bagnaia parking lot.

Shuttle Bus: A little electric shuttle bus does its laps all day from Porta San Giovanni to Piazza della Cisterna to Porta San Matteo. Route #1 runs back and forth through town; route #2—which runs only in summer—conveniently connects the three parking lots to the town center. Each route runs about hourly (€0.75 one-way, €1.50 for all-day pass, buy ticket in advance from TI or tobacco shop, possible to buy all-day pass on bus).

Self-Guided Walk

Welcome to San Gimignano

This quick walking tour will take you across town, from the bus stop at Porta San Giovanni through the town's main squares to the Duomo, and on to the Sant'Agostino Church.

• *Start, as most tourists do, at the Porta San Giovanni gate at the bottom end of town.*

Porta San Giovanni: San Gimignano lies about 25 miles from both Siena and Florence, a good stop for pilgrims en route to those cities, and on a naturally fortified hilltop that encouraged settlement. The town's walls were built in the 13th century, and gates like this helped regulate who came and went. Today, modern posts keep out all but service and emergency vehicles. The small square just outside the gate features a memorial to the town's WWII dead.

Follow the pilgrims' route (and flood of modern tourists) through the gate and up the main drag.

About 100 yards up, on the right, is a pilgrims' shelter (12th-century, Pisan Romanesque). The eight-pointed Maltese cross indicates that this was built by the Knights of Malta, whose early mission (before they became a military unit) was to provide hospitality for pilgrims. It was one of 11 such shelters in town. Today, only the wall of this shelter remains.

• *Carry on past all manner of touristy rip-off shops, up to the town's central Piazza della Cisterna. Sit on the steps of the well.*

Piazza della Cisterna: The piazza is named for the cistern that is served by the old well standing in the center of this square. A clever system of pipes drained rain-water from the nearby rooftops into the underground cistern. This square has been the center of the town since the ninth century. Turn in a slow circle and observe the commotion of rustic-yet-proud facades crowding in a tight huddle around the well. Imagine this square in pilgrimage

times, lined by inns and taverns for the town's guests. Now finger the grooves in the lip of the well and imagine generations of maids and children fetching water. Each Thursday, the square fills with a market—as it has for more than a thousand years.

• *Notice San Gimignano's famous towers.*

The Towers: Of the original 72 towers, only 14 survive. Before effective city walls were developed, rich people fortified their

own homes with these towers: They provided a handy refuge when ruffians and rival city-states were sacking the town. If under attack, tower owners would set fire to the external wooden staircase, leaving the sole entrance unreachable a story up; inside, fleeing nobles pulled up behind them the ladders that connected each level, leaving invaders no way to reach the stronghold at the tower's top. These towers became a standard part of medieval skylines. Even after town walls were built, the towers continued to rise—now to fortify noble families feuding within a town (Montague and Capulet-style).

In the 14th century, San Gimignano's good times turned very bad. In the year 1300, about 13,000 people lived within the walls. Then, in 1348, a six-month plague decimated the population, leaving the once-mighty town with barely 4,000 survivors. Once fiercely independent, now crushed and demoralized, San Gimignano came under Florence's control and was forced to tear down its towers. (The Banca CR Firenze building occupies the remains of one such toppled tower.) And, to add insult to injury, Florence redirected the vital trade route away from San Gimignano. The town never recovered, and poverty left it in a 14th-century architectural time warp. That well-preserved cityscape, ironically, is responsible for the town's prosperity today.

• *From the well, walk 30 yards uphill to the adjoining square with the cathedral.*

Piazza del Duomo: The square faces the former cathedral. The twin towers to the right are 10th century, among the first in town.

The stubby tower opposite the church is typical of a merchant's tower: main door on ground floor, warehouse upstairs, holes to hold beams that once supported wooden balconies and exterior staircases, heavy stone on the first floor, cheaper and lighter brick for upper stories.

• *On the piazza are the Civic Museum and Tower, worth checking out (see "Sights in San Gimignano," later). You'll also see the...*

Duomo (or Collegiata): Inside San Gimignano's Romanesque cathedral, Sienese Gothic art (14th century) lines the nave with parallel themes—Old Testament on the left and New Testament on the right. (For example, from back to front: Creation facing the Annunciation, the birth of Adam facing the Nativity, and the suffering of Job opposite the suffering of Jesus.) This is a classic use of art to teach. Study the fine Creation series (top left). Many scenes are portrayed with a local 14th-century "slice of life" setting, to help lay townspeople relate to Jesus—in the same way that many white Christians are more comfortable thinking of Jesus as Caucasian (€3.50, €5.50 combo-ticket includes mediocre Religious Art Museum—skip it; April-Oct Mon-Fri 10:00-19:10, Sat 10:00-17:10, Sun 12:30-19:10; Nov-March Mon-Sat 10:00-16:40, Sun 12:30-16:40; last entry 20 minutes before closing, buy ticket and enter from the courtyard around the left side).

• *From the church, hike uphill (passing the church on your left), following signs to* Rocca e Parco di Montestaffoli. *Keep walking until you enter a peaceful hilltop park and olive grove within the shell of a 14th-century fortress.*

Hilltop Views at the Rocca: On the far side, 33 steps take you to the top of a little tower (free) for the best views of San Gimignano's skyline; the far end of town and the Sant'Agostino Church (where this walk ends); and a commanding 360-degree view of the Tuscan countryside. San Gimignano is surrounded by olives, grapes, cypress trees, and—in the Middle Ages—lots of wild dangers. Back then, farmers lived inside the walls and were thankful for the protection.

• *Return to the bottom of Piazza del Duomo, turn left, and continue your walk across town, cutting under the double arch (from the town's first wall). In around 1200, this defined the end of town. The* **Church of San Bartolo** *stood just outside the wall (on the right). The Maltese cross over the door indicates that it likely served as a hostel for pilgrims. As you continue down Via San Matteo, notice that the crowds have dropped by at least half. Enjoy the breathing room as you pass a fascinating array of stone facades from the 13th and 14th centuries—now a happy cancan of wine shops and galleries. Reaching the gateway at the end of town, follow signs to the right to reach...*

Sant'Agostino Church: This tranquil church, at the far end of town (built by the Augustinians who arrived in 1260), has fewer crowds and more soul. Behind the altar, a lovely fresco cycle by Benozzo Gozzoli (who painted the exquisite Chapel of the Magi in the Medici-Riccardi Palace in Florence) tells of the life of St. Augustine, a North African monk who preached simplicity. The kind, English-speaking friars (from Britain and the US) are happy to tell you about their church and way of life, and also have Mass in English on Sundays at 11:00. Pace the peaceful cloister before heading back into the tourist mobs (free, €0.50 lights the frescoes; April-Oct daily 7:00-12:00 & 15:00-19:00; Nov-March Tue-Sun 7:00-12:00 & 15:00-18:00, Mon 16:00-18:00). Their fine little shop, with books on the church and its art, is worth a look.

Sights in San Gimignano

▲Civic Museum and Tower
(Museo Civico and Torre Grossa)

This small, fun museum, consisting of just three unfurnished rooms and a tower, is inside City Hall (Palazzo Comunale). The main room (across from the ticket desk), called the **Sala di Consiglio** (a.k.a. Dante Hall), is covered in festive frescoes, including the *Maestà* by Lippo Memmi. This virtual copy of Simone Martini's *Maestà* in Siena proves that Memmi didn't have quite the same talent as his famous brother-in-law.

Upstairs, the **Pinacoteca** displays a classy little painting collection of mostly altarpieces. The highlight is a 1422 altarpiece by Taddeo di Bartolo honoring St. Gimignano (far end of last room). You can see the saint, with the town—bristling with towers—in his hands, surrounded by events from his life.

Before going back downstairs, be sure to stop by the **Mayor's Room** (Camera del Podestà, across the stairwell from the Pinacoteca). Frescoed in 1310 by Memmo di Filippuccio, it offers an intimate and candid peek into the 14th century. The theme: profane love. As you enter, look to the left corner where a young man is ready to experience the world. He hits his parents up for a bag of money and is free. On the opposite wall (above the window), you'll see a series of bad decisions: Almost immediately he's entrapped by two prostitutes, who lead him into a tent where he loses his money, is turned out, and is beaten. Above the door, from left to right, you see a parade of better choices: marriage, the cradle of love, the bride led to the groom's house, and newlyweds bathing together and retiring happily to their bed.

The highlight for most visitors is a chance to climb the **Tower** (Torre Grossa, entrance halfway down the stairs from the Pinacoteca). The city's tallest tower, 200 feet and 218 steps up, rewards those who climb it with a commanding view. See if you can count the town's 14 towers (yes, that includes the stubby little one just below this tower). It's a sturdy, modern staircase most of the way, but the last stretch is a steep, ladder-like climb.

Coming back down to earth, you leave the complex via a delightful stony loggia and courtyard out back.

Cost and Hours: €5 includes museum and tower, daily April-Sept 9:30-19:00, Oct-March 11:00-17:30, Piazza del Duomo, tel. 0577-990-312.

San Gimignano 1300

This small but interesting attraction, located inside the Palazzo Ficarelli on a quiet street a block over from the main street, is a trip back in time. When possible, attendants like to lead visitors on individual tours around the small exhibit. The highlight is a painstakingly rendered 1:100 scale clay model of San Gimignano at the turn of the 14th century. You can see the 72 original "tower houses" and marvel at how unchanged the street plan remains today. You'll peek into cross-sections of buildings, view scenes of medieval life both within and outside the city walls, and watch videos about town history and the making of the model. After walking through a gallery of modern Italian sculpture, your visit ends in the ceramics workshop next door, where models like this one are created from wet lumps of clay. (Conveniently, the "workshop" is one corner of a ceramics shop.) While cynics might view this as little more than a gimmick to sell more little ceramic buildings, the detail of the model is truly enchanting.

Cost and Hours: €5; April-Oct daily 10:00-19:00; Nov-March Mon-Fri 10:00-17:00, Sat-Sun until 18:00; Via Berignano 23, tel. 0577-941-078, www.sangimignano1300.com.

Sleeping in San Gimignano

Although the town is a zoo during the daytime, locals outnumber tourists when evening comes, and San Gimignano becomes mellow and enjoyable. Drivers can unload near their hotels, then park outside the walls in recommended lots. Hotel websites provide instructions.

$$$ Hotel l'Antico Pozzo is an elegantly restored, 15th-century townhouse with 18 tranquil, comfortable rooms, a peaceful interior courtyard terrace, and an elite air (Sb-€95, small Db-€120, standard Db-€140, big Db-€180, includes breakfast, air-con, elevator, free Wi-Fi, near Porta San Matteo at Via San Matteo 87, tel. 0577-942-014, www.anticopozzo.com, info@anticopozzo.com; Emanuele, Elisabetta, and Mariangela). If arriving by bus, save a crosstown walk by asking for the Porta San Matteo stop (rather than getting off at the main stop near Porta San Giovanni).

$$$ Hotel la Cisterna, right on Piazza della Cisterna, feels old and stately, with 49 predictable rooms, some with panoramic view terraces—a scene from the film *Tea with Mussolini* was filmed from one (Sb-€78, Db-€100, Db with view-€125, Db with view terrace—€140, 10 percent discount with this book when you book direct, includes buffet breakfast, air-con, elevator, free Wi-Fi, good restaurant with great view, closed Jan-Feb, Piazza della Cisterna 23, tel. 0577-940-328, www.hotelcisterna.it, info@hotelcisterna.it, Alessio).

$$$ Ponte a Nappo, run by enterprising Carla Rossi (who doesn't speak English) and her sons Francesco and Andrea (who do), has seven comfortable rooms and two apartments in a kid-friendly farmhouse. Located a long half-mile below town (best for drivers, but doable for hardy walkers), this place has killer views. A picnic dinner lounging on their comfy garden furniture as the sun sets is good Tuscan living (Db-€100-130, 2-6 person apartment-€130-250, price depends on season and length of stay, for best price book direct and mention Rick Steves, air-con mid-June-mid-Sept only, free Wi-Fi, free parking, pool, free loaner bikes, lunch and dinner sometimes available to guests, 15-minute walk or 5-minute drive from Porta San Giovanni, tel. 0577-907-282, mobile 349-882-1565, www.accommodation-sangimignano.com, info@rossicarla.it). About 100 yards below the monument square at Porta San Giovanni, find Via Vecchia (not left or right, but down

Sleep Code

(€1 = about $1.30, country code: 39)
S = Single, **D** = Double/Twin, **T** = Triple, **Q** = Quad, **b** = bathroom, **s** = shower only. Unless otherwise noted, credit cards are accepted, English is spoken, and breakfast is included (but usually optional). Many towns in Italy levy a hotel tax of about €2 per person, per night, which is generally not included in the rates I've quoted.

To help you sort easily through these listings, I've divided the accommodations into three categories based on the price for a standard double room with bath:

$$$ **Higher Priced**—Most rooms €100 or more.
 $$ **Moderately Priced**—Most rooms between €70-100.
  $ **Lower Priced**—Most rooms €70 or less.

Prices can change without notice; verify the hotel's current rates online or by email. For the best prices, always book direct.

a tiny road) and follow it down a dirt road for five minutes by car. They also rent a dozen or so rooms and apartments in town (including some in the Palazzo Tortoli, a stone tower right on the main square, Db-€75-110, pay Wi-Fi, each room is described on their website).

$$ Palazzo al Torrione, on an untrampled side street just inside Porta San Giovanni, is quiet and handy, and generally better than most hotels (even though they don't have a full-time reception). Their 10 modern rooms are spacious and tastefully appointed (Db-€90, terrace Db-€110, Tb-€100, terrace Tb-€120, Qb-€120-130, 10 percent discount with this book when you book direct, breakfast-€7, communal kitchen with Wi-Fi, parking-€6/day, inside and left of gate at Via Berignano 76; operated from tobacco shop 2 blocks away, on the main drag at Via San Giovanni 59; tel. 0577-940-480, mobile 338-938-1656, www.palazzoaltorrione. com, palazzoaltorrione@palazzoaltorrione.com, Vanna and Francesco).

$ Le Vecchie Mura Camere offers three good rooms above their restaurant in the old town (Db-€65, no breakfast, air-con, free Wi-Fi, Via Piandornella 15, tel. 0577-940-270, www.vecchiemura.it, info@vecchiemura.it, Bagnai family).

$ Locanda il Pino has just seven rooms and a big living room. It's dank but clean and quiet. Run by English-speaking Elena and her family, it sits above their elegant restaurant just inside Porta San Matteo (Db-€55, no breakfast, free Wi-Fi in lobby, easy parking just outside the gate, Via Cellolese 4, tel. 0577-940-415, locanda@ ristoranteilpino.it). If you're arriving by bus, ask for the Porta San Matteo stop, rather than the main stop near Porta San Giovanni.

Eating in San Gimignano

My first two listings cling to quiet, rustic lanes overlooking the Tuscan hills (yet just a few steps off the main street); the rest are buried deep in the old center.

Dulcis in Fundo Ristorante, small and family-run, proudly serves modest portions of "revisited" Tuscan cuisine (with a modern twist and gourmet presentation) in a jazzy ambience. This enlightened place, whose menu identifies the sources of their ingredients, offers lots of vegetarian options and gladly caters to gluten-free diets—rare in Tuscany (€12 pastas, €13-16 *secondi,* meals served 12:30-14:30 & 19:15-21:30, closed Wed, Vicolo degli Innocenti 21, tel. 0577-941-919, Roberto and Cristina).

Le Vecchie Mura Ristorante has good and fast service, great prices, tasty if unexceptional home cooking, and the ultimate view. It's romantic indoors or out. They have a dressy, modern interior where you can dine with a view of the busy stainless-steel kitchen under rustic vaults, but the main reason to come is for the incredible cliffside garden terrace. Cliffside tables are worth reserving in advance by calling or dropping by: Ask for "front view" (€8-11 pastas, €12-15 *secondi,* open only for dinner from 18:00, last order at 22:00, closed Tue, Via Piandornella 15, tel. 0577-940-270, Bagnai family).

Cum Quibus ("In Company"), tucked away near Porta San Matteo, has a smallish dining room with soft music, beamed ceilings, and modern touches; it also offers al fresco tables in its interior patio in summer. Lorenzo and Fabiana produce tasty Tuscan cuisine, fresh truffle specialties, and artistic desserts (€10 pastas, €15 *secondi,* truffle dishes more expensive, Wed-Mon 12:30-14:30 & 19:00-22:00, closed Tue, reservations advised, Via San Martino 17, tel. 0577-943-199, www.cumquibus.it).

Trattoria Chiribiri, just inside Porta San Giovanni on the left, serves homemade pastas and desserts at remarkably fair prices. While its petite size and tight seating make it hot in the summer, it's a good budget option—and, as such, it's in all the guidebooks (€8 pastas, €10 *secondi,* daily 11:00-23:00, Piazza della Madonna 1, tel. 0577-941-948, Maria and Maurizio).

Locanda di Sant'Agostino spills out onto the peaceful square, facing Sant'Agostino Church. It's cheap and cheery, serving lunch and dinner daily—big portions of basic food in a restful setting. Dripping with wheat stalks and atmosphere on the inside, there's shady on-the-square seating outside (€8 pizzas, pastas, and *brus-*

chette; €9-15 *secondi*, daily 11:00-22:00, closed Tue off-season and Jan-Feb, Piazza Sant'Agostino 15, tel. 0577-943-141, Genziana and sons).

Enoteca: **diVinorum,** a cool wine bar with a small entrance right on Piazza Cisterna, has a contemporary cellar atmosphere and—best of all—a row of tables out back overlooking rolling Tuscan hills (just downhill and toward the main drag from Dulcis in Fundo, recommended earlier; at mealtimes, you'll have to order food to sit at the outdoor tables). They have local wines by the glass (€3-5) as well as snacks that can easily make a light meal (€10-15 *antipasti* plates, €7-8 *bruschette* and warm plates, daily 11:00-21:30, Nov-April until 20:00, Piazza Cisterna 30 or Via degli Innocenti 5, tel. 0577-907-192, Matteo).

Picnics: The big, modern **Co-op supermarket** sells all you need for a nice spread (Mon-Sat 8:30-20:00, Sun 8:30-12:30 except closed Sun Nov-March, at parking lot below Porta San Giovanni). Or browse the little shops guarded by boar heads within the town walls; they sell pricey boar meat *(cinghiale)*. Pick up 100 grams (about a quarter pound) of boar, cheese, bread, and wine and enjoy a picnic in the garden at the Rocca or the park outside Porta San Giovanni.

Gelato: To cap the evening and sweeten your late-night city stroll, stop by **Gelateria Dondoli** on Piazza della Cisterna (at #4). Gelato-maker Sergio was a member of the Italian team that won the official Gelato World Cup—and his gelato really is a cut above (daily 8:00-24:00, closes at 19:00 off-season, tel. 0577-942-244, Dondoli family).

San Gimignano Connections

Bus tickets are sold at the bar just inside the town gate or at the TI. Many connections require a change at Poggibonsi (poh-jee-BOHN-see, with a soft "g"), which is also the nearest train station.

From San Gimignano by Bus to: Florence (hourly, less on Sun, 1.5-2 hours, change in Poggibonsi, €6.80), **Siena** (8/day direct, on Sun must change in Poggibonsi, 1.25 hours, €6), **Volterra** (4/day Mon-Sat; on Sun only 1/day—in the late afternoon and usually crowded—with no return to San Gimignano; 2 hours, change in Colle Val d'Elsa, €6.15). Note that the bus connection to Volterra is four times as long as the drive; if you're desperate to get there faster, you can pay about €70 for a taxi.

By Car: San Gimignano is an easy 45-minute drive from Florence (take the A-1 exit marked *Firenze Certosa*, then a right past tollbooth following *Siena per 4 corsie* sign; exit the freeway at Poggibonsi). From San Gimignano, it's a scenic and windy half-hour drive to Volterra.

Volterra

Encircled by impressive walls and topped with a grand fortress, Volterra sits high above the rich farmland surrounding it. More

than 2,000 years ago, Volterra was one of the most important Etruscan cities, and much larger than we see today. Greek-trained Etruscan artists worked here, leaving a significant stash of art, particularly funerary urns. Eventually Volterra was absorbed into the Roman Empire, and for centuries it was an independent city-state. Volterra fought bitterly against the Florentines, but like many Tuscan towns, it lost in the end and was given a fortress atop the city to "protect" its citizens.

Unlike other famous towns in Tuscany, Volterra feels neither cutesy nor touristy...but real, vibrant, and almost oblivious to the allure of the tourist dollar. This probably stems from the Volterrans' feisty resistance to change. (At a recent town meeting about whether to run high-speed Internet cable to the town, a local grumbled, "The Etruscans didn't need it—why do we?") This stubbornness helps make Volterra a refreshing change of pace from its more commercial neighbors. It also boasts some particularly fine sights for a small town, from a remarkably intact ancient Roman theater, to a finely decorated Pisan Romanesque cathedral, to an excellent museum of Etruscan artifacts. All in all, Volterra is my favorite small town in Tuscany.

Orientation to Volterra

Compact and walkable, the city stretches out from the pleasant Piazza dei Priori to the old city gates.

Tourist Information

The helpful TI is on the main square, at Piazza dei Priori 19 (daily 9:00-13:00 & 14:00-18:00, tel. 0588-87257, www.volterratur.it). The TI's excellent €5 audioguide narrates 20 stops (2-for-1 discount on audioguides with this book).

Arrival in Volterra

By Public Transport: Buses stop at Piazza Martiri della Libertà in the town center. Train travelers can reach the town with a short bus ride (see "Volterra Connections," later.)

By Car: Drivers will find the town ringed with easy numbered parking lots (#5, #6, and #8 are free; #3 is for locals only). The most central lots are the pay lots at Porta Fiorentina and underground at Piazza Martiri della Libertà (€1.50/hour, €11/24 hours).

Helpful Hints

Market Day: The market is on Saturday morning near the Roman Theater (8:00-13:00, at parking lot #5; in winter, it's right on Piazza dei Priori). The TI hands out a list of other market days in the area.

Festivals: Volterra's Medieval Festival takes place the third and fourth Sundays of August. Fall is a popular time for food festivals—check with the TI for dates and events planned.

Internet Access: Web & Wine has a few terminals, fine wine by the glass, and organic vegetarian food (€3/hour, no minimum, summer daily 9:30-1:00 in the morning, closed Thu in Sept-May, Via Porta all'Arco 11-15, tel. 0588-81531, Lallo speaks English). **Enjoy Café Internet Point** has a couple terminals in their basement (€3/hour, daily 6:30-1:00 in the morning, Piazza dei Martiri 3, tel. 0588-80530).

Laundry: The handy self-service **Lavanderia Azzurra** is just off the main square (€4 wash, €4 dry, daily 7:00-23:00, Via Roma 7, tel. 0588-80030).

Tours in Volterra

▲▲Guided Volterra Walk

Annie Adair (also listed individually, next) and her colleagues offer a great one-hour, English-only introductory walking tour of Volterra for €10. The walk touches on Volterra's Etruscan, Roman, and medieval history, as well as the contemporary cultural scene (April-July and Sept-Oct daily, rain or shine, at 18:00; meet in front of alabaster shop on Piazza Martiri della Libertà, no need to reserve—just show up, they need a minimum of 3 people, or €30—to make the tour go, www.volterrawalkingtour.com or www.tuscantour.com, info@volterrawalkingtour.com). There's no better way to spend €10 and one hour in this city.

Local Guide

American **Annie Adair** is an excellent city guide. She and her husband Francesco, a sommelier, organize private history and wine tours and even Tuscan weddings for Americans (€50/hour, minimum 2 hours, tel. 0588-086-201, mobile 347-143-5004, www.tus-

HILL TOWNS

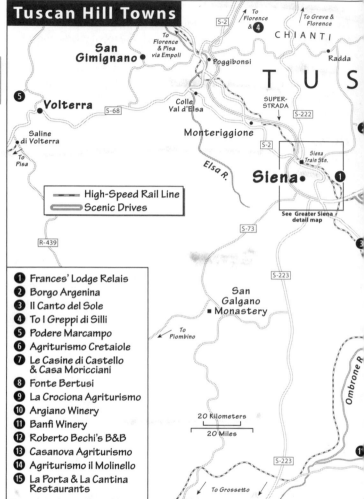

Tuscan Hill Towns

High-Speed Rail Line
Scenic Drives

1 Frances' Lodge Relais
2 Borgo Argenina
3 Il Canto del Sole
4 To I Greppi di Silli
5 Podere Marcampo
6 Agriturismo Cretaiole
7 Le Casine di Castello & Casa Moricciani
8 Fonte Bertusi
9 La Crociona Agriturismo
10 Argiano Winery
11 Banfi Winery
12 Roberto Bechi's B&B
13 Casanova Agriturismo
14 Agriturismo il Molinello
15 La Porta & La Cantina Restaurants

20 Kilometers
20 Miles

cantour.com, info@tuscantour.com). Francesco leads a crash one-hour "Wine Tasting 101" class in sampling Tuscan wines, held at a local wine bar (€50 per group plus cost of wine).

Sights in Volterra

I've arranged these sights as a handy little town walk, connected by directions on foot. Not all the sights will interest everyone, so skim the listings to decide which detours appeal to you.

• *Begin your visit of town at the Etruscan Arch. To find it, go all the way down to the bottom of Via Porta all'Arco (you'll find the top of this street*

between *Piazza Martiri della Libertà*, with the town bus stop, and the main square, *Piazza dei Priori*).

▲Etruscan Arch (Porta all'Arco)

Volterra's most famous sight is its Etruscan arch, built of massive, volcanic tuff stones in the fourth century B.C. Volterra's original wall was four miles around—twice the size of the wall that encircles it today. With 25,000 people, Volterra was a key trading center and one of 12 leading towns in the confederation of *Etruria Propria*. The three seriously eroded heads, dating from the first century B.C., show what happens when you leave something outside for 2,000 years. The newer stones are part of the 13th-century

HILL TOWNS

Otherworldly Volterra

Sitting on its stony main square at midnight, watching bats dart about as if they own the place, I sense there is something supernatural about Volterra. The cliffs of Volterra inspired Dante's "cliffs of hell." In the winter, the town's vibrancy is smothered under a deadening cloak of clouds. The name Volterra means "land that floats"—referring to the clouds that often seem to cut it off from the rest of the world below.

The people of Volterra live in a cloud of mystery, too. Their favorite cookie, crunchy with almonds, is called Ossi di Morta ("bones of the dead"). Through the 1980s, Volterra was home to Italy's second-biggest psychiatric hospital. The town's first disco was named Catacombs. Volterra's top sight—the Etruscan Museum—is filled with hundreds of ancient caskets. And in the 1970s, when Volterra was the set of a wildly popular TV horror series called *Ritratto di Donna Velata (Portrait of a Veiled Woman)*, all of Italy tuned in to Volterra every week for a good scare.

Fans of the *Twilight* books and films may recognize Volterra as the home of the powerful clan of vampires called the Volturi. Author Stephanie Meyer had never been to Volterra before setting part of her second novel, *New Moon*, in the town; she simply picked the name for its resemblance to the one she had already given to her characters, the "Volturi." Even though most scenes in the *New Moon* film (2009) were filmed in Montepulciano, a wave of *Twilight* interest swept Volterra. *Twilight* is just one more chapter in a long tale of a town that revels in being otherworldly.

city wall, which incorporated parts of the much older Etruscan wall.

A plaque just outside remembers June 30, 1944. That night, Nazi forces were planning to blow up the arch to slow the Allied advance. To save their treasured landmark, Volterrans ripped up the stones that pave Via Porta all'Arco and plugged the gate, managing to convince the Nazi commander that there was no need to blow up the arch. Today, all the stones are back in their places, and like silent heroes, they welcome you through the oldest standing Etruscan gate into Volterra. Locals claim this as the only surviving round arch of the Etruscan age; most experts believe this is where the Romans got the idea for using a keystone in their arches.

• *Go through the arch and head up Via Porta all'Arco, which I like to call...*

"Artisan Lane" (Via Porta all'Arco)

This steep and atmospheric strip is lined with interesting shops featuring the work of artisans and producers. Because of its alabaster heritage, Volterra attracted craftsmen and artists, who brought with them a rich variety of handiwork (shops generally open Mon-Sat 10:00-13:00 & 16:00-19:00, closed Sun; the TI produces a free booklet called *Handicraft in Volterra*).

From the Etruscan Arch, browse your way up the hill, checking out these shops and items (listed from bottom to top): La Mia Fattoria—a co-op of producers of cheese, salami, and olive oil lets you buy direct at farm prices (just up Via Laberinti near #52); alabaster shops (#57, #50, and #45); book bindery and papery (#26); jewelry (#25); etchings (#23); Web & Wine (Internet access; #11-15); and bronze work (#6).

• *Reaching the top of Via Porta all'Arco, turn left and walk a few steps into Volterra's main square, Piazza dei Priori. It's dominated by the...*

Palazzo dei Priori

Volterra's City Hall (c. 1209) claims to be the oldest of any Tuscan city-state. It clearly inspired the more famous Palazzo Vecchio in Florence. Town halls like this are emblematic of an era when city-states were powerful. They were architectural exclamation points declaring that, around here, no pope or emperor called the shots. Towns such as Volterra were truly city-states—proudly independent and relatively democratic. They had their own armies, taxes, and even weights and measures. Notice the horizontal "cane" cut into the City Hall wall (right of the door). For a thousand years, this square hosted a market, and the "cane" was the local yardstick. When not in use for meetings or weddings, the city council chambers—lavishly painted and lit with fun dragon lamps, as they have been for centuries of town meetings—are open to visitors.

The tower was recently opened to the public. For the adventurous, 70 or so steps take you up a tight, winding, metal staircase to a small platform with great panoramic views of the city and surrounding countryside. Be aware that this is the bell tower; expect loud chimes if you visit on the hour or half-hour.

Cost and Hours: €1.50, €2.00 additional for tower, mid-March-Oct daily 10:30-17:30, Nov-mid-March Sat-Sun only 10:00-17:00.

• *Facing the City Hall, notice the black–and–white–striped wall to the right (set back from the square). The door in that wall leads into Volterra's...*

Duomo

This church is not as elaborate as its cousin in Pisa, but the simple 13th-century facade and the interior (rebuilt in the late 16th cen-

HILL TOWNS

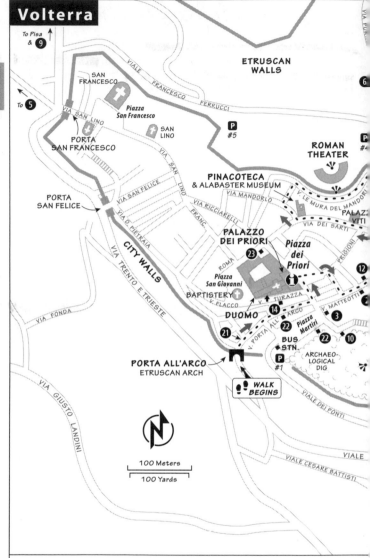

Volterra

ETRUSCAN WALLS

To Pisa & 9

To 5

SAN FRANCESCO

Piazza San Francesco

PORTA SAN FRANCESCO

SAN LINO

VIALE FRANCESCO FERRUCCI

P #5

ROMAN THEATER

P #4

6

PINACOTECA & ALABASTER MUSEUM

VIA MANDORLO

V. LE MURA DEL MANDORLI

PALAZZ. VITI

PORTA SAN FELICE

VIA SAN FELICE

VIA RICCIARELLI

VIA DEI SARTI

VIA SAN LINO

VIA D. PIETRAIA

VIA C. FRANC.

PALAZZO DEI PRIORI

Piazza dei Priori

PRIGIONI

12

CITY WALLS

VIA TRENTO E TRIESTE

ROMA

Piazza San Giovanni

BAPTISTERY

V. FLACCO

23

i

VIA DEI SARTI

V. TURAZZA

14

V. MATTEOTTI

3

2

VIA FONDA

DUOMO

21

V. PORTA ALL' ARCO

22

Piazza Martiri

22

10

PORTA ALL'ARCO
ETRUSCAN ARCH

BUS STN.

P #1

ARCHAEO-LOGICAL DIG

7

WALK BEGINS

VIALE DEI PONTI

VIA GIUSTO LANDINI

N

100 Meters
100 Yards

VIALE CESARE BATTISTI

VIALE

1 Hotel La Locanda

2 Albergo Etruria

3 Albergo Nazionale

4 To Park Hotel Le Fonti

5 To Albergo Villa Nencini & Old Etruscan Wall

6 La Primavera B&B

7 Seminario Vescovile Sant'Andrea

8 To Chiosco delle Monache Hostel, Hotel Foresteria &Trattoria da Bado

9 To Podere Marcampo

10 Ristorante Enoteca del Duca

11 Trattoria Don Beta

12 La Vecchia Lira

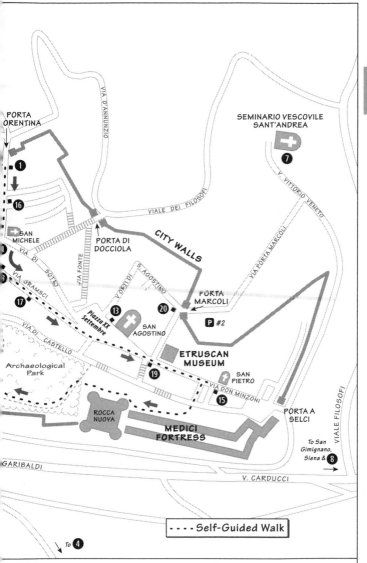

---- Self-Guided Walk

13 La Carabaccia

14 Ristorante il Sacco Fiorentino

15 La Vena di Vino Wine Bar

16 Ombra della Sera & Pizzeria Tavernetta

17 Despar Market

18 L'Isola di Gusto Gelato

19 Alab'Arte Alabaster Showroom

20 Alab'Arte Alabaster Workshop

21 "Artisan Lane"

22 Internet Cafés (2)

23 Launderette

HILL TOWNS

Italy Is Made of Tuff Stuff

Tuff (*tufo* in Italian) is a light-colored volcanic rock that is common in Italy. A part of Tuscany is even called the "Tuff Area." The seven hills of Rome are made of tuff, and quarried blocks of this stone can be seen in the Colosseum, Pantheon, and Castel Sant'Angelo. Just outside of Rome, the catacombs were carved from tuff. Sorrento rises above the sea on a tuff outcrop. Orvieto, Civita di Bagnoregio (pictured), and many other hill towns perch on bluffs of tuff.

Italy's early inhabitants, including the Etruscans and Romans, carved caves, tunnels, burial niches, and even roads out of tuff. Blocks of this rock were quarried to make houses and walls. Tuff is soft and easy to carve when it's first exposed to air, but hardens later, which makes it a good building stone.

Italy's tuff-producing volcanoes resulted from a lot of tectonic-plate bumping and grinding. This violent geologic history is reflected in Italy's volcanoes, like Vesuvius and Etna, and earthquakes such as the 2009 quake in the L'Aquila area northeast of Rome.

Tuff is actually just a big hardened pile of old volcanic ash. When volcanoes hold magma that contains a lot of water, they erupt explosively (think heat + water = steam = POW!). The exploded rock material gets blasted out as hot volcanic ash, which settles on the surrounding landscape, piles up, and over time welds together into the rock called tuff.

So when you're visiting an area in Italy of ancient caves or catacombs built out of this material, you'll know that at least once (and maybe more) upon a time, it was a site of a lot of volcanic activity.

tury), with its central nave flanked by monolithic stone columns, are beautiful examples of the Pisan Romanesque style.

Cost and Hours: Free, daily 8:00-12:30 & 15:00-18:00, Nov-March until 17:00, closed Fri 15:00-16:00 while the cleaners religiously perform their duties.

Visiting the Church: Enter through the door off Piazza dei Priori (technically the back door) and take a moment to let your eyes adjust to this dark, Romanesque space. (If you come through the main door around on Piazza San Giovanni, do this tour in reverse.) The interior was decorated mostly in the late 16th century, during Florentine rule under the Medici family. Their coat of arms, with its distinctive balls (called *palle*), is repeated multiple times throughout the building.

Head down into the nave to face the main altar. Up the stairs just to the right is a dreamy painted and gilded-wood *Deposition* (Jesus being taken down from the cross), restored to its original form. Carved in 1228, a generation before Giotto, it shows emotion and motion way ahead of its time (€1 buys some light).

The glowing **windows** in the transept and behind the altar are sheets of alabaster. These, along with the recorded Gregorian chants, add to the church's wonderful ambience.

The 12th-century marble **pulpit** is also beautifully carved. In the relief panel of the Last Supper, all the apostles are together except Judas, who's under the table with the evil dragon (his name is the only one not carved into the relief).

Just past the pulpit on the right (at the Rosary Chapel), check out the *Annunciation* by Fra Bartolomeo (who was a student of Fra Angelico and painted this in 1497). Bartolomeo delicately gives worshippers a way to see Mary "conceived by the Holy Spirit." Note the vibrant colors, exaggerated perspective, and Mary's *contrapposto* pose—all attributes of the Renaissance.

At the end of the nave, the **chapel** to the right of the doors has painted terra-cotta statue groups of the Nativity and the Adoration of the Magi, thought to be the work of master ceramists Luca and Andrea della Robbia. Luca is credited with inventing the glazing formula that makes his inventive sculptures shine even in poorly lit interiors.

To see a classically Pisan space, step outside the door into Piazza San Giovanni. A common arrangement in the Middle Ages was for the church to face the baptistery (you couldn't enter the church until you were baptized)...and for the hospital to face the cemetery (now the site of the local ambulance corps). These buildings all overlooked the same square. That's how it is in Pisa, and that's how it is here.

• *Exit the cathedral out the back door into the main square, Piazza dei Priori. Face the City Hall, and go down the street to the left; after one short block, you're standing at the head (on the left) of...*

▲Via Matteotti

The town's main drag, named after the popular Socialist leader Giacomo Matteotti (killed by the Fascists in 1924), provides a good cultural scavenger hunt.

At #1 is a typical Italian bank security door. (Step in and say, "Beam me up, Scotty.") Back outside, stand at the corner and look up and all around. Find the medieval griffin torch holder—symbol of Volterra—and imagine it holding a lit torch. The pharmacy sports the symbol of its medieval guild. Across the street from the bank, #2 is the base of what was a San Gimignano-style fortified

Tuscan tower. Look up and imagine heavy beams cantilevered out, supporting extra wooden rooms and balconies crowding out over the street. Throughout Tuscany, today's stark and stony old building fronts once supported a tangle of wooden extensions.

As you head down Via Matteotti, notice how the doors show centuries of refitting work. Doors that once led to these extra rooms are now partially bricked up to make windows. Contemplate urban density in the 14th century, before the plague thinned out the population. Be careful: There's a wild boar (a local delicacy) at #10.

At #12, notice the line of doorbells: This typical palace, once the home of a single rich family, is now occupied by many middle-class families. After the social revolution in the 18th century and the rise of the middle class, former palaces were condominiumized. Even so, like in *Dr. Zhivago,* the original family still lives here. Apartment #1 is the home of Count Guidi.

At #16, pop in to an alabaster showroom. Alabaster, mined nearby, has long been a big industry here. Volterra alabaster—softer and more porous than marble—was sliced thin to serve as windows for Italy's medieval churches.

At #19, the recommended La Vecchia Lira is a lively cafeteria. The Bar L'Incontro across the street is a favorite for pastries; in the summer, they sell homemade gelato, while in the winter they make chocolates.

Across the way, up Vicolo delle Prigioni, is a fun bakery *(panificio).* They're happy to sell small quantities if you want to try the local *cantuccini* (almond biscotti) or another treat (closed 14:00-17:30, Sat after 14:00, and all day Sun).

Continue to the end of the block. At #51, a bit of Etruscan wall is artfully used to display more alabaster art. And #56A is the alabaster art gallery of Paolo Sabatini.

Locals gather early each evening at Osteria dei Poeti (at #57) for some of the best cocktails in town—served with free munchies. The cinema is across the street. Movies in Italy are rarely in *versione originale;* Italians are used to getting their movies dubbed into Italian. To bring some culture to this little town, they also show live transmissions of operas and concerts (advertised in the window).

At #66, another Tuscan tower marks the end of the street. This noble house has a ground floor with no interior access to the safe upper floors. Rope ladders were used to get upstairs. The tiny door was wide enough to let in your skinny friends...but definitely not anyone wearing armor and carrying big weapons.

Across the street stands the ancient Church of St. Michael. After long years of barbarian chaos, the Lombards moved in from the north and asserted law and order in places like Volterra. That generally included building a Christian church on the old Roman forum to symbolically claim and tame the center of town. (Locals still call this San Michele in Foro—"in the forum.") The church standing here today is Romanesque, dating from the 12th century. Around the right side, find the crude little guy and the smiling octopus under its eaves—they've been making faces at the passing crowds for 800 years.

• *Three more sights—Palazzo Viti (fancy old palace), the Pinacoteca (gallery of gilded altarpieces), and the Alabaster Museum (within the Pinacoteca building)—are a short stroll down Via dei Sarti: From the end of Via Matteotti, turn left. If you want to skip straight down to the Roman Theater, just head straight from the end of Via Matteotti onto Via Guarnacci, then turn left when you get to the Porta Fiorentina gate. To head directly to Volterra's top sight, the Etruscan Museum, just turn around, walk a block back up Via Matteotti, turn left on Via Gramsci, and follow it all the way through Piazza XX Settembre up Via Don Minzoni to the museum.*

Palazzo Viti

Go behind the rustic, heavy stone walls of the city and see how the nobility lived (in this case, rich from 19th-century alabaster wealth). One of the finest private residential buildings in Italy, with 12 rooms open to the public, Palazzo Viti feels remarkably lived in—because it is. You'll also find Signora Viti herself selling admission tickets. It's no wonder this time warp is so popular with Italian movie directors. Remember, you're helping keep a noble family in leotards.

Cost and Hours: €5, pick up the loaner English description, April-Oct daily 10:00-13:00 & 14:30-18:30, closed Nov-March, Via dei Sarti 41, tel. 0588-84047, www.palazzoviti.it.

• *A block past Palazzo Viti, also on Via dei Sarti, is the...*

Pinacoteca and Alabaster Museum

The Pinacoteca fills a 15th-century palace with fine paintings that feel more Florentine than Sienese—a reminder of whose domain this town was in. You'll see roomfuls of gilded altarpieces and saintly statues. Head upstairs to the first floor. If you go left, you'll circle all the way around and save the best for last—but to cut to the chase, turn right at the landing and go directly into the best room, with Luca Signorelli's beautifully lit *Annunciation* (1491), an example of classic High Renaissance (from the town cathedral), and (to the right) *Deposition from the Cross* (1521), the groundbreaking Mannerist work by Rosso Fiorentino (note the elongated bodies and harsh emotional lighting and colors). In the adjacent room, see Ghirlandaio's *Christ in Glory* (1492). The two devout-looking kneeling women are actually pagan, pre-Christian Etruscan demigoddesses, Attinea and Greciniana, but the church identified them as obscure saints to make the painting acceptable. Rather than attempt to get locals to stop venerating them (as their images were all over town), the church simply sainted them. Upstairs, the second floor has three more rooms of similar art.

A new staircase leads down to the recently opened **Alabaster Museum.** With alabaster sculptures spread over four floors, the museum contains examples from Etruscan times until the present (and lacked English descriptions when I visited). The top floor shows tools used to work the stone. Etruscan pieces are on the third floor, and modern sculptures—including an intriguing alabaster fried egg—are on the lower floors. As you leave, note the fine, tranquil, cloister-like courtyard with the remains of its original well.

Cost and Hours: €6 for Pinacoteca, €8 for Alabaster, €10 combo-ticket covers both museums plus Etruscan Museum, daily 9:00-18:45, Nov-mid-March until 13:45, Via dei Sarti 1, no photos permitted, tel. 0588-87580.

• *Exiting the Pinacoteca, turn right, then right again down the Passo del Gualduccio passage into the parking-lot square; at the end of this square, turn right and walk along the wall, with fine views of the...*

Roman Theater

Built in about 40 B.C., this well-preserved theater has good acoustics. Because a fine aerial view is available from the city wall promenade, you may find it unnecessary to pay admission to enter. Belly up to the 13th-century wall and look down. The wall that you're standing on divided the theater from the town center...so, naturally, the theater became the town dump. Over time, the theater was forgotten—covered in the garbage of Volterra. Luckily, it was rediscovered in the 1950s, by an administrator (and armchair historian) at the local mental hospital. Since they couldn't secure government funding for the dig, the theater was first excavated by mental patients who found the activity therapeutic.

The stage wall was standard Roman design—with three levels from which actors would appear: one level for mortals, one for heroes, and the top one for gods. Parts of two levels still stand. Gods leaped out onto the third level for the last time around the third century A.D., which is when the town began to use the theater stones to build fancy baths instead. You can see the remains of the baths behind the theater, including the round sauna with brick supports that raise the heated floor.

From the vantage point on the city wall promenade, you can trace Volterra's vast Etruscan wall. Find the church in the distance, on the left, and notice the stones just below. They are from the Etruscan wall that followed the ridge into the valley and defined Volterra in the fourth century B.C.

Cost and Hours: €3.50, but you can view the theater free from Via Lungo le Mure; the entrance is near the little parking lot just outside Porta Fiorentina—you can see the entry to the right as you survey the theater from above; mid-March-Oct daily 10:30-17:30,

Nov–mid-March Sat–Sun only 10:00–16:00, may be closed in bad weather.

• *From the Roman Theater, make your way back to Via Matteotti (follow Via Guarnacci straight up from Porta Fiorentina). A block down Via Matteotti, you can't miss the wide, pedestrianized shopping street called Via Gramsci. Follow this up to Piazza XX Settembre, walk through that leafy square, and continue uphill on Via Don Minzoni. Watch on your left for the...*

▲▲Etruscan Museum (Museo Etrusco Guarnacci)

Filled top to bottom with rare Etruscan artifacts, this museum—even with few English explanations and its dusty, almost neglectful, old-school style—makes it easy to appreciate how advanced this pre-Roman culture was.

Cost and Hours: €8, €10 combo-ticket includes the Pinacoteca and Alabaster Museum; daily mid-March-Oct 9:00–19:00, Nov–mid-March 10:00–16:00; ask at the ticket window for mildly interesting English pamphlet, audioguide-€3, Via Don Minzoni 15, tel. 0588-86347, www.comune.volterra.pi.it/english.

Visiting the Museum: The museum's three floors feel dusty and disorganized. As there are scarcely any English explanations, consider the serious but interesting €3 audioguide; the information below hits the highlights.

Ground Floor: The collection starts with a small gathering of pre-Etruscan Villanovian artifacts (c. 1500 B.C., to the left as you enter), but its highlight is straight ahead, sprawling through several rooms: a seemingly endless collection of Etruscan **funerary urns** (dating from the seventh to the first century B.C.). Designed to contain the ashes of cremated loved ones, each urn is tenderly carved with a unique scene, offering a peek into the still-mysterious Etruscan society. Etruscan urns have two parts: The casket on the bottom contained the remains (with elaborately carved panels), while the lid was decorated with a sculpture of the departed.

First pay attention to the people on top. While contemporaries of the Greeks, the Etruscans were more libertine. Their religion was less demanding, and their women were a respected part of both the social and public spheres. Women and men alike are depicted lounging on Etruscan urns. While they seem to be just hanging out, the lounging dead were actually offering the gods a banquet—in order to gain their favor in the transition to the next life. The banquet—where Etruscans really did lounge like this in front of a table—was the epitome of their social structure. But the outcome of this particular banquet had eternal consequences. The dearly departed are often depicted holding scrolls, blank wax tablets (symbolizing blank new lives in the next world), and containers that would generally be used at banquets, including libation cups for offering wine to the gods. The women in particular are finely dressed, sometimes holding a pomegranate (symbolizing fertility) or a mirror. Look at the faces, and imagine the lives they lived and the loved ones they left behind.

Now tune into the reliefs carved into the fronts of the caskets. The motifs vary widely, from floral patterns to mystical animals (such as a Starbucks-like mermaid) to parades of magistrates. Most show journeys on horseback—appropriate for someone leaving this world and entering the next. The most evocative scenes show the fabled horseback-and-carriage ride to the underworld, where the dead are greeted by Charon, an underworld demon, with his hammer and pointy ears.

While the finer urns are carved of alabaster, most are made of limestone. Originally they were colorfully painted. Many lids are mismatched—casualties of reckless 18th- and 19th-century archaeological digs.

First Floor: You'll enter a room with a circular mosaic in the floor (a Roman original, found in Volterra and transplanted here). Turn left into a series of green rooms—the best presented (and most important) of the museum.

The first room, Sala XIV, collects scenes of Ulysses carved into the fronts of caskets. Turn left and head into Sala XV, with the museum's prize piece. Fans of Alberto Giacometti will be amazed at how the tall, skinny figure called *The Evening Shadow* (*L'Ombra della Sera,* third century B.C.) looks just like the modern Swiss sculptor's work—but is 2,500 years older. This is an exceptional example of the *ex-voto* bronze statues that the Etruscans created in thanks to the gods. With his supremely lanky frame, distinctive wavy hairdo, and inscrutable Mona Lisa smirk, this Etruscan lad captures the illusion of a shadow stretching long late in the day. Admire the sheer artistry of the statue; with its right foot shifted slightly forward, it even hints at the *contrapposto* pose that would become common in this same region during the Renaissance, two millennia later.

Continue circling clockwise, through Sala XVI (alabaster urns with more Greek myths), Sala XVII (ex-voto water-bearer statues, kraters—vases with handles, and bronze hand mirrors), and Sala XVIII (golden jewelry). Sala XIX shows off the museum's other top piece, the **Urn of the Spouses** (*Urna degli Sposi,* first century B.C.). It's unique for various reasons, including its material (it's in terra-cotta—a relatively rare material for these funerary urns) and its depiction

of two people rather than one. Looking at this elderly couple, it's easy to imagine the long life they spent together and their desire to pass eternity lounging with each other at a banquet for the gods.

The rest of this floor has black glazed pottery; thousands of Etruscan, Greek, and Roman coins; and many more bronze ex-votos and jewelry.

Top Floor: From the top of the stairs, turn right, then immediately right again to find a re-created grave site, with several neatly aligned urns and artifacts that would have been buried with the deceased. Some of these were funeral dowries (called *corredo*) that the dead would pack along. You'll see artifacts such as mirrors, coins, hardware for vases, votive statues, pots, pans, and jewelry. On the landing are fragments from Volterra's acropolis—a site now occupied by the Medici Fortress.

• *After your visit, duck across the street to the alabaster showroom and the wine bar (both described next).*

▲Alabaster Workshop

Alab'Arte offers a fun peek into the art of alabaster. Their showroom is across from the Etruscan Museum, but to find their powdery workshop, go a block downhill, in front of Porta Marcoli, where you can watch Roberto Chiti and Giorgio Finazzo at work. They are delighted to share their art with visitors. (Everything—including Roberto and Giorgio—is covered in a fine white dust.) Lighting shows off the translucent quality of the stone and the expertise of these artists. This is not a touristy guided visit, but something far more special: the chance to see busy artisans practicing their craft. For more such artisans in action, visit "Artisan Lane" (Via Porta all'Arco) described earlier, or ask the TI for their list of the town's many workshops open to the public.

Cost and Hours: Free, showroom—daily 10:30-13:00 & 15:30-19:00, Via Don Minzoni 18; workshop—March-Oct Mon-Sat 9:30-13:00 & 15:00-19:00, closed Sun, usually closed Nov-Feb—call ahead, Via Orti Sant'Agostino 28; tel. 0588-87968, www.alabarte.com.

▲La Vena di Vino (Wine-Tasting with Bruno and Lucio)

La Vena di Vino, also just across from the Etruscan Museum, is a fun *enoteca* where two guys who have devoted themselves to the wonders of wine share it with a fun-loving passion. Each day Bruno and Lucio open six or eight bottles, serve your choice by the glass, pair it with characteristic munchies, and offer fine music (guitars

Under the Etruscan Sun

Around 550 B.C.—just before the Golden Age of Greece—the Etruscan people of central Italy had their own Golden Age. Though their origins are mysterious, their mix of Greek-style art with Roman-style customs helped lay a civilized foundation for the rise of the Roman Empire. As you travel through Italy—particularly in Tuscany (from "Etruscan")—you'll find traces of this long-lost people.

Etruscan tombs and artifacts are still being discovered, often by farmers in the countryside. Museums in Volterra and Cortona house fine collections of urns, pottery, and devotional figures. You can visit several domed tombs outside Cortona.

The Etruscans first appeared in the ninth century B.C., when a number of cities sprouted up in sparsely populated Tuscany and Umbria, including today's hill towns of Cortona, Chiusi, and Volterra. Possibly immigrants from Turkey, but more likely local farmers who moved to the city, they became traders and craftsmen, and welcomed new ideas from Greece.

More technologically advanced than their neighbors, the Etruscans mined metal, exporting it around the Mediterranean, both as crude ingots and as some of the finest-crafted jewelry in the known world. They drained and irrigated large tracts of land, creating the fertile farmland of central Italy's breadbasket. With their disciplined army, warships, merchant vessels, and (from the Greek perspective) pirate galleys, they ruled central Italy and the major ports along the Tyrrhenian Sea. For nearly two centuries (c. 700-500 B.C.), much of Italy lived a Golden Age of peace and prosperity under the Etruscan sun.

Judging from the frescoes and many luxury items that have survived, the Etruscans enjoyed the good life: They look healthy and vibrant as they play flutes, dance with birds, or play party games. Etruscan artists celebrated individual people, showing their wrinkles, crooked noses, silly smiles, and funny haircuts.

Scholars today have deciphered the Etruscans' Greek-style alphabet and some individual words, but they have yet to fully crack the code. Much of what we know of the Etruscans comes from their tombs. The tomb was a home in the hereafter, complete with all of the deceased's belongings. The sarcophagus might have a statue on the lid of the deceased at a banquet—lying across a dining couch, spooning with his wife, smiles on their faces, living the good life for all eternity.

Seven decades of wars with the Greeks (545-474 B.C.) disrupted their trade routes and drained the Etruscan League, just as a new Mediterranean power was emerging: Rome. In 509 B.C., the Romans overthrew their Etruscan king, and Rome expanded, capturing Etruscan cities one by one (the last in 264 B.C.). Etruscan resisters were killed, the survivors intermarried with Romans, and their kids grew up speaking Latin. By Julius Caesar's time, the only remnants of Etruscan culture were its priests, who be-

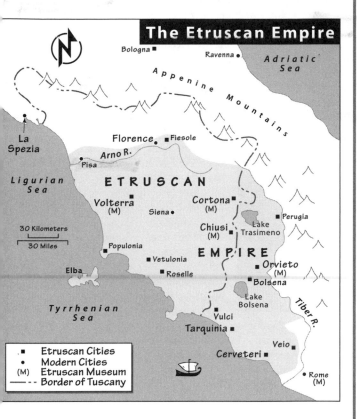

The Etruscan Empire

Bologna ■

Ravenna ●

Adriatic Sea

Appenine Mountains

La Spezia ●

Florence ● ■Fiesole

Arno R.

● Pisa

Ligurian Sea

ETRUSCAN

Volterra ■ (M) Siena ● Cortona ■ (M)

■ Perugia

Chiusi (M) ■ Lake Trasimeno

30 Kilometers

30 Miles

Populonia ●

■ Vetulonia

EMPIRE

● Orvieto (M)

Elba ■ Roselle

■ Bolsena

Lake Bolsena

Tyrrhenian Sea

Tiber R.

■ Vulci

Tarquinia ■

Veio ■

Cerveteri ■

● Rome (M)

■ Etruscan Cities
● Modern Cities
(M) Etruscan Museum
--- Border of Tuscany

came Rome's professional soothsayers. Interestingly, the Etruscan prophets had foreseen their own demise, having predicted that Etruscan civilization would last 10 centuries.

But Etruscan culture lived on in Roman religion (pantheon of gods, household gods, and divination rituals), art (realism), lifestyle (the banquet), and in a taste for Greek styles—the mix that became our "Western civilization."

Etruscan Sights in Italy

Rome: Traces of original Etruscan engineering projects (e.g., Circus Maximus), Vatican Museum artifacts, and Villa Giulia Museum, with the famous "husband and wife sarcophagus."

Orvieto: Archaeological Museum (coins, dinnerware, and a sarcophagus), necropolis, and underground tunnels and caves.

Volterra: Etruscan gate (Porta all'Arco, from fourth century B.C.) and Etruscan Museum (funerary urns).

Chiusi: Museum, tombs, and tunnels.

Cortona: Museum and dome-shaped tombs.

available for patrons) and an unusual decor (the place is strewn with bras). Hang out here with the local characters. This is your chance to try the Super Tuscan wine—a creative mix of international grapes grown in Tuscany. According to Bruno, the Brunello (€7/glass) is just right with wild boar, and the Super Tuscan (€6) is perfect for meditation. Food is served all day, including some microwaved hot dishes or a plate of meats and cheeses. Although Volterra is famously quiet late at night, this place is full of action. Downstairs is a rustic cellar that doubles on weekend nights as a sort of disco.

Cost and Hours: Pay per glass, open Wed-Mon 11:30-1:00 in the morning, closed Tue, 3- to 5-glass wine tastings, shipping options available, Via Don Minzoni 30, tel. 0588-81491, www.lavenadivino.com.

• *Volterra's final sight is perched atop the hill just above the wine bar. Climb up one of the lanes nearby, then walk (to the right) along the formidable wall to find the park.*

Medici Fortress and Archaeological Park

The Parco Archeologico marks what was the acropolis of Volterra from 1500 B.C. until A.D. 1472, when Florence conquered the pesky city and burned its political and historic center, turning it into a grassy commons and building the adjacent Medici Fortezza. The old fortress—a symbol of Florentine dominance—now keeps people in rather than out. It's a maximum-security prison housing only about 150 special prisoners. (When you're driving from San Gimignano to Volterra, you pass another big, modern prison—almost surreal in the midst of all the Tuscan wonder.) Authorities prefer to keep organized crime figures locked up far away from their family ties in Sicily.

The park sprawling next to the fortress (toward the town center) is a rare, grassy meadow at the top of a rustic hill town—a favorite place for locals to relax and picnic on a sunny day. Nearby are the remains of the acropolis (€3.50 to enter, ticket also includes the Roman Theater), but these can be viewed through a fence for free.

Cost and Hours: Park—free to enter, closes at 20:00 in summer, 17:00 in winter.

Countryside Strolls

All these sights are in a tight little zone of the old town, about a 10-minute walk from each other. But if you have time for a stroll, Volterra—perched on a ridge overlooking pristine Tuscan hills—has countryside galore to explore. Get some advice from the TI.

One popular walk is to head to the west end of town, out Porta San Francesco, into a workaday area (dubbed "Borghi," literally, "neighborhoods") that sees few tourists. Continuing downhill (past the Church of San Giusto), you'll come to a cliff with a stretch of the original fourth-century B.C. Etruscan wall. Peering over the cliff from here, you can see that Volterra sits upon orange sandy topsoil packed onto clay cliffs, called Le Balze. At various points in its history, the town has been threatened by landslides, and parts of its hilltop have simply disappeared. The big church you see in the distance was abandoned in the late 1800s for fear that it would be swallowed up by the land. The distinctive cliffs surrounding Volterra are called *calanchi* (similar to the French *calanques* that slash the Mediterranean coast).

Sleeping in Volterra

Predictably for a small town, Volterra's accommodations are limited, and all have their quirks—but there are plenty of places offering a good night's sleep at a fair price. While it's convenient to stay inside the old town, the lodgings that are a short walk away are generally a bit cheaper (and much easier for drivers).

Inside Volterra's Old Town

$$$ Hotel La Locanda feels stately and old-fashioned. This well-located place (just inside Porta Fiorentina) rents 18 decent rooms with flowery decor and modern comforts (Db-€104, less off-season, 10 percent Rick Steves discount, includes breakfast, air-con, free Wi-Fi, Via Guarnacci 24/28, tel. 0588-81547, www.hotel-lalocanda.com, staff@hotel-lalocanda.com, Giulia, Stefania, and Irina).

$$ Albergo Etruria, on Volterra's main drag, rents 21 fresh, modern, and spacious rooms within an ancient stone structure. They have a welcoming TV lounge and a peaceful rooftop garden (Sb-€75, Db-€95, Tb-€115, 10 percent discount with cash and this book when you book direct, includes breakfast, fans, free but spotty Wi-Fi, Via Matteotti 32, tel. 0588-87377, www.albergoetruria.it, info@albergoetruria.it, Lisa and Giuseppina are fine hosts).

$$ Albergo Nazionale, with 38 big rooms, is simple, a little musty, short on smiles, popular with school groups, and steps from the bus stop. While the place feels dated, it's an exceptionally handy location (Sb-€55-70, Db-€70-90, Tb-€90-105, 10 percent discount with cash and this book if you book direct, reception closes at midnight, includes breakfast, free Wi-Fi, Via dei Marchesi 11, tel. 0588-86284, fax 0588-84097, www.hotelnazionale-volterra.it, info@hotelnazionale-volterra.it).

Just Outside the Old Town

These accommodations are within a 5- to 15-minute walk of the city walls.

$$$ Park Hotel Le Fonti, a dull 10-minute walk downhill from Porta all'Arco, can't decide whether it's a business hotel or a resort. The spacious, imposing building feels old and stately, and has 64 rooms, many with views. While generally overpriced (the management knows it's the only hotel of its kind in Volterra), it can be a good value if you manage to snag a deal. In addition to the swimming pool, guests can use a small spa with sauna, hot tub, and an intriguing "emotional shower" (Db-€89-165, average is about Db-€129 but prices vary wildly depending on season, "superior" room is identical to others but has a view for €20 extra, "deluxe" room with terrace costs €30 extra, includes breakfast, elevator, pay Wi-Fi in lobby, on-site restaurant, wine bar, free parking, Via di Fontecorrenti 5, tel. 0588-85219, www.parkhotellefonti.com, info@hotellefonti.com).

$$ Albergo Villa Nencini, just outside of town, is big, professional, and older-feeling, with 36 cheaply furnished rooms. A few rooms have terraces, and many have views. Guests also enjoy the large pool and free parking (Sb-€67, Db-€88, Tb-€115, 10 percent discount with cash and this book, includes breakfast, pay Wi-Fi, Borgo Santo Stefano 55, a 15-minute uphill walk to main square, tel. 0588-86386, www.villanencini.it, info@villanencini.it, Nencini family).

$ La Primavera B&B is a great value just a few minutes' walk outside Porta Fiorentina (near the Roman Theater). Silvia rents five charming, tidy rooms that share a cutesy-country, heavily perfumed lounge. The house is along a fairly busy road, but set back along a pleasant courtyard (Db-€75, Tb-€100, includes breakfast, free Wi-Fi, free parking, Via Porta Diana 15, tel. 0588-87295, mobile 328-865-0390, www.affittacamere-laprimavera.com, info@affittacamere-laprimavera.com).

$ Seminario Vescovile Sant'Andrea has been training priests for more than 500 years. Today, the remaining eight priests still train students, but when classes are over, their 16 rooms—separated by vast and holy halls in an echoing old mansion—are rented very cheaply. Look for the 15th-century Ascension ceramic by Andrea della Robbia, tucked away in a corner upstairs (S-€17, Sb-€22, D-€32, Db-€40, T-€48, Tb-€60, no breakfast, closed Oct-March, elevator, closes at 24:00, groups welcome, free parking, 10-minute walk from Etruscan Museum, Viale Vittorio Veneto 2, tel. 0588-86028, semvescovile@diocesivolterra.it; Alberto, Angela, and Sergio).

$ Chiosco delle Monache, Volterra's youth hostel, fills a wing of the restored Convent of San Girolamo with 68 beds in 23 rooms.

It's modern, spacious, and very institutional, with lots of services and a tranquil cloister to wander. However, it's about a 20-minute hike out of town, in a boring area near deserted hospital buildings (bed in 6-bed dorm-€18, breakfast-€6 extra, lockers; Db-€69, includes breakfast; reception closed 13:00-15:00 and after 22:00, elevator, pay Wi-Fi, free parking, Via dell Teatro 4, look for hospital sign from main Volterra-San Gimignano road, tel. 0588-86613, www.ostellovolterra.it, info@ostellovolterra.it). Nearby and run by the same organization, **$ Hotel Foresteria** has 35 big, utilitarian, new-feeling rooms with great prices but the same location woes as the hostel; it's worth considering for budget travelers, families, and drivers (Sb-€58, Db-€82, Tb-€103, Qb-€122, includes breakfast, air-con, elevator, pay Wi-Fi, restaurant, free parking, Borgo San Lazzaro, tel. 0588-80050, www.foresteriavolterra.it, info@foresteriavolterra.it).

Near Volterra

$$ Podere Marcampo is a newer *agriturismo* about 2.5 miles outside Volterra on the road to Pisa. Run by Genuino (owner of the recommended Ristorante Enoteca del Duca), his wife Ivana, and their English-speaking daughter Claudia, this peaceful spot has three well-appointed rooms and three apartments, plus a swimming pool with panoramic views. Genuino produces his award-winning Merlot on site and offers €20 wine-tastings with cheese and homemade salami. Cooking classes at their restaurant in town are also available (Db-€94, apartment-€118-195, more expensive mid-July-Aug, includes breakfast with this book, air-con, free Wi-Fi, free parking, tel. 0588-85393, Claudia's mobile 328-174-4605, www.agriturismo-marcampo.com, info@agriturismo-marcampo.com).

Eating in Volterra

Menus feature a Volterran take on regional dishes. *Zuppa alla Volterrana* is a fresh vegetable-and-bread soup, similar to *ribollita* (except that it isn't made from leftovers). *Torta di ceci*, also known as *cecina*, is a savory pancake-like dish made with garbanzo beans. Those with more adventurous palates dive into *trippa* (tripe; comes in a bowl like stew), the traditional breakfast of the alabaster carvers. *Fegatelli* are meatballs made with liver.

Ristorante Enoteca del Duca, with a locally respected chef named Genuino, serves well-presented and creative Tuscan cuisine. You can dine under a medieval arch with walls lined with wine bottles, in a sedate, high-ceilinged dining room (with an Etruscan statuette at each table), on a nice little patio out back, or in their little *enoteca* (wine cellar). It's a good place for truffles, and has a friendly staff and a fine wine list (which includes Genuino's own merlot, plus several much pricier options—choose carefully). The spacious seating, dressy clientele, and calm atmosphere make this a good choice for a romantic splurge (€42 food-sampler fixed-price meal, €10-15 pastas, €15-22 *secondi,* Wed-Mon 12:30-15:00 & 19:30-22:00, closed Tue, near City Hall at Via di Castello 2, tel. 0588-81510, www.enoteca-delduca-ristorante.it).

Trattoria da Bado, a 10-minute hike out of town, is every local's favorite for its *tipica cucina Volterrana.* Giacomo and family offer a rustic atmosphere and serve food with no pretense—"the way you wish your mamma cooks" (meals from 12:30 and 19:30, closed Wed, Borgo San Lazzero 9, tel. 0577-80402, reserve before you go as it's often full).

Don Beta is a family-run trattoria on the main drag, popular with travelers for its stylish home cooking. Mirko supervises the lively young team as they whisk out steaming plates of pasta and homemade desserts (€6-10 pastas, €12-18 *secondi,* daily 12:00-14:30 & 19:00-23:00, reservations smart, Via Matteotti 39, tel. 0588-86730, www.donbeta.it).

La Vecchia Lira, bright and cheery, is a classy self-serve eatery that's a hit with locals as a quick and cheap lunch spot by day (with €5-10 meals) and a fancier restaurant at night (€9-10 pastas, €11-18 *secondi;* Fri-Wed 11:30-14:30 & 19:00-22:30, closed Thu, Via Matteotti 19, tel. 0588-86180, Lamberto and Massimo).

La Carabaccia feels like an old-school Italian eatery, with a 1950s turquoise color scheme, a deli up front, and a country-rustic dining room in back. They serve only two pastas and two *secondi* on any given night, so check the menu by the door to be sure you like the choices. Committed to tradition, on Fridays they serve only fish. They whip up €3-4 take-away sandwiches at the deli up front (€7-9 pastas and *secondi,* Tue-Sun 12:30-14:30 & 19:30-22:00, closed Mon, Piazza XX Settembre 4/5, tel. 0588-86239).

Ristorante il Sacco Fiorentino is a local favorite for traditional cuisine and seasonal seafood specials (€8-10 pastas, €10-15 *secondi,* Thu-Tue 12:00-15:00 & 19:00-22:00, closed Wed, Via Giusto Turazza 13, tel. 0588-88537).

La Vena di Vino is an *enoteca* serving up simple and traditional dishes and the best of Tuscan wine in a fun atmosphere. As their hot dishes are microwaved (there's no real kitchen), come here more for the wine and ambience than for the food (€8-12 meals, closed Tue, Via Don Minzoni 30, tel. 0588-81491).

Pizzerias: **Ombra della Sera** dishes out what local kids consider the best pizza in town. At €6-9 a pop, their pizzas make for a cheap date (Tue-Sun 12:00-15:00 & 19:00-22:00, closed Mon, Via Guarnacci 16, don't confuse this with their second, pricier location on Via Gramsci; tel. 0588-85274). **Pizzeria Tavernetta,** next door, is more romantic, with delightful indoor and on-the-street seating. Its romantically frescoed dining room upstairs is the classiest I've seen in a pizzeria. Marco, who looks like a younger Billy Joel,

serves €5-8 pizzas (Thu-Tue 12:00-16:00 & 18:30-22:00, closed Wed, Via Guarnacci 14, tel. 0588-87630).

Picnic: You can assemble a picnic at the few *alimentari* around town (try Despar Market at Via Gramsci 12, Mon-Sat 7:30-13:00 & 16:00-20:00, Sun 8:30-13:00) and eat in the breezy Archaeological Park.

Gelato: Of the many ice-cream stands in the center, I've found **L'Isola di Gusto** to be reliably high quality (daily 11:00-late, Via Gramsci 3).

Volterra Connections

In Volterra, buses come and go from Piazza Martiri della Libertà (buy tickets at the tobacco shop right on the piazza; if it's closed, purchase on board for small extra charge). Most connections—except to Pisa—are with the C.P.T. bus company (www.cpt.pisa.it) through Colle Val d'Elsa ("koh-leh" for short), a workaday town in the valley (4/day Mon-Sat, 1/day Sun, 50 minutes, €2.75). Once in Colle, you must buy another ticket (from another bus company) at the newsstand near the bus stop, or from the blue automated machine at the bus stop (press "F" to toggle to English, then punch in the number for your destination). I've listed total journey fares below. The nearest train station is in Saline di Volterra, a 15-minute bus ride away (7/day, 2/day Sun); however, trains from Saline run only to the coast, not to the major bus destinations listed next.

From Volterra by Bus to: Florence (4/day Mon-Sat, 1/day Sun, 2 hours, change in Colle Val d'Elsa, €8.35), **Siena** (4/day Mon-Sat, no buses on Sun, 2 hours, change in Colle Val d'Elsa, €6.15), **San Gimignano** (4/day Mon-Sat, 1/day Sun, 2 hours, change in Colle Val d'Elsa, €6.15), **Pisa** (9/day, 2 hours, change in Pontedera, €5.50).

South of Siena

Just an hour south of Siena (or two hours south of Florence), you'll find a trio of inviting hill towns, with an emphasis on good wine and scenic country drives: The biggest and most interesting, Montepulciano, has an engaging medieval cityscape draped in a Renaissance coat, wine cellars that plunge deep down into the cliffs it sits upon, and a classic town square. Pienza is a tidily planned Renaissance town that once gave the world a pope. And mellow Montalcino is (even more than most towns around here) all about its wine: Brunello di Montalcino. All three are within about a half-hour drive of each other, making any one of them a good home base for the entire region. Just to the north are the rippling hills of the Crete Senese. Dressed in vibrant green in spring and parched brown in fall, this area is blessed with quintessential Tuscan scenery and dotted with worthwhile countryside accommodations. While my favorite home base for the region is the most interesting town, Montepulciano, you can't go wrong staying in the countryside or in Montalcino.

Montepulciano

Curving its way along a ridge, Montepulciano (mohn-teh-pull-chee-AH-noh) delights visitors with *vino* and views. Alternately

under Sienese and Florentine rule, the city still retains its medieval *contrade* (districts), each with a mascot and flag. The neighborhoods compete the last Sunday of August in the Bravio delle Botti, where teams of men push large wine casks uphill from Piazza Marzocco to Piazza Grande, all hoping to win a banner and bragging rights. The entire last week of August is a festival: Each *contrada* arranges musical entertainment and serves food at outdoor eateries along with generous tastings of the local *vino*.

The city is a collage of architectural styles, but the elegant San Biagio Church, at the base of the hill, is its best Renaissance building. Most visitors ignore the architecture and focus more on the city's other creative accomplishment, the tasty Vino Nobile di Montepulciano red wine.

Orientation to Montepulciano

The commercial action in Montepulciano centers in the lower town, mostly along Via di Gracciano nel Corso (nicknamed "Corso"). This stretch begins at the town gate called Porta al Prato (near the TI, bus station, and some parking) and winds slowly up, up, up through town—narrated by my self-guided walk, later. Strolling here, you'll find eateries, gift shops, and tourist traps. The back streets are worth exploring. The main square, at the top of town (up a steep switchback lane from Corso), is Piazza Grande. Standing proudly above all the touristy sales energy, it has a noble, Florentine feel.

Tourist Information

The helpful TI is just outside the Porta al Prato city gate, directly underneath the small tree-lined parking lot. It offers a paltry town map for €0.50, books hotels and rooms for no fee, sells train tickets (€1 fee), has an Internet terminal (€3.50/hour), and can book one of the town's few taxis (Mon-Sat 9:30-12:30 & 15:00-18:00, Sun 9:30-12:30, daily until 20:00 in July-Aug, Piazza Don Minzoni, tel. 0578-757-341, www.prolocomontepulciano.it, info@prolocomontepulciano.it).

Note that on the main square there is an office that looks like a TI, but this is actually a privately run "Strada del Vino" (Wine Road) agency. They don't have city info, but they do provide wine-road maps, organize **wine tours** in the city, and lead minibus winery tours farther afield. They also offer other tours (olive oil, cheese, and slow food), cooking classes, and more, depending on season and demand (Mon-Fri 10:00-13:00 & 15:00-18:00, closed Sat-Sun but likely open both days in summer, Piazza Grande 7, tel. 0578-717-484, www.stradavinonobile.it).

Arrival in Montepulciano

Buses leave passengers at the station on Piazza Nenni, steeply downhill from the Porta al Prato gate. From the station, cross the street and head inside the modern orange-brick structure burrowed into the hillside, where there's an elevator. Ride to level 1, walk straight ahead down the corridor (following signs for *centro storico*), and ride another elevator to level 1. You'll pop out at the Poggiofanti Gardens; walk to the end of this park and hook left to find the gate. From here, it's a 15-minute walk uphill along the Corso, the bustling main drag, to the main square, Piazza Grande (following my self-guided walk, described later). Alternatively, you can wait for the orange shuttle bus that takes you all the way up to Piazza Grande (2/hour, €1.10, buy tickets at bars or tobacco shops); it's a good strategy to take the bus up and walk back down. There's a bus stop just before the TI, beside a gray metal canopy over a hotel-booking booth.

Drivers arriving by car should park outside the walls. The city center is a "ZTL" zone—marked with a red circle—where you'll be fined if you drive; even if you were allowed, you wouldn't want to tackle the tiny roads inside the city. In general, white lines indicate free parking and blue lines mean pay parking. (If you're sleeping in town, your hotelier will give you a permit to park within the walls; be sure to get very specific instructions.) Well-signed pay-and-display parking lots ring the city center, usually €1.30/hr. To get the full Montepulciano experience of walking the entire length of the town up the Corso, park just outside the Porta al Prato gate (#1 is handiest, but may be full; #2, #3, and #4 are nearby—#3 has a maximum of 1 hour; #5 is near the bus station—you can ride up to the gate on the elevator described earlier). For a quick surgical strike, make a beeline to the lots up at the top end of town. Follow signs for *centro storico, duomo,* and *Piazza Grande,* and use the *Fortezza* or *San Donato* lots (flanking the fortress at the top of town). Drivers, be aware that Montepulciano is a very vertical town, and it's easy to get turned around. Mercifully, it's also a small town, so backtracking isn't too time-consuming. Just avoid the ZTL areas, and don't park on yellow lines.

Helpful Hints

Market Day: It's on Thursday morning (8:00-13:00), near the bus station.

Services: There's no official **baggage storage** in town, but the TI might let you leave bags with them if they have space and you ask nicely. Public **WCs** are located at the TI, to the right of Palazzo Comunale, and at the Sant'Agostino Church.

Laundry: A self-service launderette is at Via del Paolino 2, just around the corner from the recommended **Camere Bellavista** (€4 wash, €4 dry, daily 8:00-22:00, tel. 0578-717-544).

Taxis: To reach the English-speaking **Eurospin** taxi hotline, call 330-732-723 (€10 for short trips up or down hill; they also provide rides to other towns). For a private taxi, try 348-702-4124. Montepulciano has only a few taxis, so be sure to book well in advance.

Self-Guided Walk

Welcome to Montepulciano

This two-part walk traces the spine of the town, from its main entrance up to its hilltop seat of power. Part 1 begins at Porta al Prato (where you'll enter if arriving at the bus station, parking at certain lots, or visiting the TI). Note that this part of the walk is uphill;

if you'd rather skip straight to the more level part of town, ride the twice-hourly shuttle bus up, or park at one of the lots near the Fortezza. In that case, you can still do Part 1, backwards, on the way down.

Part 1: Up the Corso

This guided stroll takes you up through Montepulciano's commercial (and touristic) gamut, which curls ever so gradually from the bottom of town to the top. While the street is lined mostly with gift shops, you'll pass a few relics of an earlier, less commercial age.

Begin in front of the imposing Porta al Prato, one of the many stout city gates that once fortified this highly strategic town. Facing the gate, find the sign for the Porta di Bacco *"passagio secreto"* on the left. While Montepulciano did have secret passages tunneled through the rock beneath it for coming and going in case of siege, this particular passage—right next to the city's front door—was probably no *secreto*...though it works great for selling salami.

Walk directly below the entrance to the **Porta al Prato,** and look up to see the slot where the portcullis (heavily fortified gate) could slide down to seal things off. Notice that there are two gates, enabling defenders to trap would-be invaders in a no-man's land where they could be doused with hot tar (sticky and painful). Besides having a drop-down portcullis, each gate also had a hinged door—effectively putting four barriers between the town and its enemies.

Pass through the gate and head a block uphill to reach the **Colona dell' Marzocco.** This column, topped with a lion holding the Medici shield, is a reminder that Montepulciano existed under the auspices of Florence—but only for part of its history. Originally the column was crowned by a she-wolf suckling human twins, the civic symbol of Siena. At a strategic crossroads of mighty regional powers (Florence, Siena, and the papal states), Montepulciano often switched allegiances—and this column became a flagpole where the overlords du jour could tout their influence.

The column is also the starting point for Montepulciano's masochistic tradition, **Bravio delle Botti,** held on the last Sunday of August, in which each local *contrada* (fiercely competitive neighborhood, like Siena's) selects its two stoutest young men to roll a 180-pound barrel up the hill through town. If the vertical climb through town wears you out, be glad you're only toting a camera.

A few steps up, on the right (at #91), is one of the many fine noble palaces that front Montepulciano's main strip. The town is fortunate to be graced with so many bold and noble palazzos—Florentine nobility favored Montepulciano as a breezy and relaxed place for a secondary residence. Grand as this palace is, with its stylized lion heads, it's small potatoes—the higher you go

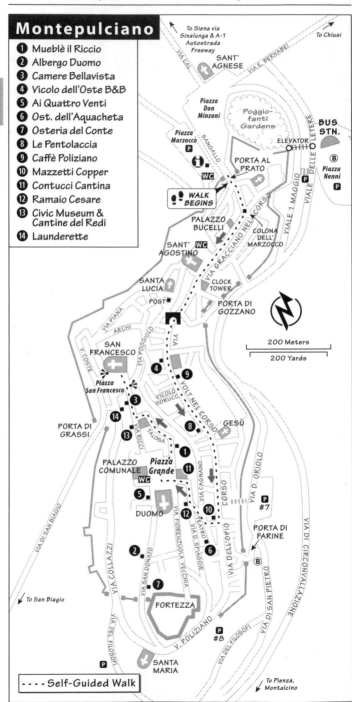

Montepulciano

1. Mueblè il Riccio
2. Albergo Duomo
3. Camere Bellavista
4. Vicolo dell'Oste B&B
5. Ai Quattro Venti
6. Ost. dell'Aquacheta
7. Osteria del Conte
8. Le Pentolaccia
9. Caffè Poliziano
10. Mazzetti Copper
11. Contucci Cantina
12. Ramaio Cesare
13. Civic Museum & Cantine del Redi
14. Launderette

To Siena via Sinalunga & A-1 Autostrada Freeway

To Chiusi

SANT' AGNESE

VIALE BERNABEI

VIA CALI

Piazza Don Minzoni

Poggio-fanti Gardens

SANGALLO

BUS STN.

ELEVATOR

Piazza Marzocco

P

PORTA AL PRATO

VIALE DELLE LETERE

VIALE 1 MAGGIO

P

Piazza Nenni

B

P

WC

WALK BEGINS

PALAZZO BUCELLI

VIA GRACCIANO NEL CORSO

COLONA DELL' MARZOCCO

SANT' AGOSTINO WC

SANTA LUCIA

CLOCK TOWER

POST

PORTA DI GOZZANO

VIA PIANA

ARCHI

VIA POGGIOLO

VIA

200 Meters

200 Yards

N

SAN FRANCESCO

V. COSTE

Piazza San Francesco

4

9

VICOLO SDRUCC.

VOLT. NEL CORSO

PORTA DI GRASSI

14

3

8

GESÙ

13

VIA TALOSA

VIA RICCI

1

11

VIA CAGNANO

CORSO

P #7

PALAZZO COMUNALE

Piazza Grande

WC

5

10

PORTA DI FARINE

VIA D. ORIOLO

DUOMO

VIA FIORENZUOLA VECCHIA

VIA D. SPIAGGIE

12

VIA TEATRO

VIA DELL'OPIO

6

B

2

VIA SAN DONATO

VIA DI CIRCONVALAZIONE

To San Biagio

7

FORTEZZA

VIA COLLAZZI

VIA DEL FILOSOFI

V. POLIZIANO

P #8

VIA DEL FILOSOFI

VIA DI SAN PIETRO

P

SANTA MARIA

VIA DI SAN BIAGIO

To Pienza, Montalcino

- - - - Self-Guided Walk

in Montepulciano, the closer you are to the town center...and the fancier the mansions.

Farther up on the right, at #75 (Palazzo Bucelli), take a moment to examine the **Etruscan and Roman fragments** embedded in the wall (left here by a 19th-century antiques dealer). You can quickly distinguish which pieces came from the Romans and those belonging to the earlier Etruscans by the differences in their alphabets: The "backwards" Etruscan letters (they read from right to left) look closer to Greek than the more modern Roman letters. Many of the fragments show a circle flanked by a pair of inward-facing semicircular designs. The circle represents the libation cup used for drinking at an Etruscan banquet. Banquets were at the center of Etruscan social life, and burial urns depict lounging nobles presenting a feast for the gods.

At the top of the block on the right, pass by the Baroque-style Church of Sant'Agostino. Huff up a few more steps (imagine pushing a barrel now), then take a breather to look back and see the **clock tower** in the middle of the street. The bell ringer at the top takes the form of the character Pulcinella, one of the wild and carefree revelers familiar from Italy's comedy theater *(commedia dell'arte)*.

Keep on going, bearing right (uphill) at the fork. At the *alimentari* on the right (at #23), notice the classic old sign advertising milk, butter, margarine, and olive and canola oil. Soon after, you'll pass under another sturdy **gateway**—indicating that this city grew in concentric circles. Passing through the gate and facing the loggia (with the Florentine Medici seal—a shield with balls), turn left and keep on going.

As you huff and puff, notice (on your right, and later on both sides) the steep, narrow, often-covered lanes called *vicolo* ("little street"). You're getting a peek at the higgledy-piggledy medieval Montepulciano. Only when the rationality of Renaissance aesthetics took hold was the main street realigned, becoming symmetrical and pretty. Beneath its fancy suit, though, Montepulciano remains a rugged Gothic city.

On the left, watch for the hulking former palace (I told you they'd get bigger) that's now home to Banca Etruria. "Etruria"—a name you'll see everywhere around here—is a term for the Etruscan territory of today's Tuscany.

Just after is a fine spot for a coffee break (on the left, at #27): **Caffè Poliziano,** the town's most venerable watering hole (from 1868). Step inside to soak in the genteel atmosphere, with a busy espresso machine, newspapers on long sticks, and a little terrace with spectacular views (open long hours daily; it also has free Wi-Fi). It's named for a famous Montepulciano-born 15th-century poet who was a protégé of Lorenzo the Magnificent de Medici and tutored his two sons. So important is he to civic pride that towns-people are nicknamed *poliziani*.

A bit farther up and on the right, notice the precipitous Vicolo dello Sdrucciolo—literally, "slippery lane." Any *vicolo* on the right can be used as a steep shortcut to the upper part of town, while those on the left generally lead to fine views. Many of these side lanes are spanned by brick arches, allowing the centuries-old buildings to lean on each other for support rather than toppling over—a fitting metaphor for the tight-knit communities that vitalize Italian small towns.

Soon the street levels out. Near the end, on the right (at #64), look for the **Mazzetti** copper shop, crammed full of both decorative and practical items. Because of copper's unmatched heat conductivity, it's a favored material in premium kitchens. The production of hand-hammered copper vessels like these is a dying art; in this shop, you can meet gregarious Cesare, who makes them in his workshop just up the street.

To get there, go up the covered lane just after the copper shop (Vicolo Benci, on the right). You'll emerge partway up the steep street just below the main square. Cesare's workshop and museum are across the street and a bit to the left (look for *Ramaio*). Steeply uphill, on the right just before reaching the square, Cesare's buddy Adamo loves to introduce travelers to Montepulciano's fine wines at the Contucci Cantina. Visit Cesare and Adamo now, or head up to the square for Part 2 of this walk before coming back down.

Either way, Montepulciano's main square is just ahead. You made it!

Part 2: Piazza Grande and Nearby

This pleasant, lively piazza is surrounded by a grab bag of architectural sights. If the medieval **Palazzo Comunale,** or town hall, reminds you of Palazzo Vecchio in Florence, it's because Florence dominated Montepulciano in the 15th and 16th centuries. The

crenellations along the roof were never intended to hide soldiers—they're just meant to symbolize power. But the big, square central tower makes it clear that the city is keeping an eye out in all directions.

Take a moment to survey the square, where the town's four great powers stare each other down. Face the Palazzo Comunale, and keep turning to the right to see: the one-time building of the courts

(Palazzo del Capitano); the noble Palazzo Tarugi, a Renaissance-arcaded confection; and the aristocratic Palazzo Contucci, with its 16th-century Renaissance facade. (The Contucci family still lives in their palace, producing and selling their own wine.) Continuing your spin, you see the unfinished Duomo looking glumly on, wishing the city hadn't run out of money for its facade. (Its interior, described later under "Sights and Experiences in Montepulciano," looks much better.)

A cistern system fed by rainwater draining from the roofs of surrounding palaces supplied the fine **well** in the corner. Check out its 19th-century pulleys, the grills to keep animals from contaminating the water supply, and the Medici coat of arms (with lions symbolizing the political power of Florence).

Climbing the town hall's **tower** rewards you with a windy but commanding view from the terrace below the clock. Go into the Palazzo Comunale, head up the stairs to your left, and pay on the second floor (€3, daily 10:00-18:00, closed in winter).

The street to the left as you face the tower leads to the **Fortezza, or fortress**. While you might expect the town to be huddled protectively around its fortress, in Montepulciano's case, it's built on a distant ledge at the very edge of town. That's because this fort wasn't meant to protect the townspeople, but to safeguard its rulers by keeping an eye on those townspeople.

Detour to the Church of San Francesco and Views: From the main square, it's a short, mostly level walk to a fine viewpoint. You could head down the wide street to the right as you face the tower. But for a more interesting look at Montepulciano behind its pretty Renaissance facades, go instead up the narrow lane between the two Renaissance palaces in the corner of the square. Within just a few steps, you'll be surrounded not by tidy columns and triangles, but by a mishmash of brick and stone. Pause at the Mueblè il Riccio B&B (with a fine courtyard—peek inside) and look high up across the street to see how centuries of structures have been stitched together, sometimes gracelessly.

Follow along this lane as it bends left, and eventually you'll pop out just below the main square, facing the recommended Cantine del Redi wine cellar (described later). Turn right and head down toward the church. At #21 (on the left), look for a red-and-gold shield, over a door, with the name *Talosa*. This marks the home of one of Montepulciano's *contrade*, or neighborhoods; birth and death announcements for the *contrada* are posted on the board next to the door.

Soon you'll come to a viewpoint (on the right) that illustrates Montepulciano's highly strategic position. The ancient town sitting on this high ridge was surrounded by powerful forces—everything you see in this direction was part of the Papal States, ruled from

Rome. In the distance is Lake Trasimeno, once a notorious swampland that made it even harder to invade this town.

Continue a few steps farther to the big parking lot in front of the church. Head out to the terrace for a totally different view: the rolling hills that belonged to Siena. And keep in mind that Montepulciano itself belonged to Florence. For the first half of the 16th century, those three formidable powers—Florence, Siena, and Rome (the papacy)—vied to control this small area. Take in the view of Montepulciano's most impressive church, San Biagio—well worth a visit for drivers or hikers (described later).

From here, you can head back up to the main square, or drop into Cantine del Redi to spelunk its wine cellars.

Sights and Experiences in Montepulciano

These are listed in the order you'll reach them on the self-guided walk, above. For me, Montepulciano's best "experiences" are personal: dropping in on either Adamo, the winemaker at Contucci Cantina; or Cesare, the coppersmith at Ramaio Cesare. Either one will greet you with a torrent of cheerful Italian; just smile and nod, pick up what you can from gestures, and appreciate this rare opportunity to meet a true local character.

▲▲Contucci Cantina

Montepulciano's most popular attraction isn't made of stone...it's the famous wine, Vino Nobile. This robust red can be tasted in any of the cantinas lining Via Ricci and Via di Gracciano nel Corso, but the cantina in the basement of Palazzo Contucci is both historic and fun. Skip the palace's formal wine-tasting showroom facing the square, and instead head down the lane on the right to the actual cellars, where you'll meet lively Adamo (ah-DAH-moh), who has been making wine since 1953 and welcomes tourists into his cellar. While at the palace, you may meet Andrea Contucci, whose family has lived here since the

11th century. He loves to share his family's products with the public. Adamo and Signor Contucci usually have a dozen bottles open.

After sipping a little wine with Adamo, explore the palace basement, with its 13th-century vaults. Originally part of the town's wall, these chambers have been filled since the 1500s with huge barrels of wine. Dozens of barrels of Croatian, Italian, and French oak (1,000-2,500 liters each) cradle the wine through a two-year in-the-barrel aging process, while the wine picks up the personality of the wood. After about 35 years, an exhausted barrel has nothing left to offer its wine, so it's retired. Adamo explains that the French oak gives the wine "pure elegance," the Croatian is more masculine, and the Italian oak is a marriage of the two. Each barrel is labeled with the size in liters, the year the wine was barreled, and the percentage of alcohol (determined by how much sun shone in that year). "Nobile"-grade wine needs a minimum of 13 percent alcohol.

Cost and Hours: Free drop-in tasting, daily 8:30-12:30 & 14:30-18:30, Sat-Sun from 9:30, Piazza Grande 13, tel. 0578-757-006, www.contucci.it.

▲Ramaio Cesare

Cesare (CHEH-zah-ray) the coppersmith is an institution in Montepulciano, carrying on his father's and grandfather's trade by hammering into existence an immense selection of copper objects in his cavernous workshop. Though his English is limited, he's happy to show you photos of his work—including the copper top of the Duomo in Siena and the piece he designed and personally delivered to Pope Benedict. Next door, he has assembled a fine museum with items he and his relatives have made, as well as pieces from his personal collection. Cesare is evangelical about copper, and if he's not too busy, he'll create personalized mementoes for visitors—he loves meeting people from around the world who apprcciatc his handiwork (as his brimming photo album demonstrates). Cesare's justifiable pride in his vocation evokes the hardworking, highly skilled craft guilds that once dominated small-town Italy's commercial and civic life.

Cost and Hours: Demonstration and museum are free; Cesare is generally in his workshop Mon-Sat 8:00-12:30 & 14:30-18:30, Piazzetta del Teatro, tel. 0578-758-753, www.rameria.com. Cesare's shop *(negozio)* is on the main drag, just downhill at Corso #64—look for Rameria Mazzetti, open long hours daily.

Duomo

This church's unfinished facade—rough stonework left waiting for the final marble veneer—is not that unusual. Many Tuscan churches were built just to the point where they had a functional interior, and then, for various practical reasons, the facades were left unfinished. But step inside and you'll be rewarded with some fine art. A beautiful Andrea della Robbia blue-and-white, glazed-terra-cotta *Altar of the Lilies* is behind the baptismal font (on the left as you enter). The high altar, with a top like a pine forest, features a luminous, early-Renaissance Assumption triptych by the Sienese artist Taddeo di Bartolo. Showing Mary in her dreamy eternal sleep as she ascends to be crowned by Jesus, it illustrates how Siena clung to the Gothic aesthetic—elaborate gold leaf and lacy pointed arches—to show heavenly grandeur at the expense of realism.

Cost and Hours: Free, daily 9:00-13:00 & 15:00-18:30.

▲Cantine del Redi

The most impressive wine cellars in Montepulciano sit below the Palazzo Ricci, just a few steps off the main square (toward the Church of San Francesco). Enter through the unassuming door and find your way down a spiral staircase—with rounded steps designed to go easy on fragile noble feet, and lined with rings held in place by finely crafted tiny wrought-iron goat heads. You'll wind up in the dramatic cellars, with gigantic barrels under even more gigantic vaults—several stories high. As you go deeper and deeper into the cellars, high up, natural stone seems to take over the brick. At the deepest point, the atmospheric cave, surrounding a filled-in well, a warren of corridors holds fine wine aging in bottles. Finally you wind up in the shop, where you're welcome to taste two or three Redi wines for free—or, if you show them this book, they'll offer you the free wines along with some light food in their spacious tasting room.

Cost and Hours: Free tasting, €7-20 bottles, affordable shipping, daily 10:30-19:00, next to Palazzo Ricci, tel. 0578-757-166, www.dericci.it.

Civic Museum (Museo Civico)

Eclectic and surprisingly modern, but small and ultimately forgettable, this museum collects bits and pieces of local history with virtually no English explanation. The ground floor and cellar hold ancient artifacts and vases, including some Etruscan items. The next two floors are the pinacoteca (art gallery); the highlight is the first-floor room filled with colorful Andrea della Robbia ceramic altarpieces. You'll find a similar della Robbia altarpiece in situ, in the Duomo, for free.

Cost and Hours: €5, Tue-Sun 10:00-13:00 & 15:00-18:00, closed Mon, Via Ricci 10, tel. 0578-717-300.

Just Outside Montepulciano

San Biagio Church

At the base of Montepulciano's hill, down a picturesque driveway lined with cypresses, this church—designed by Antonio da Sangallo and built of locally quarried travertine—is Renaissance perfection. The proportions of the Greek cross floor plan give the building a pleasing rhythmic quality. Bramante, who designed St. Peter's at the Vatican in 1516, was inspired by this dome. The lone tower was supposed to have a twin, but it was never built. The soaring interior, with a high dome and lantern, creates a fine Renaissance space. Walk around the building to study the freestanding towers, and consider a picnic or snooze on the grass in back. The street called Via di San Biagio, leading from the church up into town, makes for an enjoyable, if challenging, walk.

Cost and Hours: Free, normally open daily 8:30-18:30.

Sleeping in Montepulciano

$$$ Mueblè il Riccio ("Hedgehog") is medieval-elegant, with 10 modern and spotless rooms, an awesome roof terrace, and friendly owners. Five are new "superior" rooms with grand views across the Tuscan valleys (Sb-€80, Db-€100, view Db-€110, superior Db-€150, superior Db with balcony-€160, Tb-€116, superior Tb-€180, superior Qb-€200, breakfast-€8, air-con, guest computer and Wi-Fi, limited free parking—request when you reserve, a block below the main square at Via Talosa 21, tel. 0578-757-713, www.ilriccio.net, info@ilriccio.net, Gió and Ivana speak English). Gió and his son Iacopo give tours of the countryside (€50/hour) in one of their classic Italian cars; for details, see their website. Ivana makes wonderful breakfast tarts.

$$ Albergo Duomo is big, modern, and nondescript, with 13 rooms (with small bathrooms) and a comfortable lounge downstairs (small Db-€75, standard Db-€95, Tb-€115, family deals, elevator, air-con in some rooms for €5 extra, free Wi-Fi, loaner laptops, free parking nearby, Via di San Donato 14, tel. 0578-757-473, www.albergoduomo.it, albergoduomo@libero.it, Elisa and Saverio).

$$ Camere Bellavista has 10 charming, tidy rooms. True to its name, each room has a fine view—though some are better than others. Room 6 has a view terrace worth reserving (Db-€80, terrace Db-€100, cash only, optional €3-10 breakfast at a bar in the piazza, lots of stairs with no elevator, free Wi-Fi, Via Ricci 25, no reception—call before arriving or ring bell, mobile 347-823-2314, www.camerebellavista.it, bellavista@bccmp.com, Gabriella speaks only a smidgen of English).

$$ Vicolo dell'Oste B&B, just off the main drag halfway up through town, has five modern rooms with fully outfitted kitchenettes (Db-€95-100, Tb-€130, Qb-€140, includes breakfast at nearby café, free Wi-Fi, on Via dell'Oste 1—an alley leading right off the main drag just after Caffè Poliziano and opposite the *farmacia* at #47, tel. 0578-758-393, www.vicolodelloste.it, info@vicolodelloste.it, Luisa and Giuseppe).

Countryside Options near Montepulciano: If you'd rather be in the country than in town, don't miss the nearby options listed under "Sleeping near Pienza," later—about a 15-minute drive from Montepulciano.

Eating in Montepulciano

Ai Quattro Venti is fresh, flavorful, fun, and right on Piazza Grande, with a simple dining room and outdoor tables right on the square. It distinguishes itself by offering reasonable portions of tasty, unfussy Tuscan food in an unpretentious setting. Try their very own organic olive oil and wine (€8-9 pastas, €9-10 *secondi*, Fri-Wed 12:30-14:30 & 19:30-22:30, closed Thu, next to City Hall on Piazza Grande, tel. 0578-717-231, Chiara).

Osteria dell'Aquacheta is a carnivore's dream come true, famous among locals for its excellent beef steaks. Its long, narrow room is jammed with shared tables and tight seating, with an open fire in back and a big hunk of red beef lying on the counter like a corpse on a gurney. Giulio, with a pen tucked into his ponytail, whacks off slabs with a cleaver, confirms the weight and price with the diner, and tosses the meat on the grill—seven minutes per side. Steaks are sold by weight (€3/100 grams, or *etto*, one kilo is about the smallest they serve, two can split it for €30). They also serve hearty €6 pastas and salads and a fine house wine. In the tradition of old trattorias, they serve one glass, which you use  alternately for wine and water (Wed-Mon 12:30-15:00 & 19:30-22:30, closed Tue, Via del Teatro 22, tel. 0578-758-443 or 0578-717-086).

Osteria del Conte, an attractive but humble family-run bistro, offers a €30 *menù del Conte*—a four-course dinner of local specialties including wine—as well as à la carte options and cooking like mom's. While the interior is very simple, they also have outdoor tables on a stony street at the edge of the historic center (€7-8 pastas, €9-14 *secondi*, Thu-Tue 12:30-14:30 & 19:30-21:30, closed Wed, Via San Donato 19, tel. 0578-756-062).

Le Pentolaccia is a small, family-run restaurant at the upper, relatively untouristy end of the main drag. With both indoor and outdoor seating, they make tasty traditional Tuscan dishes as well as daily fish specials. Cristiana serves, and husband-and-wife team Jacobo and Alessia stir up a storm in the kitchen (€8-10 pastas, €8-15 *secondi*, Fri-Wed 12:00-15:00 & 19:30-22:30, closed Thu, Corso 86, tel. 0578-757-582).

Near Montepulciano, in Monticchiello

If you'd enjoy getting out of town for dinner—but not too far—consider the 15-minute drive to the smaller, picturesque hill town of Monticchiello. Just inside the town's gate is the highly regarded

La Porta restaurant, where Daria pleases diners either indoors or out with well-executed traditional Tuscan dishes (€9 pastas, €12-15 *secondi,* reservations smart; seatings at 12:30, 14:00, 19:30, and 21:30; closed Thu, Via del Piano 1, tel. 0578-755-163, www.osteri-alaporta.it). If La Porta is closed, or you want a bit more contemporary preparation in a modern atmosphere, continue 50 yards up into town and turn right to find **La Cantina,** run by daughter Deborah (similar prices, Tue-Thu 12:30-15:00 & 19:30-22:00, closed Wed, Via San Luigi 3, tel. 0578-755-280).

Getting There: It's a straight shot to Monticchiello, but finding the road is the hard part. At the base of Montepulciano, head toward Pienza. Shortly after passing the road to San Biagio Church (on the right), watch on the left for the Albergo San Biagio. Turn off and take the road that runs up past the left side of this big hotel, and follow it all the way to Monticchiello. This is a rough (gravel at times), middle-of-nowhere drive. As a bonus, right near Monticchiello is a twisty serpentine section lined with stoic cypress trees—one of those classic Tuscan images you'll see on calendars and postcards. It's also possible to reach Monticchiello more directly from Pienza (ask locals for directions).

Montepulciano Connections

Schedule information and bus tickets are available at the TI. All buses leave from Piazza Pietro Nenni. The bus station seems to double as the town hangout, with a lively bar and locals chatting inside. In fact, there's no real ticket window—you'll buy your tickets at the bar. Check www.sienamobilita.it for schedules.

From Montepulciano by Bus to: Florence (2/day, 2 hours, LFI bus, €11.20, www.lfi.it), **Siena** (8/day, none on Sun, 1.25 hours, €6.60), **Pienza** (8/day, 30 minutes, €2.50), **Montalcino** (4/day Mon-Fri, 3/day Sat, none Sun, change in Torrenieri, 1-1.25 hours total, €4.90). There are hourly bus connections to **Chiusi,** a town on the main Florence-Rome rail line (40 minutes, €3.40); Chiusi is a much better bet than the distant Montepulciano station (5 miles away), which is served only by milk-run trains, but it is handy on Sundays if you want to go to Siena. Buses connect Montepulciano's bus station and its train station (6/day, none on Sun).

To Montalcino: This connection is problematic by public transportation—consider asking at the TI for a **taxi,** or call **Eurospin** taxi company, listed under "Helpful Hints" earlier. Although expensive (about €70), a taxi could make sense for two or more people. Otherwise you can take a bus to Torrenieri, then change to get to Montalcino (2 hours). **Drivers** find route S-146 to Montalcino particularly scenic. **Cortona** is another awkward connection, involving a bus to Chiusi, then a 30-minute train ride to the Camuccia-Cortona train station, four miles below town with poorly timed bus connections to Cortona itself. Consider taking a taxi (about €40).

Pienza

Set on a crest and surrounded by green, rolling hills, the small town of Pienza packs a lot of Renaissance punch. In the 1400s,

locally born Pope Pius II of the Piccolomini family decided to remodel his birthplace in the style that was all the rage: Renaissance. Propelled by papal clout, the town of Corsignano was transformed—in only five years' time—into a jewel of Renaissance architecture. It was renamed Pienza, after Pope Pius. The plan was to remodel the entire town, but work ended in 1464 when both the pope and his architect, Bernardo Rossellino, died. Their vision—what you see today—was completed a century later. The architectural focal point is the square, Piazza Pio II, surrounded by the Duomo and the pope's family residence, Palazzo Piccolomini. While Piazza Pio II is Pienza's pride and joy, the entire town—a mix of old stonework, potted plants, and grand views—is fun to explore, especially with a camera or sketchpad in hand. You can walk every lane in the tiny town in a few minutes.

Cute as the town is, it's far from undiscovered; tourists can flood Pienza in peak season, and boutiques selling gifty packages of pecorino cheese and local wine greatly outnumber local shops. While it offers fine views of the surrounding countryside, Pienza is situated on a relatively flat plateau rather than the steep pinnacle of more dramatic towns like Montepulciano and Montalcino. For these reasons, it's made to order as a stretch-your-legs break to enjoy the setting, and perhaps tour the palace, but it's not ideal for lingering overnight.

Nearly every shop sells the town's specialty: pecorino cheese. This pungent sheep's cheese is available fresh *(fresco)* or aged *(secco)*, and sometimes contains other ingredients, such as truffles or peppers. Look on menus for warm Pecorino *(al forno* or *alla griglia)*, often topped with honey or pears and served with bread. Along with a glass of local wine, this just might lead you to a new understanding of *la dolce vita*.

Orientation to Pienza

Tourist Information: The TI is 10 yards up the street from Piazza Pio II, inside the Diocesan Museum (Wed-Mon 10:00-13:00 & 14:30-18:00, closed Tue, Sat-Sun only in Nov-March, Corso il Rossellino 30, tel. 0578-749-905). Ignore the kiosk just outside the gate, labeled *Informaturista*, which is a private travel agency.

Arrival in Pienza: Buses drop you just a couple of blocks directly in front of the town's main entrance. If **driving**, read signs carefully—some parking spots are reserved for locals, others require the use of a cardboard clock, and others are pay-and-display. Parking is tight, so if you don't see anything quickly, head for the large lot at Piazza del Mercato near Largo Roma outside the old town: As you approach town and reach the "ZTL" cul-de-sac (marked with a red circle) surrounding the park right in front of the town gate, head up the left side of town and look for the turn-off on the left for parking (€1.50/hour, closed Fri morning during market).

Helpful Hints: Market day is Friday morning at Piazza del Mercato, just outside the town walls. A public **WC,** marked *gabinetti pubblici*, is on the right as you face the town gate from outside, on Piazza Dante Alighieri (down the lane next to the faux TI).

Sights in Pienza

▲Piazza Pio II

One of Italy's classic piazzas, this square is famous for its elegance and artistic unity. The square and the surrounding buildings were

all designed by Rossellino to form an "outdoor room." Spinning around clockwise, you'll see City Hall (13th-century bell tower with a Renaissance facade and a fine loggia), the Bishop's Palace (now the Diocesan Museum), the Duomo, and the Piccolomini family palace. Just to the left of the church, a lane leads to the best viewpoint in town (described later).

Duomo

Its classic, symmetrical Renaissance facade—dated 1462 with the Piccolomini family coat of arms immodestly front and center—dominates Piazza Pio II. The interior is charming, with several Gothic altarpieces and painted arches. Windows feature the crest of Pius II, with five half-moons advertising the number of crusades that his family funded. The interior art is Sienese Gothic, on the cusp of the Renaissance. As the local clay and *tufo* stone did not make an ideal building foundation, the church is slouching. The church's cliff-hanging position bathes the interior in light, but also makes it feel as if the building could break in half if you jumped up and down. See the cracks in the apse walls, and get seasick behind the main altar.

Cost and Hours: Free, generally open daily 7:00-13:00 & 14:30-19:00.

▲Palazzo Piccolomini

The home of Pius II and the Piccolomini family (until 1962) can only be visited on an escorted audioguide tour (about 30 minutes total). You'll see six rooms (dining room, armory, bedroom, library, and so on), three galleries (art-strewn hallways), and the panoramic loggia before being allowed to linger in the beautiful hanging gardens. The drab interiors, faded paintings, coffered ceilings, and scuffed furniture have a mothballed elegance that makes historians wish they'd seen it in its heyday. The audioguide very dryly identifies each item in each room but (sadly) does little to muster enthusiasm for this small-town palace that once hosted a big-name player in European politics. While it's not quite the fascinating slice of 15th-century aristocratic life that it could be (I'd like to know more about the pope's toilet), this is still the best small-town palace experience I've found in Tuscany (it famously starred as the Capulets' home in Franco Zeffirelli's 1968 Academy Award-winning *Romeo and Juliet*). You can peek inside the door for free to check out the well-preserved, painted courtyard. In Renaissance times, most buildings were covered with elaborate paintings like these.

Cost and Hours: €7, Tue-Sun 10:00-13:00 & 14:00-18:30, first tour departs at 10:30, last tour at 18:00, closed Mon, Piazza Pio II 2, tel. 0578-748-392, www.palazzopiccolominipienza.it.

Diocesan Museum (Museo Diocesano)

This measly collection of religious paintings, ecclesiastical gear, altarpieces, and old giant hymnals from local churches fills one room of the cardinal's Renaissance palace. The art is provincial Sienese, displayed in chronological order from the 12th through 17th centuries (but with no English information).

Cost and Hours: €4.50, same hours as TI—which is where you'll buy the ticket, Corso il Rossellino 30.

View Terrace

As you face the church, the upper lane leading left brings you to the panoramic promenade. Views from the terrace include the Tuscan countryside and, in the distance, Monte Amiata, the largest mountain in southern Tuscany. You can exit the viewpoint down the first alley, Via del'Amore—the original Lover's Lane—which leads back to the main drag.

Sleeping near Pienza

While I wouldn't hang my hat in sleepy Pienza itself, some fine countryside options sit just outside town—including one of my favorite Italian *agriturismo* experiences, Cretaiole. Location-wise, this is an ideal home base: midway between Montepulciano and Montalcino, and immersed in Tuscan splendor. Three or four of *the* iconic Tuscan landscape vistas are within 10 or 15 minutes' drive of Pienza; you'll make your sightseeing commute along extremely scenic roads with plenty of strategically located pullouts.

$$$ Agriturismo Cretaiole, in pristine farmland just outside Pienza, is a terrific value if you want to call Tuscany home for a long stay. It's warmly run by reformed city-slicker Isabella, her country-boy husband Carlo, and their family. This family-friendly farm welcomes visitors for weeklong stays (generally Sat-Sat) in six comfortable apartments. Eager

to share their local traditions, they offer travelers a rich cultural education. Carlo is a professional olive-oil taster. Carlo's father, Luciano, is in charge of the grappa and tends the vegetable garden (take your pick of the free veggies). And Isabella is a tireless Jill-of-all-trades, who prides herself on personally assisting each of her guests to find exactly the Tuscan experience they're dreaming of. While there's no swimming pool—for philosophical reasons—many thoughtful touches and extras, such as Wi-Fi, mountain bikes, and loaner mobile phones, are provided. Isabella also organizes fairly priced optional activities such as pasta-making and olive-oil tasting classes, family-style Tuscan dinners, winery tours, truffle hunts and grape and olive harvesting (in season), visits to the studios of local artisans, side-trips to Siena, watercolor classes, dinner at a local monastery, and more (Db-€825/week, small Db apartment-€990/week, large Db apartment-€1,290/week, same apartment for four-€1,595/week, these prices promised with this book in 2014, fewer activities and lower prices mid-Nov-mid-March, tel. 0578-748-083, Isabella's mobile 338-740-9245, www. cretaiole.it, info@cretaiole.it). It's on the Montalcino-Pienza road (S-146), about 11 miles out of Montalcino, and about 2.5 miles from Pienza. While they prefer weeklong stays, when things are slow they may accept guests for as few as three nights (for this you must book less than a month in advance, Db-€120, 3-night minimum). The same family runs two other properties, with the same activities and personal attention as the main *agriturismo:* **Le Casine di Castello** is a townhouse with two units and the same prices as Cretaiole, but guests have more independence. The more upscale **Casa Moricciani** is a swanky villa featuring dreamy views, plush interiors, loads of extras, and pure Tuscan luxury (€2,900/week upstairs or €3,900/week downstairs, each with 2 bedrooms and 2 bathrooms). Both properties are in the untouristy medieval village of Castelmuzio, five miles north of Pienza; for details, see www.buongiornotoscana.com.

$$$ Fonte Bertusi, nearly across the road from Cretaiole, is well-run by young couple Manuela and Andrea, Andrea's father Eduardo, and their attention-starved cats. This imaginative family has scattered vivid, whimsical bits and pieces of artwork around the grounds and in the rooms. The eight apartments are simple—mixing rustic decor with avant-garde creations—and a bit pricey, but the setting is sublime (nightly rate: 1-bedroom apartment-€130, 2-bedroom apartment-€260, includes breakfast; weekly rate: €710-1,010, €40 extra per person for breakfast all week; free Wi-Fi, laundry service, swimming pool, communal BBQ and outdoor kitchen, just outside Pienza toward San Quirico d'Orcia on the right—don't confuse it with the turnoff for "Il Fonte" just before, tel. 0578-748-077, www.fontebertusi.it, info@fontebertusi.it).

Pienza Connections

Bus tickets are sold at the bar/café (marked *Il Caffè*, closed Tue) just outside Pienza's town gate (or pay a little extra and buy tickets from the driver). Buses leave from a few blocks up the street, directly in front of the town entrance. Montepulciano is the nearest transportation hub to other points.

From Pienza by Bus to: Siena (6/day, none on Sun, 1.5 hours, €4.40), **Montepulciano** (8/day, 30 minutes, €2.50), **Montalcino** (4/day Mon-Fri, 3/day Sat, none sun, change in Torrenieri, 45-60 minutes total, €3.40).

Montalcino

On a hill overlooking vineyards and valleys, Montalcino—famous for its delicious and pricey Brunello di Montalcino red wines—is a must for wine lovers. It's a pleasant, low-impact town with a fine ambience but little sightseeing. Everyone touring this area seems to be relaxed and in an easy groove...as if enjoying a little wine buzz.

In the Middle Ages, Montalcino (mohntahl-CHEE-noh) was considered Siena's biggest ally. Originally aligned with Florence, the town switched sides after the Sienese beat up Florence in the Battle of Montaperti in 1260. The Sienese persuaded the Montalcini to join their side by forcing them to sleep one night in the bloody Florentine-strewn battlefield.

Montalcino prospered under Siena, but like its ally, it waned after the Medici family took control of the region. The village became a humble place. Then, in the late 19th century, the Biondi Santi family created a fine, dark red wine, calling it "the brunette" (Brunello). Today's affluence is due to the town's much-sought-after wine.

If you're not a wine lover, you may find Montalcino a bit too focused on *vino,* but one sip of Brunello makes even wine skeptics believe that Bacchus was onto something. Note that Rosso di Montalcino (a younger version of Brunello) is also very good, at half the price. Those with a sweet tooth will enjoy crunching the Ossi di Morta ("bones of the dead") cookies popular in Tuscany.

Orientation to Montalcino

Sitting atop a hill amidst a sea of vineyards, Montalcino is surrounded by walls and dominated by the Fortezza (a.k.a. "La Rocca"). From here, roads lead down into the two main squares: Piazza Garibaldi and Piazza del Popolo.

Tourist Information: The helpful TI, just off Piazza Garibaldi in City Hall, can find you a room for no fee. They sell bus tickets; can call ahead to book a visit at a countryside winery (€1-per-person service fee); and have information on taxi service to nearby towns, abbeys, and monasteries (daily 10:00-13:00 & 14:00-17:30, tel. 0577-849-331, www.prolocomontalcino.com).

Arrival in Montalcino: The **bus** station is on Piazza Cavour, about 300 yards from the town center. From here, simply follow Via Mazzini straight into town.

Drivers coming in for a short visit should drive around the old gate under the fortress, take the first right (follow signs to *Fortezza;* it looks almost forbidden), and grab a spot in the pay lot at the fortress (€1.50/hour, free 20:00-8:00). If you miss this lot—or if it's full—follow the town's western wall toward the Madonna del Socorrso church and a long pay lot with the same prices. Otherwise, park for free a short walk away.

Helpful Hints: Market day is Friday (7:00-13:00) on Viale della Libertà (near the Fortezza). Day-trippers be warned: Montalcino has **no baggage storage.**

HILL TOWNS

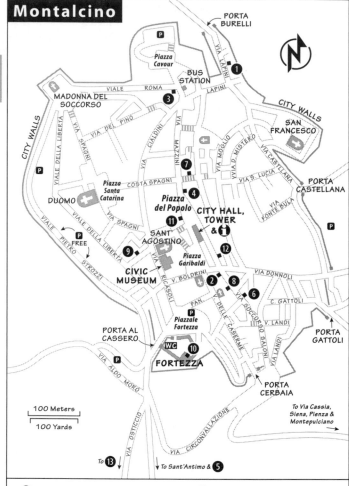

Montalcino

1 Hotel Dei Capitani
2 Palazzina Cesira
3 Albergo Giardino
4 Affittacamere Mariuccia
5 To La Crociona Agriturismo
6 Re di Macchia Ristorante
7 Taverna il Grappolo Blu
8 Ristorante-Pizzeria San Giorgio
9 Co-op Supermarket
10 Enoteca la Fortezza di Montalcino
11 Caffè Fiaschetteria Italiana
12 Enoteca di Piazza
13 To Banfi & Argiano Wineries

Sights in Montalcino

Fortezza

This 14th-century fort, built under the rule of Siena, is now little more than an empty shell. People visit for its wine bar. You can climb the ramparts to enjoy a panoramic view of the Asso and Orcia valleys, or enjoy a picnic in the park surrounding the fort.

Cost and Hours: €4 for rampart walk—buy ticket and enter in the wine bar, €6 combo-ticket includes Civic Museum (sold only at museum), daily 9:00-20:00, until 18:00 Nov-March, last entry 30 minutes before closing.

Piazza del Popolo

All roads in tiny Montalcino seem to lead to the main square, Piazza del Popolo ("People's Square").

Since 1888, the recommended **Caffè Fiaschetteria Italiana** has been *the* elegant place to enjoy a drink. Its founder, inspired by Caffè Florian in Venice, brought fine coffee to this humble town of woodcutters.

City Hall was the fortified seat of government. It's decorated by the coats of arms of judges who, in the interest of fairness, were from outside of town. Like Siena, Montalcino was a republic in the Middle Ages. When Florentines took Siena in 1555, Siena's ruling class retreated here and held out for four more years. The Medici coat of arms (with the six pills), which supersedes all the others, is a reminder that in 1559 Florence finally took Montalcino.

The one-handed **clock** was the norm until 200 years ago. For five centuries the arcaded **loggia** hosted the town market. And, of course, it's fun to simply observe the *passeggiata*—these days mostly a parade of tourists here for the wine.

Montalcino Museums (Musei di Montalcino)

While it's technically three museums in one (archaeology, medieval art, and modern art), and it's surprisingly big and modern for this little town, Montalcino's lone museum ranks only as a decent bad-weather activity. The archaeology collection, filling the cellar, includes interesting artifacts from the area dating back as far as—gulp—200,000 B.C. With good English explanations, this section also displays a mannequin dressed as an Etruscan soldier and a model of the city walls in early Roman times. The ground, first, and second floors hold the medieval and modern art collections, with an emphasis on Gothic sacred art (with works from Montalcino's heyday, the 13th to 16th centuries). Most of the art was created by local artists. The ground floor is best, with a large collection of crucifixes and the museum's highlights, a glazed-terra-cotta altarpiece and statue of St. Sebastian, both by Andrea della Robbia.

Cost and Hours: €4.50, €6 combo-ticket includes rampart

walk at Fortezza, Tue-Sun 10:00-13:00 & 14:00-17:50, closed Mon, Via Ricasoli 31, to the right of Sant'Agostino Church, tel. 0577-846-014.

Sleeping in Montalcino

$$$ Hotel Dei Capitani, at the end of town near the bus station, has plush public spaces, an inviting pool, and a cliffside terrace offering plenty of reasons for lounging. About half of the 29 rooms come with vast Tuscan views for the same price (request a view room when you reserve), the nonview rooms are bigger, and everyone has access to the terrace (Db-€138 with this book in 2014, extra bed-€40, air-con, elevator, free guest computer and Wi-Fi, limited free parking—first come, first served, Via Lapini 6, tel. 0577-847-227, www.deicapitani.it, info@deicapitani.it).

$$ Palazzina Cesira, right in the heart of the old town, is a gem renting five spacious and tastefully decorated rooms in a fine 13th-century residence with a palatial lounge and a pleasant garden. You'll enjoy a refined and tranquil ambience, a nice breakfast (with eggs), and the chance to get to know Lucilla and her American husband Roberto, who are generous with local advice (Db-€105, suites-€125, cash only, 2-night minimum, 3-night minimum on holiday weekends, air-con, free guest computer and Wi-Fi, free off-street parking, Via Soccorso Saloni 2, tel. 0577-846-055, www.montalcinoitaly.com, p.cesira@tin.it).

$ Affittacamere Mariuccia has three small, colorful, good-value, Ikea-chic rooms on the main drag over a heaven-scented bakery (Sb-€40, Db-€50, air-con, breakfast-€10 extra, check in across the street at Enoteca Pierangioli before 20:00 or let them know arrival time, Piazza del Popolo 16, rooms at #28, tel. 0577-849-113, mobile 348-392-4780, www.affittacameremariuccia.it, enotecapierangioli@hotmail.com, Alessandro and Stefania speak English).

$ Albergo Giardino, old and basic, has nine big simple rooms, no public spaces, and a convenient location near the bus station (Db-€55-60, 10 percent discount with this book outside May and Sept, no breakfast, Piazza Cavour 4, tel. 0577-848-257, mobile 338-684-3163, albergoilgiardino@virgilio.it; Roberto speaks English; dad Mario doesn't).

Near Montalcino

$$ La Crociona, an *agriturismo* farm and working vineyard, rents seven fully equipped apartments. Fiorella Vannoni and Roberto and Barbara Nannetti offer cooking classes and tastes of the Brunello wine grown and bottled on the premises (Db-€95, or €65 in Oct-mid-May; Qb-€130, or €95 in Oct-mid-May; lower weekly rates, metered gas heating, laundry-€8/load, covered pool, hot tub, fitness room, La Croce 15, tel. 0577-847-133 or 0577-848-007, www.lacrociona.com, info@lacrociona.com). The farm is two miles south of Montalcino on the road to the Sant'Antimo Monastery; don't turn off at the first entrance to the village of La Croce—wait for the second one, following directions to Tenuta Crocedimezzo e Crociona). A good restaurant is next door.

Eating in Montalcino

Restaurants

Re di Macchia is an invitingly intimate restaurant where Antonio serves up the Tuscan fare Roberta cooks. Look for their seasonal menu and Montalcino-only wine list. Try the €25 fixed-price meal, and for €17 more, have it paired with local wines carefully selected to accompany each dish (€9-10 pastas, €16 *secondi*, Fri-Wed 12:00-14:00 & 19:00-21:00, closed Thu, reservations strongly recommended, Via Soccorso Saloni 21, tel. 0577-846-116).

Taverna il Grappolo Blu is unpretentious, friendly, and serious about its wine, serving local specialties and vegetarian options to an enthusiastic crowd (€8-9 pastas, €9-14 *secondi*, daily 12:00-15:00 & 19:00-22:00, reservations smart, near the main square, a few steps off Via Mazzini at Scale di Via Moglio 1, tel. 0577-847-150, Luciano, www.grappoloblu.it).

Ristorante-Pizzeria San Giorgio is a homey trattoria/pizzeria with kitschy decor and reasonable prices. It's a reliable choice for a simple meal (€4-7 pizzas, €8 pastas, €8-12 *secondi*, daily 12:00-15:00 & 19:00-22:30, Via Soccorso Saloni 10-14, tel. 0577-848-507, Mara).

Picnic: Gather ingredients at the **Co-op supermarket** on Via Sant'Agostino (Mon-Sat 8:30-13:00 & 16:00-20:00, closed Sun, just off Via Ricasoli in front of Sant'Agostino Church), then enjoy your feast up at the Madonna del Soccorso Church, with vast territorial views.

Wine Bars: Note that two of the places listed under "Wine Bars *(Enoteche)* in Town," later, also serve light food.

Wine Tasting and Wineries

There are two basic approaches for sampling Montalcino's wines: at an *enoteca* in town, or at a countryside winery. Serious wine connoisseurs will enjoy a day of winery-hopping, sipping the wines right where they were created. But if you don't have the time, or want to try more than one producer's wines, you might prefer to simply visit a wine bar in town, where you can comfortably taste a variety of vintages before safely stumbling back to your hotel.

Wine Bars *(Enoteche)* in Town

Enoteca la Fortezza di Montalcino offers a chance to taste top-end wines by the glass, each with an English explanation. While wine snobs turn up their noses, the medieval setting inside Montalcino's fort is a hit for most visitors. Spoil yourself with Brunello in the cozy *enoteca* or at an outdoor table (€13 for 3 tastings, or €22 for 3 "top-end" tastings; €10-18 two-person sampler plates of cheeses, *salumi*, honeys, and olive oil; daily 9:00-20:00, closes at 18:00 Nov-March, inside the Fortezza, tel. 0577-849-211, www.enotecalafortezza.com, info@enotecalafortezza.com).

Caffè Fiaschetteria Italiana, a classic, venerable café/wine bar, was founded by Ferruccio Biondi Santi, the creator of the famous Brunello wine. The wine library in the back of the café boasts many local choices. A meeting place since 1888, this grand café also serves light lunches and espresso to tourists and locals alike (€6-12 Brunellos by the glass, €3-5 light snacks, €8-12 plates; same prices inside, outside, or in back room; daily 7:30-23:00, closed Thu Nov-Easter, free Wi-Fi, Piazza del Popolo 6, tel. 0577-849-043). And if it's coffee you need, this place—with its classic 1961 espresso machine—is considered the best in town.

Enoteca di Piazza is one of a chain of wine shops with a system of mechanical dispensers. A "drink card" (like a debit card) keeps track of the samples you take, for which you'll pay from €1 to €9 for each 50-milliliter taste of the 100 different wines, including some whites—rare in this town. The only nibbles are saltine-type crackers. They hope you'll buy a bottle of the samples you like and are happy to educate you in English. (Rule of thumb: A bottle costs about 10 times the cost of the sample. If you buy a bottle, the sample of that wine is free.) While the place feels a little formulaic, it can be fun—the wine is great, and the staff is casual and helpful (daily 9:00-20:00, near Piazza del Popolo at Via Matteotti 43, tel. 0577-848-104, www.enotecadipiazza.com). Confusingly, there are three similarly named places in this same area—this tasting room is a block below the main square.

Wineries in the Countryside

The surrounding countryside is littered with wineries, some of which offer tastings. A few require an appointment, but many are happy to serve a glass to potential buyers and show them around. The Montalcino TI can give you a list of more than 150 regional wineries and will call ahead for you (€1 fee per person). Or check with the vintners' consortium (tel. 0577-848-246, www.consorziobrunellodimontalcino.it, info@consorziobrunellodimontalcino.it). These two places listed below are big and capable of handling a steady flow of international visitors; they don't offer an "authentic" Tuscan or cozy experience, but they are convenient and user-friendly.

Argiano claims to be one of the oldest working wineries in the region, dating back to 1580. About a 10-minute drive south of Montalcino at Sant'Angelo in Colle, their one-hour tour in English includes the vineyards, the exterior of a historic villa, and ancient moldy cellars full of wine casks. They also rent on-site apartments—handy for those who have oversampled (€20 tour includes 6 wine samples, reserve in advance, tel. 0577-844-037, www.argiano.net, coming by car the last 2 miles are along a rough-but-drivable track through vineyards).

Banfi, run by the Italian-American Mariani brothers, is huge and touristy. While it's not an intimate family winery, the grounds are impressive and they're well set up to introduce the passing hordes to their wines (€15 for 3 tastings, €3.50-25 per glass, daily 10:00-19:00, free tours Mon-Fri at 16:00—reserve in advance, 10-minute drive south of Montalcino in Sant'Angelo Scalo, tel. 0577-877-500, www.castellobanfi.com, reservations@banfi.it).

Bus Tour: If you lack a car (or don't want to drive), you can take a tour on the **Brunello Wine Bus,** which laces together a variety of wineries (€25, mid-June-Oct Tue, Thu, and Sat, departs at 9:00, returns at 20:00, tel. 0577-846-021, www.lecameredibacco.com, info@lecameredibacco.com).

Montalcino Connections

Montalcino is poorly connected to just about everywhere except Siena— making it a good day trip if Siena is your base—but other connections are generally workable. Montalcino's bus station is on Piazza Cavour, within the town walls. Bus tickets are sold at the bar on Piazza Cavour, at the TI, and at some tobacco shops, but not on board (except for the bus to Sant'Antimo). Check schedules at the TI, at the bus station, or at www.sienamobilita.it. The nearest train station is a 20-minute bus ride away, in Buonconvento (bus runs nearly hourly, €2.05).

From Montalcino by Bus: The handiest direct bus is to **Siena** (6/day Mon-Sat, 4/day Sun, 1.5 hours, €4.90). To reach **Pienza** or **Montepulciano,** ride the bus to Torrenieri (5/day Mon-Sat, none on Sun, 20 minutes), where you'll switch to line #114 for the rest of the way (from Torrenieri: 25 minutes and €3.40 total to Pienza; 45 minutes and €4.90 total to Montepulciano). A local bus runs to **Sant'Antimo** (3/day Mon-Fri, 2/day Sat, none on Sun, 15 minutes, €1.50, buy tickets on board). Anyone going to **Florence** by bus changes in Siena; since the bus arrives at Siena's train station, it's handier to go the rest of the way to Florence by train. Alternatively, you could take the bus to Buonconvento (described earlier), and catch the train there to Florence.

The Crete Senese

Between Siena and the trio of towns I've described (Montepulciano, Pienza, Montalcino), the hilly area known as the "Sienese Clay Hills" is full of colorful fields and curvy, scenic roads. The Crete Senese (KRAY-teh seh-NAY-zeh) begins at Siena's doorstep and tumbles south through some of the most eye-pleasing scenery in Italy. You'll see an endless parade of classic Tuscan scenes, rolling hills topped with medieval towns, olive groves, rustic stone farmhouses, and a skyline punctuated with cypress trees. You won't find many wineries here, since the clay soil is better for wheat and sunflowers, but you will find the pristine, panoramic Tuscan countryside featured on countless calendars and postcards.

During the spring, the fields are painted in yellow and green with fava beans and broom, dotted by red poppies on the fringes. Sunflowers decorate the area during June and July, and expanses of windblown grass fill the landscape for much of the early spring and summer.

Most roads to the southeast of Siena will give you a taste of this area, but one of the most scenic stretches is the Lauretana road (Siena-Asciano-San Giovanni d'Asso, S-438, S-451, and SP-60a on road maps; the numbering changes as you drive, but it feels like the same road). To find the Lauretana road from Siena, follow signs for the A-1 expressway; you'll turn off onto S-438 (look for the sign for *Asciano*) well before you reach the expressway. You'll come across plenty of turnouts for panoramic photo opportunities on this road, as well as a few roadside picnic areas and several good accommodations (see "Sleeping in the Crete Senese," later).

For a break from the winding road, about 15 miles from Siena, you'll find the quaint and non-touristy village of **Asciano.** With a medieval town center and several interesting churches and museums, this town offers a rare look at everyday Tuscan living—and it's a great place for lunch (TI open Tue-Sun 10:30-13:00 & 15:00-18:00, Mon 10:00-13:00, at Corso Matteotti 18, tel. 0577-718-811). If you're in town on Saturday, gather a picnic at the outdoor market (Via Amendola, 8:00-13:00).

A bit farther along, in **Chiusure** (about 6 miles south of Asciano, on S-451), follow signs up a steep driveway to the *casa di reposo* (nursing home) for a fine viewpoint over the Crete Senese, including classic views of jagged *calanchi* cliffs. From that hilltop,

The Beauty of Tuscany's Geology (and Vice Versa)

While North Americans have romanticized notions of the "Tuscan" landscape, there's a surprisingly wide variety of land forms in the region. Never having been crushed by a glacier, Tuscany is anything but flat. The hills and mountains scattered around the area are made up of different substances, each of which is ideal for very different types of cultivation.

The Chianti region (between Florence and Siena) is rough and rocky, with an inhospitable soil that challenges grape vines to survive while coaxing them to produce excellent wine grapes.

Farther south, the soil switches from rock to clay, silt, and sand. The region called the Crete Senese is literally translated as the "Sienese Clay Hills"—a perfect description of the landscape. Seen from a breezy viewpoint, it's easy to imagine that these clay hills were once at the bottom of the sea floor. The soil here is the yin to Chianti's yang: not ideal for wine, but perfect for truffles and for vast fields of cereal crops such as wheat, fava beans, and sun-yellow rapeseed (for canola oil). In the spring and summer, the Crete Senese is blanketed with brightly colorful crops and flowers. But by the fall, after the harvest, it's a brown and dusty desolate wasteland punctuated with pointy cypress trees—still picturesque, but in a surface-of-the-moon way. Within the Crete Senese, you can distinguish two types of hills shaped by erosion: smooth, rounded *biancane* and pointy, jagged *calanchi*.

The area around Montepulciano and Montalcino is more varied, with rocky protuberances breaking up the undulating clay hills (and providing a suitable home for wine grapes). Even farther south is the Val d'Orcia, the valley of the Orcia River, with its own beauty that mixes clay hills and jutting rock.

You'll see many hot springs in this part of Tuscany, as well as town names with the word *Terme* (for "spa" or "hot spring"). These generally occur where clay meets rock: Water moving through the clay encounters a barrier and gets trapped. Aside from hot water, another byproduct of this change in landscapes is travertine, explaining the quarries you may see in or near spa towns.

you can also see the **Abbey of Monte Oliveto Maggiore.** Located 1.5 miles west of Chiursure, the abbey houses a famous fresco cycle of the life of St. Benedict, painted by Renaissance masters Il Sodoma and Luca Signorelli (free, daily 9:15-12:00 & 15:15-18:00, Nov-March until 17:00, Gregorian chanting Sat-Sun at 18:30, Sun also at 11:00, Mon-Fri at 18:15, call to confirm, tel. 0577-707-611, www.monteolivetomaggiore.it).

Once you reach the town of **San Giovanni d'Asso**—in the

heart of the truffle region—it's a short drive southwest to Montalcino, or southeast to Pienza (each about 12 miles away).

Another scenic drive is the lovely stretch between Montalcino and Montepulciano. This route (S-146 on road maps) alternates between the grassy hills of the Crete Senese and sunbathed vineyards of the Orcia River valley. Stop by Pienza en route.

Sleeping in the Crete Senese

If pastoral landscapes and easy access to varied towns are your goals, you can't do much better than sleeping in the Crete Senese. These countryside options sit between Siena, Montepulciano, Pienza, and Montalcino (a 15- to 45-minute drive from any of them). These options line up on (or just off) the scenic roads (S-438 and S-451) south of Siena; I've listed them from north to south.

$$$ Recommended local guide **Roberto Bechi** has designed and built a new house from scratch that's immersed in gorgeous Crete Sense scenery (about 15 minutes south of Siena). With five spacious rooms, the house is entirely "green," with a zero-carbon footprint (Db-€100, mobile 328-425-5648, www.toursbyroberto. com, toursbyroberto@gmail.com). It's just off road S-438; take the turnoff for Fontanelle.

$ **Casanova Agriturismo** is for people who *really* want to stay on an authentic, working farm. This rustic place comes with tractors, plenty of farm smells and noises, and a barn full of priceless Chianina cows. If the five simple rooms and one apartment take a back seat to the farm workings, the lodgings are accordingly inexpensive, and you'll appreciate the results of their hard work when you dig into one of their fine farm-fresh dinners (€20/person). German Wiebke (who speaks great English and runs the accommodations), her Tuscan husband Bartolo (who works the fields), his mama Paola (who cooks), and the rest of the Conte clan make this a true *agriturismo* experience (Db-€60, apartment-€80 for 2 and €10 per additional person up to 4, breakfast-€8, free Wi-Fi in some areas, swimming pool, just outside Asciano on road S-451 toward Chiusure, tel. 0577-718-324, mobile 346-792-0859, www. agriturismo-casanova.it, info@agriturismo-casanova.it).

$$ **Agriturismo il Molinello** ("Little Mill") rents six apartments, two built over a medieval mill, on the grounds of a working farm with organic produce, olives, and a truffle ground. Hardworking Alessandro and Elisa share their organic produce and offer weekly wine and olive-oil tastings for a minimum of four people; they also lead cooking classes on request. From May through October, they give free guided tours of Siena on Tuesday afternoons. More rustic than romantic, and lacking the dramatic views of some places, this is a nice mix of farm and style. With children, friendly dogs, toys, and a swimming pool, it's ideal for families (Db-€50-80, Qb-€70-100, apartment for up to 8-€160-200 depending on season and number of people, optional organic breakfast-€9.50, one-week stay required in July-Aug, discounts and no minimum stay off-season, free Wi-Fi in public areas, mountain-bike rentals, biking maps and guided bike tours, between Asciano and the village of Serre di Rapolano—on the road toward Rapolano, 30 minutes southeast of Siena, tel. 0577-704-791, mobile 335-692-5720, www.molinello.com, info@molinello.com).

Cortona

Cortona blankets a 1,700-foot hill surrounded by dramatic Tuscan and Umbrian views. Frances Mayes' book *Under the Tuscan Sun*

placed this town in the touristic limelight, just as Peter Mayle's books popularized the Luberon region in France. But long before Mayes ever published a book, Cortona was popular with Romantics and considered one of the classic Tuscan hill towns. Although it's unquestionably touristy, unlike San Gimignano, Cortona maintains a rustic and gritty personality—even with its long history of foreigners who, enamored with its Tuscan charm, made this their adopted home.

The city began as one of the largest Etruscan settlements, the remains of which can be seen at the base of the city walls, as well as in the nearby tombs. It grew to its present size in the 13th to 16th centuries, when it was a colorful and crowded city, eventually allied with Florence. The farmland that fills almost every view from the city was marshy and uninhabitable until about 200 years ago, when it was drained and turned into some of Tuscany's most fertile land.

Art lovers know Cortona as the home of Renaissance painter Luca Signorelli, Baroque master Pietro da Cortona (Berretini), and the 20th-century Futurist artist Gino Severini. The city's museums and churches reveal many of the works of these native sons.

Orientation to Cortona

Most of the main sights, shops, and restaurants cluster around the level streets on the Piazza Garibaldi-Piazza del Duomo axis, but Cortona will have you huffing and puffing up some steep hills. From Piazza Garibaldi, it's a level five-minute walk down bustling shop-lined Via Nazionale to Piazza della Repubblica, the heart of the town, which is dominated by City Hall (Palazzo del Comune). From this square, a two-minute stroll leads you past the TI, the interesting Etruscan Museum, and the theater to Piazza del Duomo, where you'll find the recommended Diocesan Museum. These sights are along the more-or-less level spine that runs through the bottom of town; from here, Cortona sprawls upward. Steep streets, many of them stepped, go from Piazza della Repubblica up to the San Niccolò and Santa Margherita churches and the Medici Fortress (a 30-minute climb from Piazza della Repubblica). In this residential area, you'll see fewer tourists and get a better sense of the "real" Cortona.

In the flat valley below Cortona sprawls the modern, workaday town of Camucia (kah-moo-CHEE-ah), with the train station and other services (such as launderettes) that you won't find in the hill town itself.

Tourist Information

To reach the helpful TI, head to Piazza Signorelli, then walk through the courtyard of the Etruscan Museum and up a short flight of steps, at the back (mid-May-Oct Mon-Sat 9:00-13:00 & 15:00-18:00, Sun 9:00-13:00, Nov-mid-May Mon-Fri 9:00-13:00 & 15:00-18:00, Sat 9:00-13:00, closed Sun, tel. 0575-637-223 or 0575-637-276, www.turismo.provincia.arezzo.it).

Arrival in Cortona

Cortona is challenging but doable by public transportation. There are few intercity buses, so your best bet for reaching the town is by train or by car.

By Train: Trains arrive at the unstaffed Camucia station, in the valley four miles below Cortona. Sporadic local buses connect the train station and Piazza Garibaldi in Cortona in about 10 minutes. (If you choose to walk, it's a long, steep climb, and there are no sidewalks.) From the station, walk out the front door and look left to find the bus shelter (with schedules posted). Unfortunately, buses depart only about once per hour—and only twice daily on Sundays—and the schedule is not well-coordinated with train times (purchase €1.60 from driver; you want a bus marked for Cortona rather than the opposite direction, Terontola). On the schedule, departures marked with S do not run during school vacations; those marked with N run only during school vacations. Buses usually drop off at Piazza Garibaldi, but may stop instead at Piazza del Mercato (just outside the city walls near Porta Santa Maria), requiring a 10-minute uphill walk to Piazza Signorelli (for the TI and the Etruscan Museum).

If you'd rather not wait, consider taking a taxi into town (€10,

call for Dejan and his seven-seater cab, mobile 348-402-3501—
Dejan also arranges day trips, see "Local Guides," later; or you can
ask your hotel to arrange a taxi).

By Car: You'll find several lots ringing the walls; some are free
(white lines), others require payment (blue lines), and still others
are for local residents only (yellow lines), so check signs carefully.
Your best bet is the large, free lot on Viale Cesare Battisti, just after
the big Santo Spirito Church. From here, a series of stairs and escalators take you steeply up to Piazza Garibaldi. Piazza Garibaldi
itself may have a handful of pay spots available (marked by blue
lines, pay & display, free 20:00-8:00). The small town is actually
very long, and it can be smart to drive to the top for sightseeing up
there (free parking at Santa Margherita Basilica).

Helpful Hints

Market Day: The market is on Saturday on Piazza Signorelli (from
early morning until 14:00).

Services: The town has **no baggage storage,** so try asking nicely at
a hotel to leave your bag there. The best public **WC** is located
in Piazza del Duomo, under Santa Margherita's statue.

Tuscan Cooking School: Husband-and-wife team **Romano and
Agostina** hold morning hands-on cooking and cheesemak-
ing classes, as well as wine-, cheese-, and oil-tasting courses,
six mornings a week in the converted cellar of a 16th-century
monastery, just behind their recommended Ristorante La Bucaccia (closed Mon). In the five-hour class, you'll prepare two
antipasti, two types of pasta, an entrée, and a dessert, which
you then get to eat (roughly €90/person, price includes wine,
5 percent discount if you show this book, classes start at 9:30).
A three-hour version starts at 11:00 (€70/person; try to book
at least a month in advance, evening and personalized classes
available). They also offer Italian snack tastings with Romano's
homemade cheeses and cold meats (17:00-23:00, €15—includes a free glass of wine with this book; Via Ghibellina 17,
tel. 0575-606-039, www.labucaccia.it, info@labucaccia.it).

Local Guides: Giovanni Adreani exudes energy and a love of his
city and Tuscan high culture. He is great at bringing the fine
points of the city to life and can take visitors around in his car
for no extra charge. As this region is speckled with underap-
preciated charms, having Giovanni for a day as your driver/
guide promises to be a fascinating experience (€110/half-day,
€200/day, tel. 0575-630-665, mobile 347-176-2830, www.
adreanigiovanni.com, adreanigiovanni@libero.it). Reliable,
English-speaking taxi driver **Dejan** (DAY-zhan) **Prvulovic**
can also take you on full-day tours to Pienza, Montalcino,
Siena, Assisi, and Chianti—email him and devise your own

itinerary (€250/day depending on number of passengers, mobile 348-402-3501, dejanprvi70@yahoo.it).

Self-Guided Walk

Welcome to Cortona

This introductory walking tour will take you from Piazza Garibaldi and up the main strip to the town center, its piazzas, and the Duomo.

• *Start at the bus stop in...*

Piazza Garibaldi: Many visits start and finish in this square, thanks to its bus stop. While the piazza, bulging out from the town fortifications like a big turret, looks like part of an old rampart, it's really a souvenir of those early French and English Romantics—the ones who first created the notion of a dreamy, idyllic Tuscany. During the Napoleonic Age, the French built this balcony (and the scenic little park behind the adjacent San Domenico Church) simply to enjoy a commanding view of the Tuscan countryside.

With Umbria about a mile away, Cortona marks the end of Tuscany. This is a major cultural divide, as Cortona was the last town in Charlemagne's empire and the last under Medici rule. Umbria, just to the south, was papal territory for centuries. These deep-seated cultural disparities were a great challenge for the visionaries who unified the fractured region to create the modern nation of Italy during the 1860s. An obelisk in the center of this square honors one of the heroes of the struggle for Italian unification—the brilliant revolutionary general, Giuseppe Garibaldi.

Enjoy the commanding view from here. Assisi is just over the ridge on the left. Lake Trasimeno peeks from behind the hill, looking quite normal today. But, according to legend, it was blood-red after Hannibal defeated the Romans here in 217 B.C., when 15,000 died in the battle. The only sizable town you can see, on the right, is

Montepulciano. Cortona is still defined by its Etruscan walls—remnants of these walls, with stones laid 2,500 years ago, stretch from here in both directions.

Frances Mayes put Cortona on the map for many Americans with her book (and later movie) *Under the Tuscan Sun.* The book describes her real-life experience buying, fixing up, and living in a run-down villa in Cortona with her husband, Ed. The movie romanticized the story, turning Frances into a single, recently divorced writer who restores the villa and her peace of mind. Mayes' villa isn't "under the Tuscan sun" very often; it's named "Bramasole"—literally, "craving sun." On the wrong side of the hill, it's in the shade after 15:00. She and her husband still live there part of each year and are respected members of their adopted community (outside the walls, behind the hill on the left—a 20-minute walk away; ask at the TI for directions if you'd like to see it up close).

• *From this square, head into town along...*

Via Nazionale: The only level road in town, locals have nicknamed Via Nazionale the *ruga piana* (flat wrinkle). This is the main commercial street in this town of 2,500, and it's been that way for a long time. Every shop seems to have a medieval cellar or an Etruscan well. Notice the crumbling sandstone door frames. The entire town is constructed from this grainy, eroding rock.

• *Via Nazionale leads to...*

Piazza della Repubblica: City Hall faces Cortona's main square. Note how City Hall is a clever hodgepodge of twin medieval towers, with a bell tower added to connect them, and a grand staircase to lend some gravitas. Notice also the fine wood balconies on the left. In the Middle Ages, wooden extensions like these were common features on the region's stone buildings. These balconies (not original, but rebuilt in the 19th century) would have fit right into the medieval cityscape. These days, you usually see only the holes that once supported the long-gone wooden beams.

This spot has been the town center since Etruscan times. Four centuries before Christ, an important street led from here up to the hill-capping temple. Later, the square became the Roman forum. Opposite City Hall is the handy, recommended Despar Market Molesini, good for cheap sandwiches. Above that is the loggia—once a fish market, now the recommended Ristorante La Loggetta.

• *The second half of the square, to the right of City Hall, is...*

Piazza Signorelli: Dominated by Casali Palace, this square was the headquarters of the Florentine captains who used to control the city. Peek into the palace entrance (under the MAEC sign) for a look at the coats of arms. Every six months, Florence would send a new captain to Cortona, who would help establish his rule by inserting his family coat of arms into the palace's wall. These date from the 15th to the 17th century, and were once painted with bright colors. Cortona's fine Etruscan Museum (described later, under "Sights in Cortona") is in the Casali Palace courtyard, which is lined with many more of these family coats of arms. The inviting Caffè del Teatro fills the loggia of the theater that is named for the town's most famous artist, Luca Signorelli.

• *Head down the street, just to the right of the museum, to...*

Piazza del Duomo: Here you'll find the Diocesan Museum (listed later, under "Sights in Cortona"), cathedral, and (closer to the top of the square) a statue of Santa Margherita. The cathedral's

facade, though recently renovated, still seems a little underwhelming and tucked away. Cortona so loves its hometown saint, Margherita, that it put the energy it would otherwise have invested in its cathedral into the Santa Margherita Basilica, at the top of the hill (at the other end of town—not visible from here). Margherita was a 13th-century rich girl who took good care of the poor and was an early follower of St. Francis and St. Clare. Many locals believe that Margherita protected Cortona from WWII bombs.

The Piazza del Duomo terrace comes with a commanding view of the Tuscan countryside. Notice the town cemetery in the foreground. If you were standing here before the time of Napoleon, you'd be surrounded by tombstones. But Cortona's graveyards—like other urban graveyards throughout Napoleon's realm—were cleaned out in the early 1800s to reclaim land and improve hygiene.

• *Next, enter the...*

Duomo: The Cortona cathedral is not, strictly speaking, a cathedral, because it no longer has a bishop. The white-and-gray Florentine Renaissance-style interior is mucked up with lots of Ba-

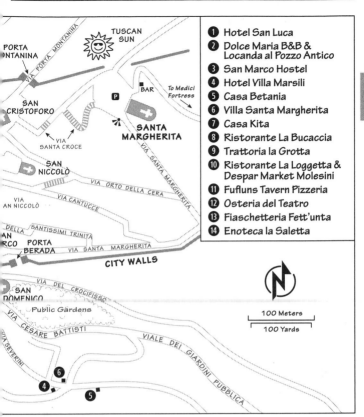

1. Hotel San Luca
2. Dolce Maria B&B & Locanda al Pozzo Antico
3. San Marco Hostel
4. Hotel Villa Marsili
5. Casa Betania
6. Villa Santa Margherita
7. Casa Kita
8. Ristorante La Bucaccia
9. Trattoria la Grotta
10. Ristorante La Loggetta & Despar Market Molesini
11. Fufluns Tavern Pizzeria
12. Osteria del Teatro
13. Fiaschetteria Fett'unta
14. Enoteca la Saletta

roque chapels filling once-spacious side niches. In the rear (on the right) is an altar cluttered with relics. Technically, any Catholic altar, in order to be consecrated, needs a relic embedded in it. Gently lift up the tablecloth (go ahead—the priest here doesn't mind), and you'll see a little marble patch that holds a bit of a saint (daily in summer 7:30-13:00 & 15:00-18:30, daily in winter 8:00-12:30 & 15:00-17:30, closed during Mass).

• *From here, you can visit the nearby Diocesan Museum, or head back toward Piazza della Repubblica to visit the Etruscan Museum in Piazza Signorelli (both listed next) or to get a bite to eat (see "Eating in Cortona," later).*

Sights in Cortona

▲Etruscan Museum (Museo dell'Accademia Etrusca e della Città di Cortona)

Located in the 13th-century Casali Palace and called MAEC for short, this fine gallery (established in 1727) is one of the first dedicated to artifacts from the Etruscan civilization. (In the logo, notice the E is backwards—in homage to the Etruscan alphabet.) This sprawling collection is nicely installed on four big floors with plenty of English information. The bottom two floors (underground) are officially the "Museum of the Etruscan and Roman City of Cortona." You'll see an exhibit on the Roman settlement and take a virtual tour of the Etruscan "Il Sodo" tombs (in the nearby countryside). The Cortona Tablet (*Tabula Cortonensis,* second century B.C.), a 200-word contract inscribed in bronze, contains dozens of Etruscan words archaeologists had never seen before its discovery in 1992. Along with lots of gold and jewelry, you'll find a seventh-century B.C. grater (for some *very* aged Parmesan cheese). The top two floors, called the "Accademia," display an even more eclectic collection, including more Etruscania, Egyptian artifacts, fine Roman mosaics, and a room dedicated to 20th-century abstract works by Severini, all lovingly described in English. A highlight is the magnificent fourth-century B.C. bronze oil lamp chandelier with 16 spouts. On the top floor, peek into the classic old library of the Etruscan Academy, founded in 1727 to promote an understanding of the city through the study of archaeology.

Cost and Hours: €10, €13 combo-ticket includes Diocesan Museum; April-Oct daily 10:00-19:00; Nov-March Tue-Sun 10:00-17:00, closed Mon; Casali Palace on Piazza Signorelli, tel. 0575-637-235, www.cortonamaec.org.

▲Diocesan Museum (Museo Diocesano)

This small collection contains some very choice artworks from the town's many churches, including works by Fra Angelico and Pietro Lorenzetti, and masterpieces by hometown hero and Renaissance master Luca Signorelli.

Cost and Hours: €5, €13 combo-ticket includes Etruscan Museum, helpful audioguide-€3; April-Oct daily 10:00-19:00; Nov-March Tue-Sun 10:00-17:00, closed Mon; Piazza del Duomo 1, tel. 0575-62-830.

Visiting the Museum: From the entrance, head straight into the Signorelli Room (Sala 4). Signorelli was a generation ahead of Michelangelo and, with his passion for painting ideas, was an inspiration for the younger artist (for more on Signorelli, visit the San Niccolò Church, described later). Take a slow stroll past his very colorful canvases, mostly relocated here from local churches. Among the most striking is *Lamentation over the Dead Christ* (*Compianto sul Cristo Morto,* 1502). Everything in Signorelli's painting has a meaning: The skull of Adam sits under the sacrifice of Jesus; the hammer represents the Passion (the Crucifixion leading to the Resurrection); the lake is blood; and so on. I don't understand all the medieval symbolism, but it is intense.

Then cut across the top of the stairwell into Sala 3, which was once the nave of the Gesù Church (look up at the beautiful wood-carved ceiling). In Fra Angelico's sumptuous *Annunciation* (c. 1430), Mary says "Yes," consenting to bear God's son. The angel's words are top and bottom, while Mary's answer is upside down (logically, since it's directed to God, who would be reading while looking down from heaven). Notice how the house sits on a pillow of flowers...the new Eden. The old Eden, featuring the expulsion of Adam and Eve from Paradise, is in the upper left. The bottom edge of the painting comes with comic strip-like narration of scenes from Mary's life. On the wall to the right, the crucifix (by Pietro Lorenzetti, c. 1325) is striking in its severity. Notice the gripping realism—even the tendons in Jesus' arms are pulled tight.

Now head back to the stairwell, which is lined with colorful Stations of the Cross scenes by another local but much later artist, the 20th-century's Gino Severini. These are actually "cartoons," models used to create permanent pieces for the approach up to the Santa Margherita Basilica. Downstairs, the lower refectory (Sala 6) has a vault with beautiful frescoes (1545) designed by Giorgio Vasari. Back up near the entrance, another staircase leads down to an important but dull collection of vestments and ecclesiastical gear.

San Francesco Church

Established by St. Francis' best friend, Brother Elias, this church dates from the 13th century. The wooden beams of the ceiling are original. While the place was redecorated in the Baroque age, some of the original frescoes that once wallpapered the church peek through the whitewash in the second chapel on the left. Francis fans visit for its precious Franciscan relics. To the left of the altar, you'll find one of Francis' tunics, his pillow (inside a fancy cover), and his gospel book. Notice how the entire high altar seems designed to frame its precious relic—a piece of the cross Elias brought back from his visit to the patriarch in Constantinople. You're welcome to climb the altar for a close-up look. In the humble choir area behind the main altar is Elias' very simple tomb (just a stone slab in the middle of the floor—on a nearby slab, see the *Frate Elia da Cortona* plaque).

Cost and Hours: Free, daily 9:00-17:30, often open until 19:00 in summer, check with TI; Mass on Sun at 10:00, Mon-Sat at 17:30.

San Niccolò Church

Although this tiny church is rarely open, Signorelli enthusiasts may want to make the pilgrimage—a steep 10-minute walk above the San Francesco Church. While it's not worth going out of the way for (the picturesque neighborhood surrounding it is, for many, more interesting), it's an easy detour if you're hiking up to Santa Margherita. The highlight of this humble church is an altarpiece painted on both sides by Signorelli; it's usually pulled halfway open so you can see both sides.

Cost and Hours: €1 donation, check with TI before making the trip to make sure it's open.

Santa Margherita Basilica

From San Niccolò Church, another steep path leads uphill 10 minutes to this basilica, which houses the remains of Margherita, the town's favorite saint. The red-and-white-striped interior boasts some colorfully painted vaults. Santa Margherita, an unwed mother from Montepulciano, found her calling with the Franciscans in Cortona, tending to the sick and poor. The well-preserved and remarkably emotional 13th-century crucifix on the right is the cross that, according to legend, talked to Margherita.

Cost and Hours: Free, daily 9:00-12:00 & 15:00-19:00 except closed Mon morning, tel. 0575-603-116.

Nearby: Still need more altitude? Head uphill five more minutes to the **Medici Fortezza Girifalco** (though may be closed—check with TI; if open, likely to be €3, daily late April-Sept 9:00-13:00 & 15:00-18:00, often later in July-Aug, closed Oct-late April, sometimes closed for rehearsals by Italian rock legend Jovanotti, who lives in a villa beyond San Niccolò Church). The views are stunning, stretching all the way to distant Lago Trasimeno.

Etruscan Tombs near Cortona

Guided tours to the tombs (called *melone* for their melon-like shape), in the locality of Sodo, are complicated to arrange. But the excavation site and bits of the ruins are easy to visit and can be seen even from outside the fence. In the mornings, the guardian often opens the gates for a closer inspection (8:30-13:30). It's just a couple of miles northwest of Cortona on the Arezzo road (R-71), at the foot of the Cortona hill; ask anyone for "Il Sodo."

Sleeping in Cortona

Inside the Old Town

$$$ Hotel San Luca, perched on the side of a cliff, has 54 impersonal business-class rooms, half with stunning views of Lago Trasimeno. While the hotel feels tired and the rooms have seen better days, it's friendly and conveniently located, right on Piazza Garibaldi at the entrance to the Old Town (Sb-€70, Db-€100, Tb-€130, request a view room when you reserve for no extra charge, popular with Americans and groups, air-con, elevator, free Wi-Fi, Piazza Garibaldi 2, tel. 0575-630-460, www.sanlucacortona.com, info@sanlucacortona.com). If driving, you might find a spot at the small public parking lot at the hotel; otherwise you can park at the big lot down below and ride the escalator up.

$$ Dolce Maria B&B is located in a 16th-century building with high-beamed ceilings. The six rooms are good-value, luminous, and spacious, with tasteful period furnishings and modern bathrooms. The B&B is run by warm and efficient Paola, who also runs the Antico Pozzo restaurant next door—the two businesses share a patio (Db-€80-100, air-con, free Wi-Fi, Via Ghini 12, tel. 0575-601-577, www.cortonastorica.com, info@cortonastorica.com).

$ San Marco Hostel, at the top of town, is housed in a remodeled 13th-century palace (bunk in 4- to 6-bed dorm-€18, in 2-bed room-€25, includes breakfast, lunch or dinner-€11, lockout 10:00-13:00; from Piazza Garibaldi head up steep Via Santa Margherita, then turn left to find Via Maffei 57; tel. 0575-601-765, www.cortonahostel.com, ostellocortona@libero.it).

Outside the Old Town

These accommodations line up along the road that angles downhill from Piazza Garibaldi, within a 10-minute (uphill) walk to the entrance to the Old Town. Drivers may find these handier than the places in town.

$$$ Hotel Villa Marsili is a comfortable splurge just below town. It was originally a 15th-century church, then an elegant 18th-century home. Its 26 rooms and public areas have been recently redecorated and restored, and come with lots of thoughtful little touches. Guests can enjoy an evening aperitif with free snacks on the panoramic terrace. In general, the higher up the room, the fancier the decor and the higher the price. Diane Lane slept in one of the suites while filming *Under the Tuscan Sun* (Sb-€110, small standard Db-€150, superior Db-€180, deluxe Db-€230, Db suite-€350, extra bed-€25/child or €50/adult, Jacuzzi in deluxe room and suites, air-con, elevator, free guest computer and Wi-Fi, free street parking nearby—first come, first served, otherwise €12, Viale Cesare Battisti 13, tel. 0575-605-252, fax 0575-605-618, www.villamarsili.net, info@villamarsili.net, Marina).

$ Casa Betania, a big, wistful convent with an inviting view terrace, rents 30 fine rooms (mostly twin beds) for the best price in town. While it's primarily for "thoughtful travelers," anyone looking for a peaceful place to call home will feel welcome in this pilgrims' resort. Marco, a big-city lawyer escaping from the rat race, has taken over this place and turned it into an impressive retreat facility, with conference rooms, a chapel, wine cellar, cooking classes, and more (S-€32, D-€44, Db-€48, Tb-€66, extra bed-€20, breakfast-€4, free Wi-Fi, free parking, about a third of a mile out of town, a few minutes' walk below Piazza Garibaldi and through iron gates on the right at Via Gino Severini 50, tel. 0575-630-423, www.casaperferiebetania.com, info@casaperferiebetania.com).

$ Villa Santa Margherita, run by the Serve di Maria Riparatrici sisters, rents 22 nicely renovated rooms in a smaller and more traditional-feeling convent just up the street from Casa Betania (Sb-€50, Db-€66, Tb-€86, Qb-€98, elevator, pay Wi-Fi, free parking, Viale Cesare Battisti 17, tel. 0575-178-7203 or 0575-630-336, fax 0575-630-549, www.villasm.it, info@villasm.it).

$ Casa Kita, renting five slightly quirky rooms, is a homey place just below Piazza Garibaldi with fine views from its terrace. You'll really feel like you're staying in someone's home, but the prices are good (Db-€65, free Wi-Fi, 100 yards below Piazza Garibaldi at Vicolo degli Orti 7, tel. 389-557-9893, www.casakita.com, info@casakita.com, Lorenzini family).

Eating in Cortona

Ristorante La Bucaccia is a family-run eatery set in a rustic medieval wine cellar. It's dressy and romantic. Taking an evangelical pride in their Chianina beef dishes and homemade pastas, Romano hosts and his wife Agostina cooks. Reservations are required for dinner—and worth making (€8-9 pastas, €12-15 *secondi*, Tue-Sun 12:30-15:30 & 19:00-23:00, closed Mon, show this book for a 5 percent discount and a small free appetizer, Via Ghibellina 17, tel. 0575-606-039, www.labucaccia.it).

Trattoria la Grotta, just off Piazza della Repubblica, is a traditional place serving daily specials to an enthusiastic clientele under grotto-like vaults (€7-9 pastas, €7-20 *secondi*, good wine by the glass, Wed-Mon 12:00-14:30 & 19:00-22:00, closed Tue, Piazza Baldelli 3, tel. 0575-630-271).

Locanda al Pozzo Antico offers an affordable menu of Tuscan fare, with a focus on fresh, quality produce, and using their own homemade olive oil. Eat in a classy, minimalist dining room or tucked away in a tranquil secret courtyard. Paola is a charming hostess; ask about her cooking classes (€6-9 pastas, €10-16 *secondi*, Fri-Wed 12:30-14:30 & 19:30-22:00, closed Thu, Via Ghini 12, tel. 0575-62091 or 0575-601-577; Paola, husband Franco, and son Gianni).

Ristorante La Loggetta serves up big portions of well-presented Tuscan cuisine on the loggia overlooking Piazza della Repubblica. While they have fine indoor seating under stone vaults, I'd eat here for the chance to gaze at the square over a meal (€8-10 pastas, €8-15 *secondi*, Thu-Tue 12:30-15:00 & 19:30-23:00, closed Wed, Piazza Pescheria 3, tel. 0575-630-575).

Fufluns Tavern Pizzeria (that's the Etruscan name for Dionysus) is easy-going, friendly, and remarkably unpretentious for its location in the town center. It's popular with locals for its good, inexpensive Tuscan cooking, friendly staff, and stone-and-beam-cozy interior (€5-7 pizza and €6-10 pastas plus big salads, good house wine, Wed-Mon 12:15-14:30 & 19:15-22:30, closed Tue, a block below Piazza della Repubblica at Via Ghibellina 3, tel. 0575-604-140).

Osteria del Teatro tries very hard to create a romantic Old World atmosphere, and does it well. Chef and owner Emiliano serves nicely presented and tasty Italian and local cuisine (taking creative liberties with traditions). There's good outdoor seating, too. It feels upscale and a bit self-important (€8-9 pastas, €11-16 *secondi,* Thu-Tue 12:30-14:30 & 19:30-22:00, closed Wed, 2 blocks uphill from the main square at Via Maffei 2—look for the gnomes on the steps, tel. 0575-630-556, www.osteria-del-teatro.it). They also own the bright little restaurant just opposite, **Fiaschetteria Fett'unta,** which has traditional light snacks and sandwiches.

Enoteca la Saletta, dark and classy with a nice, mellow vibe, is good for fine wine and a light meal. You can sit inside surrounded by wine bottles or outside to people-watch on the town's main drag (€3-5 sandwiches and pizzas, €7-12 pastas and *secondi,* daily 7:30-24:00, meals served 12:00-24:00, closed Wed in winter, free Wi-Fi, Via Nazionale 26, tel. 0575-603-366).

Picnic: On the main square, the chic little **Despar Market Molesini** makes tasty sandwiches, served with a smile (see list on counter and order by number, or invent your own), and sells whatever else you might want for a picnic (Mon-Sat 7:00-13:30 & 16:00-20:00, Sun 9:30-13:30, Piazza della Repubblica 23). Munch your picnic across the square on the steps of City Hall, or just past Piazza Garibaldi in the public gardens behind San Domenico Church.

Cortona Connections

Cortona has good train connections with the rest of Italy through its Camucia-Cortona station. The station is usually unstaffed, but it has two ticket machines: One is in front as you enter the station, and one is outside on platform 1. They take credit cards and cash (change is given). When purchasing, choose the British flag for English, and then follow the clear instructions, delivered with a charming Italian accent. After buying your ticket, immediately validate it in one of the green boxes next to the ticket machine in the main station or on platforms 1 and 3.

To get to the train station at the foot of the hill, take a €10 taxi or hop the €1.20 bus (see "Arrival in Cortona," earlier; runs only about once hourly; buy tickets at a newsstand or tobacco shop, or buy from driver for €0.40 more). Be sure to confirm with the TI whether these buses leave from Piazza Garibaldi or Piazza del Mercato, outside Porta Santa Maria. Some buses take you only as far as the newsstand that's 200 yards in front of the station.

From Camucia-Cortona by Train to: Rome (9/day, 2.5 hours, 4 direct, others with change, €11.35), **Florence** (hourly, 1.5 hours, €9.80), **Assisi** (every 2 hours, 70 minutes, €5.55), **Montepulciano**

(9/day, 1.5-2 hours, change in Chiusi; because few buses serve Montepulciano's town center from its distant train station, it's better to go by train to Chiusi, then by hourly 40-minute bus to Montepulciano, or easier still to take a taxi for about €40), **Chiusi** (9/day, 40 minutes).

Most trains stop at the Camucia-Cortona train station, but each day, two or three high-speed trains to/from Rome, Florence, and Assisi stop at **Terontola,** 10 miles away (buses go about hourly to Terontola, leaves from Piazza Garibaldi, 25-30 minutes, €2, check the schedule at the bus stop or pick up printed bus schedule from the TI).

More Hill Towns and Sights

These are listed roughly from north to south.

▲Florence American Cemetery and Memorial

The compelling sight of endless rows of white marble crosses and Stars of David recalls the heroism of the young Americans who fought so valiantly in World War II to free Italy (and ultimately Europe) from the grip of fascism. This particular cemetery is the final resting place of more than 4,000 Americans who died in the liberation of Italy. Climb the hill past the perfectly manicured lawn lined with grave markers, to the memorial, where maps and a history of the Italian campaign detail the Allied advance.

Cost and Hours: Free, daily 9:00-17:00; 7.5 miles south of Florence, off Via Cassia, which parallels the *superstrada* between Florence and Siena, 2 miles south of Florence Certosa exit on A-1 autostrada; buses from Florence stop just outside the cemetery; tel. 055-202-0020, www.abmc.gov.

▲San Galgano Monastery

Of southern Tuscany's several evocative monasteries, San Galgano is the best. Set in a forested area called the Montagnolo ("Medium-Size Mountains"), the isolated abbey and chapel are postcard-perfect, though you'll need a car to get here. Other, more accessible Tuscan monasteries worth visiting include Sant'Antimo (6 miles south of Montalcino) and Monte Oliveto Maggiore (15 miles south of Siena, mentioned in "The Crete Senese," earlier).

Cost and Hours: €2, June-Aug daily 9:00-20:00, shoulder

season until 19:00, Nov-Feb daily 9:30-17:30, tel. 0577-756-738, www.prolocochiusdino.it; concerts sometimes held here in summer—info tel. 055-597-8309, www.festivalopera.it. For a quick snack, a small, touristy bar at the end of the driveway is your only option.

Getting There: Although a bus reportedly comes here from Siena, this sight is realistically accessible only for drivers. It's just outside Monticiano (not Montalcino), about an hour southwest of Siena. A warning to the queasy: These roads are curvy.

Visiting the Monastery: St. Galgano was a 12th-century saint who renounced his past as a knight to become a hermit. Lacking a cross to display, he created his own by miraculously burying his sword up to its hilt in a stone, à la King Arthur, but in reverse. After his death, a large Cistercian monastery complex grew. Today, all you'll see is the roofless, ruined abbey and, on a nearby hill, the Chapel of San Galgano with its fascinating dome and sword in the stone.

This picturesque Cistercian **abbey** was once a powerful institution in Tuscany. Known for their skill as builders, the Cistercians oversaw the construction of Siena's cathedral. But after losing most of its population in the plague of 1348, the abbey never really recovered and was eventually deconsecrated.

The Cistercian order was centered in France, and the architecture of the abbey shows a heavy French influence. Notice the large, high windows and the pointy, delicate arches. This is pure French Gothic, a style that never fully caught on in Italy (compare it with the chunky, elaborately decorated cathedral in Siena, built about the same time).

As you enter the church, look to the left to see a small section of the cloister wall. This used to surround the garden and was the only place where the monks were allowed to talk, for one hour each day. From inside the church, the empty windows frame the view of the chapel up on the hill.

The upper floor of the actual monks' quarters (to the side of the abbey) may now be open to the public.

A path from the abbey leads up the hill to the **Chapel of San Galgano.** The unique, beehive-like interior houses St. Galgano's sword and stone, recently confirmed to date back to the 12th century. Don't try and pull the sword from the stone—the small chapel to the left displays the severed arms of the last guy who tried. The chapel also contains some deteriorated frescoes and more interesting *sinopie* (fresco sketches). The adjacent gift shop sells a little bit of everything, from wine to postcards to herbs, some of it monk-made.

▲Urbino

If you're driving through central Italy, Urbino is worth a stop for its sprawling, fascinating Ducal Palace. Although Urbino is the hometown of the artist Raphael and the architect Donato Bramante, it's better known for the Duke of Montefeltro, a mercenary general who built the palace and turned Urbino into an important Renaissance center. For my expanded coverage of Urbino, see www.ricksteves.com/urbino.

A classic hill town, Urbino has a medieval wall with four gates and two main roads that crisscross at the town's main square, Piazza della Repubblica. The tiny **TI** is just across from the Ducal Palace (mid-March-Oct daily 9:00-13:00 & 15:00-18:30, but closed Mon afternoons; Nov-mid-March daily 9:00-13:00, Mon and Fri also 15:00-18:00; Piazza Duca Federico 35, tel. 0722-2613, www.turismo.pesarourbino.it, info@turismo.pesarourbino.it).

The **Ducal Palace** (Palazzo Ducale), which has more than 300 rooms, was built in the mid-1400s. While the rooms are fairly bare, the palace holds a few very special paintings, as well as exquisite inlaid-wood decorations. It's a monument to how one man—the Duke of Montefeltro—brought the Renaissance to his small town (€5, but sometimes €9 for special exhibits, Mon 8:30-13:00, Tue-Sun 8:30-19:00, last entry one hour before closing, tel. 072-232-2625). The highlights of the palace include great paintings such as Raphael's *Portrait of a Gentlewoman* (a.k.a. *La Muta*); the Renaissance courtyard patterned after the trendsetting Medici-Riccardi Palace in Florence; the richly paneled and inlaid-wood walls of the duke's study; and the vast cellars that include a giant stable with a clever horse-pie disposal system.

Stop by the **Oratory of St. John** to see its remarkable frescoed interior that tells the story of the life of St. John the Baptist (€2.50, Mon-Sat 10:00-13:00 & 15:00-18:00, Sun 10:00-13:00, 5-minute walk from main square—follow signs, Piazza Baricci 31; if no one's there, find attendant at the Oratory of San Giuseppe a few steps away; mobile 347-671-1181).

Finally, for the ultimate Urbino view, climb up to the grassy park surrounding the **fortress** (interior closed, but grounds open to the public). The Franciscan church spire, on the left, marks the main square.

Getting There: Urbino is easier for drivers, but public transportation is an option. Buses link Urbino with Pesaro, on the Ravenna-Pescara train line (buses run hourly, 1-hour trip). From Venice, Florence, or Rome, trains leave for Pesaro almost hourly (taking 3-5 hours). In Urbino, buses come and go from the Piazza Mercatale parking lot below the town, where an elevator lifts you up to the base of the Ducal Palace (or take a 5-minute steep walk up Via Mazzini to Piazza della Repubblica).

Sleeping in Urbino: The hotel scene is limited to a few comfortable, expensive places, including **Albergo San Domenico** (www.viphotels.it), **Hotel Raffaello** (www.albergoraffaello.com), and **Albergo Italia** (www.albergo-italia-urbino.it). The TI has a line on lots of families renting rooms.

Eating in Urbino: Try **Taverna degli Artisti** (Via Donato Bramante 52) and **Il Coppiere** (Via Santa Margherita 1), or **Ristorante/Pizzeria Le Tre Piante** (Via Voltaccia della Vecchia 1).

▲Chiusi

This small hill town (rated ▲▲ for Etruscan fans) was once one of the most important Etruscan cities. Today it's a key train junction and a pleasant, workaday Italian village with an enjoyable historic center and few tourists. The hill upon which Chiusi sits is honeycombed with Etruscan tunnels, which you can see in a variety of ways.

Tourist Information: The well-organized TI faces the main square (April-Aug daily 9:00-13:00 & 15:00-17:00, Sept daily 9:00-13:00 & 15:00-17:00, Oct-March Tue-Sun 9:30-12:30, closed Mon, Via Porsenna 79, tel. 0578-227-667, www.prolocochiusi.it).

Arrival in Chiusi: The region's **trains** (to Florence, Siena, and Rome—each of these is about an hour away) go through or change at this hub, making Chiusi an easy day trip. There's no luggage storage at the station, but the TI may be willing to take your bags for a short time. Buses link the train station with the town center two miles away (every 40 minutes, buy tickets at tobacco shop, bus doesn't run during a gap in the afternoon, taxi costs €10). All buses from the station drop off at a stop just below the center of town (follow well-marked pedestrian signs up to the TI and museums); about half continue on to a stop near the town theater, right downtown. **Drivers** follow signs for *centro storico,* then the TI. Easy and free parking lots are a five-minute walk from the center; pay spaces (marked with blue lines) are right downtown, next to the TI and museums. Hertz has a rental-car office near the train station (Via M. Buonarroti 21, tel. 057-822-3000).

Sights in Chiusi: All the town's sights are within a five-minute walk of each other and the TI.

The **Archaeological Museum** (Museo Archeologico Nazionale, a.k.a. the Etruscan Museum) thoughtfully presents a high-quality collection with plenty of explanations in English. The collection of funerary urns, some in painted terra-cotta and some in *pietra fetida* ("stinky stone"), are remarkably intact. You'll also see exhibits on two tombs in the nearby countryside: a model of the Tomba della Pellegrina, and small-scale reproductions of the frescoes from the Tomba della Scimmia—both mentioned below (€6, daily 9:00-20:00, in the stately Neoclassical-looking building just off the main square at Via Porsenna 93, tel. 0578-20177, www.archeotoscana.beniculturali.it).

The museum also arranges tours to visit the actual Pellegrina and Scimmia **tombs;** to take part, you'll need to have your own car and to join a guide (meet at the museum 15 minutes before the tour time). For the Tomba della Pellegrina (Tomb of the Pilgrim), from the Hellenistic period (4th century B.C.), tours depart daily at 11:00 and 16:00 (or 14:30 in winter). This is included in museum admission, and no reservations are necessary—just ask when you arrive. The other, the Tomba della Scimmia (Tomb of the Monkey), is a century earlier and has some well-preserved frescoes (€2;Tue, Thu, and Sat only; March-Oct at 11:00 and 16:00, Nov-Feb at 11:00 and 14:30; this tomb requires an advance reservation).

Troglodyte alert! The **Cathedral Museum** on the main square has a dark, underground labyrinth of Etruscan tunnels. The mandatory guided tour of the tunnels ends in a large Roman cistern, from which you can climb the church bell tower for an expansive view of the countryside (museum-€2, labyrinth-€3, combo-ticket-€4, daily June-mid-Oct 9:45-12:45 & 16:00-18:30, mid-Oct-May 9:45-12:45 only, 30-minute tunnel tours run every 40 minutes during museum hours, Piazza Duomo 1, tel. 0578-226-490).

Craving more underground fun? The **Museo Civico** provides hourly tours of the Etruscan water system, which includes an underground lake (€4; May-Oct Tue-Sun at 10:15, 11:30, 12:45, 15:15, 16:30, and 17:45; closed Mon, fewer tours and closed Mon-Wed off-season, call to confirm times, Via II Ciminia 1, tel. 0578-20530, mobile 334-626-6851).

▲Gubbio

This handsome town climbs Monte Ingino in northeast Umbria. Tuesday is market day, when Piazza 40 Martiri (named for 40 local martyrs shot by Nazis) bustles. Nearby are the ruins of the Roman amphitheater, and a park that's perfect for a picnic. Head up Via della Repubblica to the main square with the imposing Palazzo dei Consoli. Farther up, Via San Gerolamo leads to the funky lift that will carry you up the hill, in two-person "baskets," for a stunning view  from the top, where the Basilica of San Ubaldo is worth a look. The **TI** is at Via della Repubblica 15 (daily April-Sept 8:30-13:45 &

15:30-18:30, Oct-March closes at 18:00 daily; tel. 075-922-0693, www.gubbio-altochiascio.umbria2000.it). Buses from Gubbio run directly to Rome and Perugia (where you can transfer to Florence).

▲Bevagna

This sleeper of a town south of Assisi has Roman ruins, interesting churches, and more. Locals offer their guiding services for free (usually Italian-speaking only) and are excited to show visitors their town. Get a map at the **TI** at Piazza Silvestri 1 (daily 9:30-12:30 & 15:30-19:30, tel. 074-236-1667) and wander. Highlights are the Roman mosaics, remains of the arena, a paper-making workshop, the Romanesque Church of San Silvestro, and a gem of a 19th-century theater. Bevagna has all the elements of a hill town except one: a hill. You can see the main sights easily in a couple of hours.

▲Spello

Umbrian hill town aficionados always include Spello on their list. Just six miles south of Assisi, this town is much less touristy than its neighbor to the north. Spello will give your legs a workout. Via Consolare goes up, up, up to the top of town. Views from the terrace of the **Il Trombone** restaurant will have you singing a tune (Via Fontanello 1, tel. 074-265-1069). The **TI** is on Piazza Matteotti 3 (daily 9:30-12:30 & 16:00-18:00, afternoons 15:30-17:30 in winter, tel. 074-230-1009, www.prospello.it). Spello is on the Perugia-Assisi-Foligno train line.

SIENA

Siena was medieval Florence's archrival. And while Florence ultimately won the battle for political and economic superiority, Siena still competes for the tourists. Sure, Florence has the heavyweight sights. But Siena seems to be every Italy connoisseur's favorite town. In my office, whenever Siena is mentioned, someone exclaims, "Siena? I looove Siena!"

Once upon a time (about 1260-1348), Siena was a major banking and trade center, and a military power in a class with Florence, Venice, and Genoa. With a population of 60,000, it was even bigger than Paris. Situated on the north-south road to Rome (Via Francigena), Siena traded with all of Europe. Then, in 1348, the Black Death (bubonic plague) swept through Europe, hitting Siena and cutting the population by more than a third. Siena never recovered. In the 1550s, Florence, with the help of Philip II's Spanish army, conquered the flailing city-state, forever rendering Siena a non-threatening backwater. Siena's loss became our sightseeing gain, as its political and economic irrelevance pickled the city in a purely medieval brine. Today, Siena's population is still 60,000.

Siena, situated atop three hills, qualifies as Italy's ultimate "hill town" (though it's much larger than its cousins covered in the Hill Towns of Central Italy chapter). Its thriving historic center, with red-brick lanes cascading every which way, offers Italy's best medieval city experience. Most people do Siena, just 35 miles south of Florence, as a day trip, but it's best experienced at twilight. While Florence has the blockbuster museums, Siena has an easy-to-enjoy soul: Courtyards sport flower-decked wells, alleys dead-end at rooftop views, and the sky is a rich blue dome.

For those who dream of a Fiat-free Italy, Siena is a haven. Pedestrians rule in the old center of town, as the only drivers allowed are residents and cabbies. Sit at a café on the main square. Wander narrow streets lined with colorful flags and studded with iron rings to tether horses. Take time to savor the first European city to eliminate automobile traffic from its main square (1966), and then, just to be silly, wonder what would happen if they did it in your hometown.

Planning Your Time

On a quick trip, consider spending two nights in Siena (or three nights with a whole-day side-trip into Florence). Whatever you do, be sure to enjoy a sleepy medieval evening in Siena. The next morning, you can see the city's major sights in half a day.

Orientation to Siena

Siena lounges atop a hill, stretching its three legs out from Il Campo. This main square, the historic meeting point of Siena's

neighborhoods, is pedestrian-only—and most of those pedestrians are students from the university.

Just about everything mentioned in this chapter is within a 15-minute walk of the square. Navigate by three major landmarks (Il Campo, Duomo, and Church of San Domenico), following the excellent system of street-corner signs. The typical visitor sticks to the Il Campo-San Domenico axis. Make a point to stray from this main artery. Sienese streets go in anything but a straight line, so it's easy to get lost—but equally easy to get found. Don't be afraid to explore.

Siena itself is one big sight. Its individual sights come in two little clusters: the square (Civic Museum and City Tower) and the cathedral (Baptistery and Duomo Museum, with its surprise viewpoint). Check these sights off, and then you're free to wander.

Tourist Information

The TI on Il Campo can be an exasperating place. Think about the importance of tourism to this town—and yet this office charges €0.50 for a map and lets tour commissions color its advice (Mon-Sat 9:30-18:30, Sun 9:30-17:00, on Il Campo at #56, tel. 0577-280-551, www.terresiena.it). They hand out a few pretty booklets (including *Siena* and the regional *Terre di Siena* guide), sell maps and books, and may be able to answer a few questions. The TI also organizes walking tours (described later, under "Tours in Siena").

SIENA

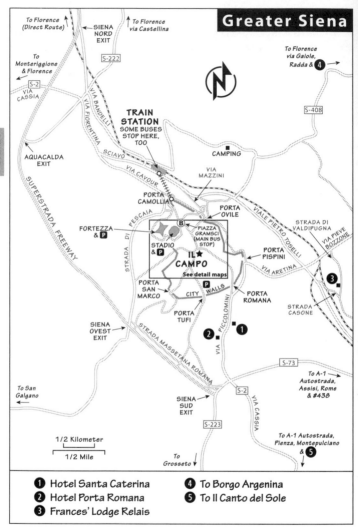

Greater Siena

- **1** Hotel Santa Caterina
- **2** Hotel Porta Romana
- **3** Frances' Lodge Relais
- **4** To Borgo Argenina
- **5** To Il Canto del Sole

Ignore the second "TI" across from the Church of San Domenico, which is a useless private agency run by the local hotel association.

Arrival in Siena

By Train

The small train station, located at the base of the hill on the edge of town, has a bar, a bus office (Mon-Fri 7:15-19:30, Sat 7:15-17:45, Sun 8:30-12:30 & 14:30-18:30), and a newsstand (which sells local bus tickets—buy one now if you're taking the city bus into town), but no baggage check or lockers (stow bags at Piazza Gramsci—

see "By Intercity Bus," later). A shopping mall with a supermarket (handy for picnic supplies) is across the plaza right in front of the station.

Getting from the Train Station to the City Center: To reach central Siena, you can hop aboard the city bus, ride a long series of escalators (which involves a bit of walking along a picturesque street), or take a taxi.

By Bus or Escalator: To reach either the bus or the escalators, head for the shopping mall across the plaza. From the tracks, go down the stairs into the tunnel that connects the platforms; this leads (with escalators) right up into the mall. Alternatively, you can exit the station out the front door, cross over to the plaza, turn left and walk to the far end of the plaza, then turn right to enter the mall's glass doors.

To ride the **city bus,** go through the shopping mall's right-hand door and use the elevator to go down to the subterranean bus stop. If you didn't buy bus tickets in the train station, you can get them from the blue machine (press "F" to toggle to English, then select "A" for type of ticket). Buses leave frequently (6/hour, fewer on Sun and after 22:00, €1.10, about a 10-minute ride into town depending on route). Smaller shuttle buses go up to Piazza del Sale, while bigger city buses head to nearby Piazza Gramsci (both are at the north end of town, walkable to most of my recommended hotels). Before boarding, double-check the destination with the driver by asking *"Centro?"* Punch your ticket in the machine onboard to validate it.

Riding the **escalator** into town takes a few minutes longer and requires more walking than the bus. From the station, follow the instructions above and enter the mall at the far-left end. Once inside, go straight ahead and ride the escalators up two floors to the food court. Continue directly through the glass doors to another escalator (marked *Porta Camollia/Centro*) that takes you gradually up, up, up into town (free). Exiting the escalator, turn left down the big street, bear left at the fork, then continue straight through the town gate. From here, landmarks are well-signed (go up Via Camollia).

By Taxi: The taxi stand is to your right as you exit the train station, but as the city is chronically short on cabs, getting one here can take a while (about €11 to Il Campo, taxi tel. 0577-49222).

Getting to the Train Station from the City Center: If you're leaving Siena by train, you can ride a smaller shuttle bus from Piazza del Sale (which goes straight to the station), or catch an orange or red-and-silver city bus from Piazza Gramsci (which may take a more roundabout route). Multiple bus routes make this trip—look for *Ferrovia* or *Stazione* on schedules and marked on the bus. City buses drop off right in front of the station. Confirm with the driver

SIENA

that the bus is going to the *stazione* (staht-see-OH-nay); remember to purchase your ticket in advance from a tobacco shop or blue machine, then validate it on board.

By Intercity Bus

Most buses arrive in Siena at Piazza Gramsci, a few blocks north of the city center. (Some buses only go to the train station; others go first to the train station, then continue to Piazza Gramsci—to find out, ask your driver, "pee-aht-sah GRAHM-chee?") The main bus companies are Sena and Tiemme/Siena Mobilità (formerly called Tra-In). Day-trippers can store baggage in the Sottopassaggio la Lizza passageway underneath Piazza Gramsci at the Tiemme/ Siena Mobilità office (€5.50/day, open daily 7:00-19:00, carry-on-sized luggage no more than 33 pounds, no overnight storage). From Piazza Gramsci, it's an easy walk into the town center—just head in the opposite direction of the tree-filled park.

By Car

Siena is not a good place to drive. Plan on parking in a big lot or garage and walking into town.

Drivers coming from the autostrada take the *Siena Ovest* exit and follow signs for *Centro,* then *Stadio* (stadium). The soccer-ball signs take you to the stadium lot (Parcheggio Stadio, €1.70/hour, pay when you leave) near Piazza Gramsci and the huge, bare-brick Church of San Domenico. The nearby Fortezza lot charges the same amount. Another good option is the underground Santa Caterina garage (you'll see signs on the way to the stadium lot, same price). From the garage, hike 150 yards uphill through a gate to an escalator on the right, which carries you up into the city. If you're staying in the south end of town, try the Il Campo lot, near Porta Tufi.

On parking spots, blue stripes mean pay and display; white stripes mean free parking. You can park for free in the lot west of the Fortezza; in white-striped spots behind the Hotel Villa Liberty (south of the Fortezza); and overnight in most city lots from 20:00 to 8:00. Watch for signs showing a street cleaner and a day of the week—that's when the street is closed to cars for cleaning.

Driving within Siena's city center is restricted to local cars and policed by automatic cameras. If you drive or park anywhere marked *Zona Traffico Limitato (ZTL),* you'll likely have a hefty ticket waiting for you in the mail back home.

Technically, hotel customers are allowed to drop off bags at their hotel before finding a place to park overnight, but getting permission to do so isn't worth the trouble.

Helpful Hints

Combo-Tickets: Siena always seems to be experimenting with different combo-tickets, but in general, only two are worth considering: the €12 Opa Si combo-ticket that includes the Duomo, Duomo Museum, Crypt, and Baptistery (a savings of at least €9 if you plan on seeing all of those sights; sold only at the ticket office just right of the Duomo, near the Duomo Museum entrance), and the €13 combo-ticket covering the Civic Museum and City Tower (a €3 savings; must purchase at City Tower on Il Campo).

Wednesday Morning Market: The weekly market (clothes, knick-knacks, and food) sprawls between the Fortezza and Piazza Gramsci along Viale Cesare Maccari and the adjacent Viale XXV Aprile. The fact that this is more local than touristy makes it, for some, even more interesting.

Internet Access: In this university town, there are lots of places to get plugged in. **Cheap Phone Center** is hidden in a small shopping mall near Il Campo (€2/hour to use terminals, €1/hour for Wi-Fi, Mon-Sat 10:00-22:00, Sun 12:00-22:00; coming from Il Campo, go uphill past recommended Albergo Tre Donzelle, turn left at Via Cecco Angiolieri, after 20 yards look for #16). **Internet Point** is located upstairs at Via di Città 80, with the entrance around the corner on Via delle Campane (€3/hour, daily 9:00-21:00).

Post Office: It's on Piazza Matteotti (Mon-Fri 8:15-19:00, Sat 8:15-13:30, closed Sun).

Books: Libreria Senese sells books (including my guidebooks), newspapers, and magazines in English, with an emphasis on Italian-related topics (Mon-Sat 9:00-20:00, Sun 10:00-20:00, Via di Città 62, tel. 0577-280-845). The **Feltrinelli** bookstore at Banchi di Sopra 52 also sells books and magazines in English (Mon-Sat 9:00-19:30, closed Sun, tel. 0577-271-104; the bigger Feltrinelli branch farther down the street at #64 has no English books).

Laundry: Onda Blu is a modern, self-service launderette just 50 yards from Il Campo (about €6 wash and dry, daily 8:00-21:15, last load at 20:15, Via del Casato di Sotto 17).

Travel Agency: Palio Viaggi, on Piazza Gramsci, sells plane tickets upstairs. Their downstairs office (go down the ramp to the door below the arch) sells train tickets, railpass reservations, and some bus tickets (only for the longer-distance Sena buses, not the regional Tiemme/Siena Mobilità buses). They charge a €1 fee per bus or train ticket, but this saves you a trip to the train station (Mon-Fri 9:00-12:45 & 15:00-18:30, Sat 9:00-12:30, closed Sun, opposite the columns of NH Excelsior Hotel at La Lizza 12, tel. 0577-280-828).

Wine Classes: The **Tuscan Wine School** gives two-hour classes in English on Italian wine and food. Morning classes (11:00) cover rotating topics: wines from all over Italy, olive-oil tasting, or a "Savor Siena" food tour that visits several vendors around town (check website for specific schedule). Afternoon classes (16:00) focus on Tuscan wines, including samples of five vintages. They also offer a one-hour "crash course" at 14:00. Rebecca and her fellow sommeliers keep things entertaining and offer classes for as few as two people (€40/person, 20 percent student discount to anyone with this book, €25 for one-hour course, classes offered Mon-Sat, closed Sun, reservations recommended—especially in peak season, Via di Stalloreggi 26, 30 yards from recommended Hotel Duomo, tel. 0577-221-704, mobile 333-722-9716, www.tuscanwineschool.com, info@tuscanwineschool.com). Their outlet store sells wine from local producers at cost (Mon-Sat 11:00-18:00, closed Sun).

Tours in Siena

Roberto's Tuscany Tours
Roberto Bechi, a hardworking Sienese guide, specializes in off-the-beaten-path, ecologically friendly minibus tours of the surrounding countryside (up to eight passengers, convenient pickup at hotel). Married to an American (Patti) and having run restaurants in Siena and the US, Roberto communicates well with Americans. His passions are Sienese culture, Tuscan history, and local cuisine. It's ideal to book well in advance, but you might be able to schedule a tour if you call the day before (seven different tours—explained on his website, €90/person for full-day tours, €60/person for off-season four-hour tours, entry fees extra, assistant Carolina can schedule city tours as well as other guides if Roberto is booked, Carolina's mobile 320-147-6590, Roberto's mobile 328-425-5648, www.toursbyroberto.com, toursbyroberto@gmail.com). Roberto also offers multiday tours. If you book any tour with Roberto, he can advise you on other aspects of your trip.

Other Local Guides
Federica Olla, who leads walking tours of Siena, is a smart, youthful guide with a knack for creative teaching (€55/hour, mobile 338-133-9525, info@ollaeventi.com).

GSO Guides Co-op is a group of 10 young professional guides who offer good tours covering all of Tuscany and Umbria (€130/half-day, €260/full day, 10 percent discount for Rick Steves readers, www.guidesienaeoltre.com). Among them, charming Stefania Fabrizi specializes in Siena (mobile 338-640-7796, stefania-fabrizi@kata.com; if unavailable call Silvia, mobile 338-611-0127).

Walking Tours

The TI offers walking tours of the old town. Guides usually conduct their walks in both English and Italian (€20, daily April-Oct at 11:00, 2 hours, no interiors, depart from TI, Il Campo 56, tel. 0577-280-551).

Bus Tours

Somehow a company called My Tour has a lock on all hotel tour-promotion space. Every hotel has a rack of their brochures, which advertise a variety of five-hour big-bus tours into the countryside (€38, depart from Piazza Gramsci).

Sights in Siena

On Il Campo, the Main Square

▲▲▲Il Campo

This square is the heart, both geographically and metaphorically, of Siena. It fans out from City Hall (Palazzo Pubblico) to create an

amphitheater. It's the only town square I've ever seen where people stretch out as if at the beach. Il Campo's shining moment is the famous Palio horse races, which take place in summer.

Originally, this area was just a field *(campo)* located outside the former city walls. Bits of those original walls, which circled the Duomo (and curved against today's square), can be seen above the pharmacy (the black-and-white stones, to the right as you face City Hall). In the 1200s, with the advent of the Sienese Republic, the city expanded—once a small medieval town circling its cathedral, it became a larger, humanistic city gathered around its towering City Hall. In this newer and relatively secular age, the focus of power shifted from the bishop to the city council.

As the city expanded, Il Campo eventually became the historic junction of Siena's various competing *contrade* (neighborhood districts) and the old marketplace. The brick surface is divided into nine sections, representing the council of nine merchants and city bigwigs who ruled medieval Siena. The square and its buildings are the color of the soil upon which they stand—a color known to artists and Crayola users as "Burnt Sienna."

City Hall: This secular building, with its 330-foot tower, dominates the square. In medieval Siena, this was the center of

Siena at a Glance

▲▲▲**Il Campo** Best square in Italy. **Hours:** Always open. See page 97.

▲▲▲**Duomo** Art-packed cathedral with mosaic floors and statues by Michelangelo and Bernini. **Hours:** March-Oct Mon-Sat 10:30-19:00, Sun 13:30-18:00; Nov-Feb Mon-Sat 10:30-17:30, Sun 13:30-17:30. See page 104.

▲▲**Civic Museum** City museum in City Hall with Sienese frescoes, the *Effects of Good and Bad Government*. **Hours:** Daily mid-March-Oct 10:00-19:00, Nov-mid-March 10:00-18:00. See page 99.

▲▲**Duomo Museum** Siena's best museum, displaying cathedral art (including Duccio's *Maestà*) and offering sweeping Tuscan views. **Hours:** Daily March-Oct 10:30-19:00, Nov-Feb 10:30-17:30. See page 110.

▲**City Tower** 330-foot tower climb. **Hours:** Daily March-mid-Oct 10:00-19:00, mid-Oct-Feb 10:00-16:00. See page 100.

▲**Pinacoteca** Fine Sienese paintings. **Hours:** Tue-Sat 8:15-19:15, Sun-Mon 9:00-13:00. See page 101.

▲**Baptistery** Cave-like building with baptismal font decorated by Ghiberti and Donatello. **Hours:** Daily March-Oct 10:30-19:00, Nov-Feb 10:30-17:30. See page 112.

▲**Santa Maria della Scala** Museum with vibrant ceiling and wall frescoes depicting day-to-day life in a medieval hospital, much of the original *Fountain of Joy*, and an Etruscan artifact exhibit. **Hours:** May be closed for renovation—if open, likely daily March-Oct 10:30-18:00, Nov-Feb 10:30-16:00. See page 112.

Crypt Site of 12th-century church, housing some of Siena's oldest frescoes. **Hours:** Daily March-Oct 10:30-19:00, Nov-Feb 10:30-17:30. See page 112.

Church of San Domenico Huge brick church with St. Catherine's head and thumb. **Hours:** Daily 7:00-18:30. See page 113.

Sanctuary of St. Catherine Home of St. Catherine. **Hours:** Daily 9:00-18:00, church closed 12:30-15:00. See page 115.

the city, and the whole focus of Il Campo still flows down to it.

The **City Tower** (Torre del Mangia) is Italy's tallest secular tower. It was named after a hedonistic watchman who consumed his earnings like a glutton consumes food. His chewed-up statue is in the courtyard, to the left as you enter. (For details on climbing the tower, see "City Tower" listing, later.)

The open **chapel** located at the base of the tower was built in 1348 as thanks to God for ending the Black Death (after it killed more than a third of the population). It should also be used to thank God that the top-heavy tower—just plunked onto the building with no extra foundation and no iron reinforcement—still stands. These days, the chapel is used solely to bless the Palio contestants, and the tower's bell rings only for the race.

Fountain of Joy (Fonte Gaia): This 15th-century work by Jacopo della Quercia marks the square's high point. The joy is all about how the Sienese Republic blessed its people with water. Notice Lady Justice with her scales (also holding a sword, right of center), overseeing the free distribution of water to all. Imagine residents gathering here in the 1400s to fill their jugs. The Fountain of Joy still reminds locals that life in Siena is good. Notice the pigeons politely waiting their turn to tightrope gingerly down slippery

spouts to slurp a drink from wolves' snouts. The relief panel on the left shows God creating Adam by helping him to his feet. It's said that this reclining Adam influenced Michelangelo when he painted his Sistine Chapel ceiling. This fountain is a copy—you can see most of the original fountain in an interesting exhibit at Siena's Santa Maria della Scala (described later).

▲▲Civic Museum (Museo Civico)

At the base of the tower is Siena's City Hall, the spot where secular government got its start in early Renaissance Europe. There you'll find city government still at work, along with a sampling of local art, including Siena's first fresco (with a groundbreaking down-to-earth depiction of the Madonna). While pricey, it's worth strolling through the dramatic halls to see fascinating frescoes and portraits extolling Siena's greats, saints, and the city-as-utopia.

Cost and Hours: €8, €13 combo-ticket with tower (must be purchased at the tower), daily mid-March–Oct 10:00–19:00, Nov–mid March 10:00–18:00, last entry 45 minutes before closing, tel. 0577-292-615, www.comune.siena.it.

Visiting the Museum: Start in the Sala del Risorgimento, with dramatic scenes of Victor Emmanuel II's unification of Italy (surrounded by statues that don't seem to care).

Passing through the chapel, where the city's governors and bureaucrats prayed, enter the Sala del Mappamondo. On opposite walls are two large frescoes. The beautiful *Maestà* (*Enthroned Virgin*, 1315), by Siena's great Simone Martini (c. 1280-1344), is groundbreaking as Siena's first fresco showing a Madonna not in a faraway, gold-leaf heaven, but under the blue sky of the real world that we inhabit. Facing the *Maestà* is the famous *Equestrian Portrait of Guidoriccio da Fogliano* (1330), which depicts a mercenary general surveying the imposing castle that his armies have just conquered.

Next is the Sala della Pace—where the city's fat cats met. Looking down on the oligarchy during their meetings was a fascinating fresco series showing the *Effects of Good and Bad Government,* by Sienese painter Ambrogio Lorenzetti. Compare the whistle-while-you-work happiness of the utopian community ruled by the utopian government (in the better-preserved fresco) against the crime, devastation, and societal mayhem of a community ruled by politicians with more typical values. The message: Without justice, there can be no prosperity.

On your way out, climb up to the loggia (using the stairs just before the Sala del Risorgimento) for a sweeping view of the city and its surroundings. (For a less impressive version of this view, you could skip the stairs and simply peek behind the curtains in the Sala della Pace.)

▲City Tower (Torre del Mangia)

Siena gathers around its City Hall more than its church. Medieval

Siena was a proud republic, and this tall tower is the exclamation point of its "declaration of independence." Its 300 steps get pretty skinny at the top, but the reward is one of Italy's best views.

Cost and Hours: €8, €13 combo-ticket with

Civic Museum, daily March-mid-Oct 10:00-19:00, mid-Oct-Feb 10:00-16:00, last entry 45 minutes before closing, closed in rain, free and mandatory bag check.

Crowd Alert: Admission is limited to 50 people at a time, so be prepared for long lines or for tickets to be sold out. Wait at the bottom of the stairs for the green *Avanti* light. Try to avoid midday crowds (up to an hour wait at peak times).

Near Il Campo
▲Pinacoteca

If you're into medieval art, you'll likely find this quiet, uncrowded, colorful museum delightful. The museum walks you through Siena's art chronologically, from the 12th through the 16th centuries, when a revolution in realism was percolating in Tuscany.

Cost and Hours: €4, Tue-Sat 8:15-19:15, Sun-Mon 9:00-13:00, last entry 30 minutes before closing, free and mandatory bag check (must leave ID); from Il Campo, walk out Via di Città and go left on Via San Pietro to #29; tel. 0577-281-161 or 0577-286-143, www.pinacotecanazionale.siena.it.

Visiting the Museum: In general, the collection lets you follow the evolution of painting styles from Byzantine to Gothic, then to International Gothic, and finally to Renaissance.

As you walk through the museum, take time to trace the delicate features with your eyes. Long after Florentine art went realistic, the Sienese embraced a timeless, otherworldly style glittering with lots of gold. But Sienese art features more than just paintings. In this city of proud craftsmen, the gilding and carpentry of the frames almost compete with the actual paintings. The exquisite attention to detail gives a glimpse into the wealth of the 13th and 14th centuries, Siena's Golden Age. The woven silk and gold clothing you'll see was worn by the very people who once walked these halls, when this was a private mansion (appreciate the colonnaded courtyard).

The core of the collection is on the second floor, in Rooms 1-19. Works by Duccio (artist of the *Maestà* in the Duomo Museum) feature groundbreaking innovations that are subtle to the layman's eyes: less gold-leaf background, fewer gold creases in robes, transparent garments, inlaid-marble thrones, and a more human Mary and Jesus. Notice that the Madonna-and-Bambino pose is eerily identical in each version.

St. Augustine of Siena, by Duccio's assistant, Simone Martini (who did the *Maestà* and possibly the Guidoriccio frescoes in the Civic Museum), sets the saint's life in pretty realistic Sienese streets, buildings, and landscapes. In each panel, the saint pops out at the oddest (difficult to draw) angles to save the day.

Also look for religious works by the hometown Lorenzetti

SIENA

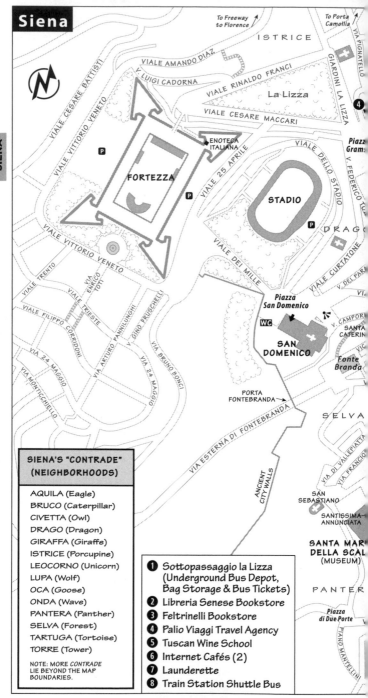

Siena

To Freeway
to Florence

To Porta
Camollia

VIA PIGNATTELLO

ISTRICE

VIALE AMANDO DIAZ

V. LUIGI CADORNA

VIALE RINALDO FRANCI

La Lizza

GIARDINI LA LIZZA

VIALE CESARE MACCARI

VIALE CESARE BATTISTI

Piazza
Gram...

VIALE VITTORIO VENETO

P

ENOTECA
ITALIANA

VIALE 25 APRILE

VIALE DELLO STADIO

V. FEDERICO TO...

FORTEZZA

P

STADIO

P

DRAGO

VIALE VITTORIO VENETO

VIALE DEI MILLE

VIALE CURTATONE

V. DEL PAR...

VIA...

VIALE TRENTO

VIA ENRICO TOTI

VIALE TRIESTE

VIALE FILIPPO CORRIDONI

VIA ARTURO PANNILUNGHI

V. GINO FRUSCHELLI

VIA GINO FRUSCHELLI

VIA BRUNO BONCI

VIA 24 MAGGIO

Piazza
San Domenico

CAMPOR...

SANTA
CATERIN...

VIC...

SAN
DOMENICO

WC

Fonte
Branda

VIA 24 MAGGIO

VIA MONTICCHELLO

PORTA
FONTEBRANDA

SELVA

VIA DI VALLEPIATTA

VIA FRANCI...

VIA ESTERNA DI FONTEBRANDA

SAN
SEBASTIANO

SANTISSIMA
ANNUNCIATA

ANCIENT
CITY WALLS

SANTA MAR...
DELLA SCAL...
(MUSEUM)

SIENA'S "CONTRADE" (NEIGHBORHOODS)

AQUILA (Eagle)
BRUCO (Caterpillar)
CIVETTA (Owl)
DRAGO (Dragon)
GIRAFFA (Giraffe)
ISTRICE (Porcupine)
LEOCORNO (Unicorn)
LUPA (Wolf)
OCA (Goose)
ONDA (Wave)
PANTERA (Panther)
SELVA (Forest)
TARTUGA (Tortoise)
TORRE (Tower)

NOTE: MORE *CONTRADE*
LIE BEYOND THE MAP
BOUNDARIES.

PANTER...

Piazza
di Due Porte

PIANO MANTELLINI

1 Sottopassaggio la Lizza
(Underground Bus Depot,
Bag Storage & Bus Tickets)
2 Libreria Senese Bookstore
3 Feltrinelli Bookstore
4 Palio Viaggi Travel Agency
5 Tuscan Wine School
6 Internet Cafés (2)
7 Launderette
8 Train Station Shuttle Bus

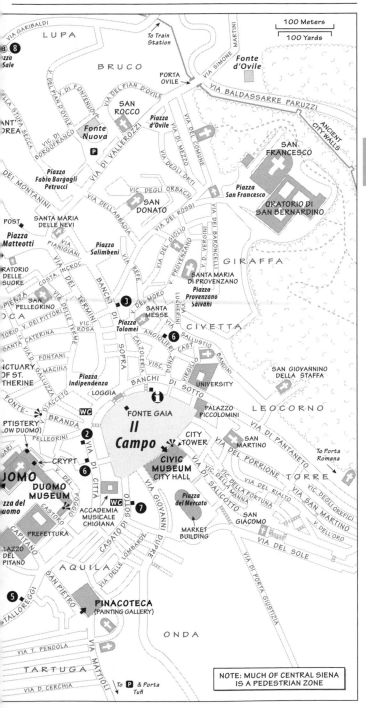

SIENA

NOTE: MUCH OF CENTRAL SIENA IS A PEDESTRIAN ZONE

brothers (Ambrogio is best known for the secular masterpiece, the *Effects of Good and Bad Government,* in the Civic Museum). *Città sul Mare (City by the Sea)* and *Castello in Riva al Lago (Castle on the Lakeshore)* feature the strange, medieval landscape Cubism seen in the work of the contemporaneous *Guidoriccio da Fogliano* (in the Civic Museum). Notice the weird, melancholy light that captures the sense of the Dark Ages. These images are replicated on postcards found throughout the city.

SIENA

Several colorful rooms on the first floor are dedicated to Domenico Beccafumi (1486-1551), who designed many of the Duomo's inlaid pavement panels (including *Slaughter of the Innocents*). With strong bodies, twisting poses, and dramatic gestures, Beccafumi's works epitomize the Mannerist style.

Cathedral Area

Each of the first four sights (Duomo, Duomo Museum, Crypt, and Baptistery) is covered by a separate ticket, or by the €12 Opa Si combo-ticket. If you're planning to visit only the Duomo and Duomo Museum, this ticket doesn't add up; but if you're curious about the Crypt and Baptistery, the combo-ticket lets you peek into those sights for just €1 more. Separate tickets and the Opa Si combo-ticket are sold only at the ticket office near the entrance to the Duomo Museum—to the right as you face the cathedral facade (no tickets sold at sight entrances).

▲▲▲Duomo

If the Campo is the heart of Siena, the Duomo (or cathedral) is its soul. The white-and-dark-green striped church, sitting on an artificial platform atop Siena's highest point, is visible for miles around. This ornate but surprisingly secular shrine to the Virgin Mary is stacked with colorful art inside and out, from the inlaid-marble floors to the stained-glass windows. The interior is a Renaissance riot of striped columns, intricate marble  inlays, Michelangelo statues, and Bernini sculptures. In the Piccolomini Library, a series of captivating frescoes by the Umbrian painter Pinturicchio tells the story of Aeneas Piccolomini, Siena's consummate Renaissance Man, who became Pope Pius II.

Cost: €4 includes cathedral and Piccolomini Library, buy ticket at Duomo Museum entrance (facing the cathedral entry, the museum is 100 yards to the right, near the south transept). To add the Duomo Museum, Crypt, and Baptistery, consider the €12 Opa Si combo-ticket. Check the line to get into the Duomo before buying tickets—if there's a long wait, you can pay an extra €1 for a (misnamed) "reservation" that lets you skip the line (not possible to book in advance—just buy it on the spot).

Hours: March-Oct Mon-Sat 10:30-19:00, Sun 13:30-18:00; Nov-Feb Mon-Sat 10:30-17:30, Sun 13:30-17:30; last entry 30 minutes before closing.

Information: Tel. 0577-286-300, www.operaduomo.siena.it. Inside the Duomo are €2 video terminals that give a history of the cathedral floor.

Dress Code: Modest dress is required, but stylish paper ponchos are provided for the inappropriately clothed.

Tours: The Porta Del Cielo ("Heaven's Gate") **guided tour** includes a 45-minute visit to the dome's cupola and roof for spectacular interior and exterior views, along with a 45-minute guided tour of the rest of the cathedral. Tours must be reserved at least 48 hours in advance and might be in Italian only (ask about English tours). When you reserve, you will be given a reference number, which you must show on arrival at the ticket office; pay before meeting your guide (€25, April-Oct Fri-Sun only; call for tour times—tel. 0577-286-300 Mon-Fri between 9:00 and 17:00).

The **videoguide** (rent in the nave) is informative but extremely dry. I'd stick with the commentary in this chapter (for Duomo only: €6, €10/2 people; for Duomo plus Duomo Museum, Crypt, and Baptistery: €8, €14/2 people).

◗ Self-Guided Tour: Grab a spot on a stone bench opposite the entry to take in this architectural festival of green, white, pink, and gold.

Exterior: Like a medieval altarpiece, the facade is divided into sections, each frame filled with patriarchs and prophets, studded with roaring gargoyles, and topped with prickly pinnacles. Imagine pilgrims arriving at this church, its facade trumpeting the coming of Christ and the correct path to salvation.

The current structure dates back to 1215, with the major decoration done during Siena's heyday (1250-1350). The lower story, by Giovanni Pisano (who worked from 1284 to 1297), features remnants of the fading Romanesque style (round arches over the doors), topped with the pointed arches of the new Gothic style that was seeping in from France. The upper half, in full-blown Gothic, was designed and built a century later.

• Step inside, putting yourself in the mindset of a pilgrim as you take in this trove of religious art. (With a maximum capacity of 700 visitors, you may have to wait—the current number is indicated on a computer screen at the turnstile. Remember, if the line is dreadfully long, you can pay €1 for a "reservation" at the ticket office and go right in.)

SIENA

SIENA

Siena's Palio

In the Palio, the feisty spirit of Siena's 17 neighborhoods lives on. Each neighborhood, or *contrada*, has a parish church, well or fountain, and sometimes even a historical museum. Each is represented by a mascot (porcupine, unicorn, wolf, etc.) and unique colors worn proudly by residents.

Contrada pride is evident year-round in Siena's parades and colorful banners, lamps, and wall plaques. (If you hear the thunder of distant drumming, run to it for some medieval action—there's a good chance it'll feature flag throwers.) You are welcome to participate in these lively neighborhood festivals. Buy a scarf in *contrada* colors, grab a glass of Chianti, munch on some *panforte*, and join in the merriment.

Contrada passion is most visible twice a year—on July 2 and August 16—when the city erupts during its world-famous horse race, the Palio di Siena. Ten of the 17 neighborhoods compete (chosen by rotation and lot), hurling themselves with medieval abandon into several days of trial races and traditional revelry. Jockeys—usually from out of town—are considered hired guns, no better than paid mercenaries. Bets are placed on which *contrada* will win...and lose. Despite the shady behind-the-scenes dealing, on the big day the horses are taken into their contrada's church to be blessed. ("Go and return victorious," says the priest.) It's considered a sign of luck if a horse leaves droppings in the church.

On the evening of the race, Il Campo is stuffed to the brim with locals and tourists. Dirt is brought in and packed down over the gray pavement of the perimeter to create the track's surface, while mattresses pad the walls of surrounding buildings. The most treacherous spots are the sharp corners, where many a rider

Nave: The heads of 172 popes—who reigned from Peter's time to the 12th century—peer down from above, looking over the fine inlaid art on the floor. With a forest of striped columns, a coffered dome, a large stained-glass window at the far end (described later), and an art gallery's worth of early Renaissance art, this is one busy interior. If you look closely at the popes, you'll see the same four faces repeated over and over.

For almost two centuries (1373-1547), 40 artists paved the marble floor with scenes from the Old Testament, allegories, and intricate patterns. The series starts near the entrance with historical allegories; the larger, more elaborate scenes surrounding the altar are mostly stories from the Old Testament. Many of the floor

has bitten the dust.

Picture the scene: Ten snorting horses and their nervous riders line up near the pharmacy (on the west side of the square) to await the starting signal. Then they race like crazy while  spectators wave the scarves of their neighborhoods. Every possible vantage point and perch is packed with people straining to see the action. One lap around the course is about a third of a mile (350 meters); three laps make a full circuit. In this literally no-holds-barred race—which lasts just over a minute—a horse can win even without its rider (jockeys perch precariously without saddles on the sweaty horses' backs, and often fall off).

When the winner crosses the line, 1/17th of Siena—the prevailing neighborhood—goes berserk. Winners receive a *palio* (banner), typically painted by a local artist and always featuring the Virgin Mary. But the true prize is proving that your *contrada* is *numero uno* and mocking your losing rivals.

All over town, sketches and posters depict the Palio. This is not some folkloric event—it's a real medieval moment. If you're packed onto the square with 60,000 people, all hungry for victory, you won't see much, but you'll feel it. Bleacher and balcony seats are expensive, but it's free to join the masses in the square. Be sure to go with an empty bladder as there are no WCs, and be prepared to surrender any sense of personal space.

While the actual Palio packs the city, you could side-trip in from Florence to see the horse-race trials—called *prove* (prohvay)—on any of the three days before the main event (usually at 9:00 and after 19:00, free seats in bleachers). For more information, visit www.ilpalio.org.

panels are roped off—and occasionally even covered—to prevent further wear and tear.

• *Look for the marble altarpiece decorated with statues.*

Piccolomini Altar: This was designed for the tomb of the Sienese-born Pope Pius III (born Francesco Todeschini Piccolomini). It was commissioned when he was the cardinal of Siena, but because he later became a pope (see the fresco of his coronation with Pius wearing the golden robe—above and to the right of the Michelangelo statue), he was buried in the Vatican, and this fancy tomb was never used. It's most interesting for its statues: one by Michelangelo, and three by his students. Michelangelo was originally contracted to do 15 statues, but another sculptor had started the marble blocks, and Michelangelo's heart was never in the project. He personally finished only one—the figure of St. Paul (lower right, clearly more interesting than the bland, bored popes above him).

• *Now grab a seat under the...*

Dome: The dome sits on a 12-sided base, but its "coffered" ceiling is actually a painted illusion. Get oriented to the array of sights by thinking of the church floor as a big 12-hour clock. You're the middle, and the altar is high noon: You'll find the *Slaughter of the Innocents* roped off on the floor at 10 o'clock, Pisano's pulpit between two pillars at 11 o'clock, a copy of Duccio's round stained-glass window at 12 o'clock, Bernini's chapel at 3 o'clock, the Piccolomini Altar at 7 o'clock, the Piccolomini Library at 8 o'clock, and a Donatello statue at 9 o'clock.

Pisano's Pulpit: The octagonal Carrara marble pulpit (1268) rests on the backs of lions, symbols of Christianity triumphant.

Like the lions, the Church eats its catch (devouring paganism) and nurses its cubs. The seven relief panels tell the life of Christ in rich detail. The pulpit is the work of Nicola Pisano (c. 1220-1278), the "Giotto of sculpture," whose revival of classical forms (columns, sarcophagus-like relief panels) signaled the coming Renaissance. His son Giovanni (c. 1240-1319) carved many of the panels, mixing his dad's classicism and realism with the decorative detail and curvy lines of French Gothic—a style that would influence Donatello and the other Florentines.

Duccio's Stained-Glass Rose Window: This is a copy of the original window, which was moved to the Duomo Museum a couple of years ago. The famous rose window was created in 1288 and dedicated to the Virgin Mary.

Slaughter of the Innocents: This pavement panel shows Herod (left), sitting enthroned amid Renaissance arches, as he orders the massacre of all babies to prevent the coming of the promised Messiah. It's a chaotic scene of angry soldiers, grieving mothers, and dead babies, reminding locals that a republic ruled by a tyrant will experience misery.

• *Step into the chapel just beyond the pavement panel (next to the Piccolomini Library) to see the...*

St. John the Baptist **Statue:** The statue of the rugged saint in his famous rags was created by Donatello. The aging Florentine sculptor, whose style was now considered passé in Florence, came here to build bronze doors for the church (similar to Ghiberti's in

Florence). He didn't complete the door project, but he did finish this bronze statue (1457). Notice the cherubs high above it, playfully dangling their feet.

• *Cross beneath the dome to find the Chigi Chapel, also known as the...*

Chapel of the Madonna del Voto: To understand why Gian Lorenzo Bernini (1598-1680) is considered the greatest Baroque sculptor, step into this sumptuous chapel (designed in the early 1660s for Fabio Chigi, a.k.a. Pope Alexander VII). Move up to the altar and look back at the two Bernini statues: Mary Magdalene in a state of spiritual ecstasy, and St. Jerome playing the crucifix like a violinist lost in beautiful music. It's enough to make even a Lutheran light a candle.

The painting over the altar is the *Madonna del Voto,* a Madonna and Child adorned with a real crown of gold and jewels (painted by an unknown Italian master in the mid-13th century). In typical medieval fashion, the scene is set in the golden light of heaven. Mary has the almond eyes, long fingers, and golden folds in her robe that are found in orthodox icons of the time. Still, this Mary tilts her head and looks out sympathetically, ready to listen to the prayers of the faithful. This is the Mary to whom the Palio is dedicated, dear to the hearts of the Sienese. In thanks, they give **offerings** of silver hearts and medallions, many of which hang now on the wall just to the left as you exit the chapel.

• *Cross back to the other side of the church to find the...*

Piccolomini Library: Brilliantly frescoed, the library captures the exuberant, optimistic spirit of the 1400s, when humanism and the Renaissance were born. The never-restored frescoes look nearly as vivid now as the day they were finished 550 years ago. (With the bright window light, candles were unnecessary in this room—and didn't sully the art with soot.) The painter Pinturicchio (c. 1454-1513) was hired to celebrate the life of one of Siena's hometown boys—a man many call "the first humanist," Aeneas Piccolomini (1405-1464), who became Pope Pius II. Each of the 10 scenes is framed with an arch, as if Pinturicchio were opening a window onto the spacious 3-D world we inhabit.

The library also contains intricately decorated, illuminated music scores and a statue (a Roman copy of a Greek original) of the Three Graces, who almost seem to dance to the beat. The oddly huge sheep-skin sheets of music are from the days before individual hymnals—they had to be big so that many singers could read the music at the same time from a distance. Appreciate the fine painted decorations on the music—the gold-leaf highlights, the newly discovered (and quite expensive) cobalt for blue tones, and the miniature figures. All of this exquisite detail was lovingly crafted by Benedictine monks for the glory of God. Find your favorite—I like the blue, totally wild god of wind with the big hair (in the fourth case).

• *Exit the Duomo and make a U-turn to the left, walking alongside the church to Piazza Jacopo della Quercia.*

Unfinished Church: After rival republic Florence began its grand cathedral (1296), proud Siena planned to build one even bigger, the biggest church in all Christendom.

Construction began in the 1330s on an extension off the right side of the existing Duomo (today's cathedral would have been used as a transept). The nave of the Duomo was supposed to be where the piazza is today. Worshippers would have entered the church from the far end of the piazza through the unfinished wall. (Look way up at the highest part of the wall. That's the viewpoint accessible from inside the Duomo Museum.) Some of the nave's green-and-white-striped columns were built, and are now filled in with a brick wall. White stones in the pavement mark where a row of pillars would have been.

The vision was grand, but it underestimated the complexity of constructing such a building without enough land for it to sit upon. That, coupled with the devastating effects of a plague, killed the city's ability and will to finish the project. Look through the unfinished entrance facade, note blue sky where the stained-glass windows would have been, and ponder the struggles, triumphs, and failures of the human spirit.

▲▲Duomo Museum (Museo dell'Opera e Panorama)

Located in a corner of the Duomo's grand but unfinished extension (to the right as you face the main facade), Siena's most enjoyable museum was built to house the cathedral's art. Here you can stand eye-to-eye with the saints and angels who once languished unknown in the church's upper reaches (where copies are found today).

Cost and Hours: €7, covered by

Opa Si combo-ticket, buy tickets near Duomo Museum entry, daily March-Oct 10:30-19:00, Nov-Feb 10:30-17:30, last entry 30 minutes before closing, videoguide-€4 (€6/2 people); next to the Duomo, in the skeleton of the unfinished part of the church on the Il Campo side—look for the white banner, tel. 0577-286-300, www.operaduomo.siena.it.

Audioguides: You can rent a videoguide on a tablet computer for €4 (€6/2 people). A pricier option also covers the Duomo and other sights, but you have to pick it up and drop it off inside the cathedral.

SIENA

◗ **Self-Guided Tour:** Start your tour at the bottom and work your way up.

Ground Floor: This floor is filled with the cathedral's original Gothic sculptures by Giovanni Pisano, who spent 10 years in the late 1200s carving and orchestrating the decoration of the cathedral with saints, prophets, sibyls, animals, and the original she-wolf with Romulus and Remus.

On the ground floor you'll also find Donatello's fine, round *Madonna and Child* carved relief. A slender, tender Mary gazes down at her chubby-cheeked baby, as her sad eyes say that she knows the eventual fate of her son.

On the opposite side of the room is Duccio's original stained-glass window, which until recently was located above and behind the Duomo's altar. Now the church has a copy, and art lovers can enjoy a close-up look at this masterpiece. The rose window—20 feet across, made in 1288—is dedicated (like the church and the city itself) to the Virgin Mary. The work was designed by Siena's most famous artist, Duccio di Buoninsegna (c. 1255-1319), and combines elements from rigid Byzantine icons (Mary's almond-shaped bubble, called a *mandorla*, and the full-frontal saints that flank her) with a budding sense of 3-D realism (the throne turned at a three-quarter angle to simulate depth, with angels behind).

Duccio's *Maestà*: Upstairs awaits a private audience with the *Maestà* (*Enthroned Virgin*, 1311), whose panels were once part of the Duomo's main altarpiece. Although the former altarpiece was disassembled (and the frame was lost), most of the pieces are displayed here, with the front side (*Maestà*, with Mary and saints) at one end of the room, and the back side (26 Passion panels) at the other.

The *Maestà* was revolutionary for the time in its sheer size and opulence, and in Duccio's budding realism, which broke standard conventions. Duccio, at the height of his powers, used every innovative arrow in his quiver. He replaced the standard gold-leaf background (symbolizing heaven) with a gold, intricately patterned curtain draped over the throne. Mary's blue robe opens to reveal her body, and the curve of her knee suggests real anatomy beneath the robe. Baby Jesus wears a delicately transparent garment. Their faces are modeled with light—a patchwork of bright flesh and shadowy valleys, as if lit from the left (a technique he likely learned from his contemporary Giotto during a visit to Florence).

The flip side of the *Maestà* featured 26 smaller panels—the medieval equivalent of pages—showing colorful scenes from the Passion of Christ.

Panorama dal Facciatone: About 60 claustrophobic spiral stairs take you to the first viewpoint. You can continue up another similar spiral staircase to reach the very top. Standing on the wall from this high point in the city, you're rewarded with a stunning view of Siena...and an interesting perspective. Look toward the Duomo and consider this: If Siena's grandiose plans to expand the cathedral had come to fruition, you'd be looking straight down the nave toward the altar.

▲Baptistery

Siena is so hilly that there wasn't enough flat ground on which to build a big church. What to do? Build a big church anyway and prop up the overhanging edge with the Baptistery. This dark and quietly tucked-away cave of art is worth a look for its cool, tranquil bronze panels and angels by Ghiberti, Donatello, and others that adorn the pedestal of the baptismal font.

Cost and Hours: €4, covered by Opa Si combo-ticket, buy tickets near Duomo Museum entry, daily March-Oct 10:30-19:00, Nov-Feb 10:30-17:30, last entry 30 minutes before closing.

Crypt

The cathedral "crypt" is archaeologically important. The site of a small 12th-century Romanesque church, it was filled in with dirt a century after its creation to provide a foundation for the huge church that sits atop it today. Recently excavated, the several redis-covered frescoed rooms show off what are likely the oldest frescoes in town. Religious art exhibitions are sometimes held here.

Cost and Hours: €6, €8 during special exhibitions, covered by Opa Si combo-ticket, buy tickets near Duomo Museum entry, daily March-Oct 10:30-19:00, Nov-Feb 10:30-17:30, last entry 30 minutes before closing, entrance is halfway up the stairs between the Baptistery and Duomo Museum.

▲Santa Maria della Scala

This museum, opposite the Duomo entrance, was used as a hospital until the 1980s (though it may be closed for renovation during your visit). Its labyrinthine 12th-century cellars—carved out of volcanic tuff and finished with brick—go down several floors and during medieval times were used to store supplies for the hospital upstairs. Today, the hospital and its cellars are filled with exhibits (well-described in English) and can be a welcome refuge from the hot streets. Stop in for a cool and quiet break in the air-conditioned lobby, which offers a fine bookshop and big, comfy couches, all under great 15th-century timbers.

Cost and Hours: If open, likely around €6, daily March-Oct 10:30-18:00, Nov-Feb 10:30-16:00, last entry 30 minutes before closing, bookstore, tel. 0577-534-511, www.santamariadellascala.com.

Visiting the Museum: It's easy to get lost in this gigantic complex, so stay focused on the main attractions—the fancily frescoed Pellegrinaio Hall (ground floor), most of the original *Fountain of Joy* (first basement), and the Etruscan collection in the Archaeological Museum (second basement). Just inside the complex (enter from the square) is the Church of the Santissima Annunziata.

From the entrance, walk down the lengthy hall to the long room with the colorful frescoes. The sumptuously frescoed walls of **Pellegrinaio Hall** show medieval Siena's innovative health care and social welfare system in action (c. 1442, wonderfully described in English). Starting in the 11th century, the hospital nursed the sick and cared for abandoned children, as is vividly portrayed in these frescoes. The good works paid off, as bequests and donations poured in, creating the wealth that's evident throughout this building.

Head down the stairs, then continue straight into the darkened rooms with pieces of Siena's landmark fountain—follow signs to *Fonte Gaia*. An engaging exhibit explains Jacopo della Quercia's early 15th-century ***Fountain of Joy (Fonte Gaia)***—and displays the disassembled pieces of the original fountain itself. In the 19th century, after serious deterioration, the ornate fountain was dismantled, and plaster casts were made. (From these casts, they formed the replica that graces Il Campo today.) Here you'll see the eroded original panels paired with their restored casts, along with the actual statues that once stood on the edges of the fountain.

Descend into the cavernous second basement. Under the groin vaults of the **Archaeological Museum,** you're alone with piles of ancient Etruscan stuff excavated from tombs dating centuries before Christ (displayed in a labyrinthine exhibit). Remember, the Etruscans dominated this part of Italy before the Roman Empire swept through—some historians think even Rome originated as an Etruscan town.

San Domenico Area
Church of San Domenico

This huge brick church is worth a quick look. The spacious, plain interior (except for the colorful flags of the city's 17 *contrade,* or neighborhoods) fits the austere philosophy of

SIENA

SIENA

St. Catherine of Siena
(1347-1380)

The youngest of 25 children born to a Sienese cloth dyer, Catherine began experiencing heavenly visions as a child. At  16 she became a Dominican nun, locking herself away for three years in a room in her family's house. She lived the life of an ascetic, which culminated in a vision wherein she married Christ. Catherine emerged from solitude to join her Dominican sisters, sharing her experiences, caring for the sick, and gathering both disciples and enemies. At age 23, she lapsed into a spiritual coma, waking with the heavenly command to spread her message to the world. She wrote essays and letters to kings, dukes, bishops, and popes, imploring them to find peace for a war-ravaged Italy. While visiting Pisa during Lent of 1375, she had a vision in which she received the stigmata, the wounds of Christ.

Still in her twenties, Catherine was invited to Avignon, France, where the pope had taken up residence. With her charm, sincerity, and reputation for holiness, she helped convince Pope Gregory XI to return the papacy to the city of Rome. Catherine also went to Rome, where she died young. She was canonized in the next generation (by a Sienese pope), and her relics were distributed to churches around Italy.

Because of her intervention in the papal schism, today Catherine is revered (along with St. Benedict) as the patron saint of Europe and remembered as a rare outspoken medieval woman still appreciated for her universal message: that this world is not a gift from our fathers, but a loan from our children.

the Dominicans and invites meditation on the thoughts and deeds of St. Catherine. Walk up the steps in the rear to see paintings from her life. Halfway up the church on the right, find a metal bust of St. Catherine, a small case housing her thumb (on the left), and a glass box on the lowest shelf containing the chain she used to scourge herself. In the chapel (15 feet to the left) surrounded with candles, you'll see Catherine's actual head atop the altar. Through the door just beyond are the sacristy and the bookstore.

Cost and Hours: Free, daily 7:00-18:30, gift shop tel. 0577-286-848, www.basilicacateriniana.com. A WC (€0.50) is at the far end of the parking lot, to the right as you face the church entrance.

Sanctuary of St. Catherine (Santuario di Santa Caterina)
Step into the cool and peaceful site of Catherine's home. Siena remembers its favorite hometown gal, a simple, unschooled, but mystically devout soul who, in the mid-1300s, helped convince the pope to return from France to Rome. Pilgrims have visited this place since 1464, and architects and artists have greatly embellished what was probably once a humble home (her family worked as wool dyers). You'll see paintings throughout showing scenes from her life.

Enter through the courtyard, and walk down the stairs at the far end. The church on your right contains the wooden crucifix upon which Catherine was meditating when she received the stigmata. Take a pew, gaze at it, and try to imagine the scene. Back outside, the oratory across the courtyard stands where the kitchen once was. Go down the stairs (left of the gift shop) to reach the saint's room. Catherine's bare cell is behind wrought-iron doors.

Cost and Hours: Free, daily 9:00-18:00, church closed 12:30-15:00, a few downhill blocks toward the center from San Domenico—follow signs to *Santuario di Santa Caterina*—at Costa di Sant'Antonio 6, tel. 0577-288-175.

Shopping in Siena

The main drag, Via Banchi di Sopra, is a cancan of fancy shops. Here are some things to look for:

Flags: For easy-to-pack souvenirs, get some of the large, colorful scarves/flags that depict the symbols of Siena's 17 different neighborhoods (such as the wolf, the turtle, or the snail). They're good for gifts or to decorate your home (sold in varying sizes at souvenir stands).

Sweets: All over town, Prodotti Tipici shops sell Sienese specialties. Siena's claim to caloric fame is its *panforte*, a rich, chewy concoction of nuts, honey, and candied fruits that impresses even fruitcake haters. There are a few varieties: *Margherita*, dusted in powdered sugar, is more fruity, while *panpepato* has a spicy, peppery crust. Locals prefer a chewy, white macaroon-and-almond cookie called *ricciarelli*.

Sleep Code

(€1 = about $1.30, country code: 39)
S = Single, **D** = Double/Twin, **T** = Triple, **Q** = Quad, **b** = bathroom, **s** = shower only.

Unless otherwise noted, credit cards are accepted, English is spoken, and breakfast is included. If your hotel doesn't provide breakfast, eat at a bar on Il Campo or near your hotel. Many cities in Italy levy a hotel tax of €2 per person, per night, which must be paid in cash (not included in the rates I've quoted).

To help you easily sort through these listings, I've divided the accommodations into three categories based on the price for a standard double room with bath during high season:

$$$ Higher Priced—Most rooms €130 or more.
$$ Moderately Priced—Most rooms between €90-130.
$ Lower Priced—Most rooms €90 or less.

Prices can change without notice; verify the hotel's current rates online or by email. For the best prices, always book direct.

Sleeping in Siena

Finding a room in Siena is tough during Easter (April 20 in 2014) or the Palio (July 2 and Aug 16). Many hotels won't take reservations until the end of May for the Palio, and even then they might require a four-night stay. While day-tripping tour groups turn the town into a Gothic amusement park in midsummer, Siena is basically yours in the evenings and off-season.

Part of Siena's charm is its lively, festive character—this means that all hotels can be plagued with noise, even (and sometimes especially) the hotels in the pedestrian-only zone. If tranquility is important for your sanity, ask for a room that's off the street, or consider staying at one of the recommended places outside the center.

Fancy Sleeps, Southwest of Il Campo

These well-run places are a 10-minute walk from Il Campo.

$$$ Pensione Palazzo Ravizza is elegant and friendly, with 38 rooms and an aristocratic feel—fitting, as it was once the luxurious residence of a noble. Guests enjoy a peaceful garden set on a dramatic bluff, along with a Steinway in the upper lounge (Sb-€180, small loft Db-€140, standard Db-€180, superior Db-€220, Tb-€255, family suites-€300, rates can vary, see website for room differences, rooms in back overlook countryside, air-con, elevator, free Wi-Fi, Via Piano dei Mantellini 34, tel. 0577-280-462, www.palazzoravizza.it, bureau@palazzoravizza.it). As parking is free and the hotel is easily walkable from the center, this is a particularly good value for drivers.

$$$ Hotel Duomo has 20 spacious but slightly dated rooms, a picnic-friendly roof terrace, and a bizarre floor plan (Sb-€105, Db-€130, Db suite-€180, Tb-€180, Qb-€230, elevator with some stairs, air-con, free Wi-Fi, discounted parking-€20/day; follow Via di Città, which becomes Via di Stalloreggi, to #38; tel. 0577-289-088, www.hotelduomo.it, booking@hotelduomo.it, Alessandro). If you're arriving by train, take a taxi (€12) or ride bus #3 to the Porta Tufi stop, just a few minutes' walk from the hotel; you can also arrange to have Alessandro take you to/from the train station or airport (with this book: train station-€10, Florence's Vespucci Airport-€105, Pisa's Galilei Airport-€165; he'll also take you to nearby hill towns, e.g. Florence-€105 and Pisa-€165). If you're driving, go to Porta San Marco, turn right, and follow signs to the hotel—drop your bags, then park in the nearby Il Campo lot near Porta Tufi.

Simple Places near Il Campo

Most of these listings are forgettable but well-priced, and just a horse wreck away from one of Italy's most wonderful civic spaces.

$$ Piccolo Hotel Etruria, with 20 simple, recently redecorated rooms, is well-located and restful (S-€50, Sb-€60, Db-€90-110, Tb-€120-138, Qb-€145 166, higher rates are for peak-of-peak times, 10 percent discount with this book, optional breakfast-€5, air-con May-Oct only, elevator, Wi-Fi, next to recommended Albergo Tre Donzelle at Via delle Donzelle 1-3, tel. 0577-288-088, www.hoteletruria.com, info@hoteletruria.com, friendly Conti family).

$ Albergo Tre Donzelle is a fine budget value with 20 plain, well-worn rooms. Although the showers have seen better days, these may be the cheapest rooms in the center. Don't hang out here...think of Il Campo, a block away, as your terrace (S-€38, D-€49, Db-€60, T-€70, Tb-€85, no rooms available for Palio, breakfast-€5, free Wi-Fi; with your back to the tower, head away from Il Campo toward 2 o'clock to Via delle Donzelle 5; tel. 0577-280-358, www.tredonzelle.com, info@tredonzelle.com).

$ Hotel Cannon d'Oro, a few blocks up Via Banchi di Sopra, is a labyrinthine slumbermill renting 30 institutional, overpriced rooms (Sb-€71, Db-€90, Tb-€115, Qb-€136, these discounted prices good with this book through 2014, fans, free Wi-Fi in lobby and some rooms, a couple of blocks from the bus hub at Via dei Montanini 28, tel. 0577-44-321, www.cannondoro.com, info@cannondoro.com; Maurizio, Tommaso, and Rodrigo).

SIENA

SIENA

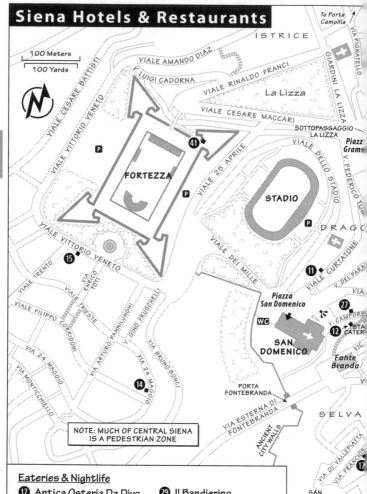

Siena Hotels & Restaurants

100 Meters
100 Yards

ISTRICE

To Porta
Camollia

VIALE AMANDO DIAZ

V. LUIGI CADORNA

VIALE RINALDO FRANCI

La Lizza

VIALE CESARE MACCARI

SOTTOPASSAGGIO
LA LIZZA

Piazz
Grams

VIALE DELLO STADIO

V. FEDERICO TO

FORTEZZA

VIALE 25 APRILE

STADIO

DRAGO

VIALE DEI MILLE

VIALE CURTATONE

V. DEL PARA

VIA

🕚 **11**

VIALE VITTORIO VENETO

🕟 **15**

Piazza
San Domenico

27

V. CAMPORE

STA
CATER

WC

12

VIC

**SAN
DOMENICO**

Fonte
Branda

🕝 **14**

PORTA
FONTEBRANDA

VIA ESTERNA DI
FONTEBRANDA

ANCIENT
CITY WALLS

SELVA

VIA DI VALLEPIATTA

17

VIA FRANCE

NOTE: MUCH OF CENTRAL SIENA
IS A PEDESTRIAN ZONE

SAN
SEBASTIANO

SANTISSIMA
ANNUNCIATA

**SANTA MARI
DELLA SCAL**
(MUSEUM)

PANTER

Piazza
di Due Porte

8

1

PIANO MANTELLIN

To **9**

Eateries & Nightlife

17 Antica Osteria Da Divo
18 Taverna San Giuseppe
19 Compagnia dei Vinattieri
20 Hostaria Il Carroccio
21 Trattoria La Torre,
   Ciao Cafeteria &
   Spizzico Pizza
22 Osteria del Gatto
23 Ristorante Guidoriccio
24 Trattoria Papei
25 Osteria Trombicche
26 La Taverna Di Cecco
27 Il Pomodorino
28 Rist. Alla Speranza
   & Bar Paninoteca
   San Paolo

29 Il Bandierino
30 Bar Il Palio
31 Osteria Liberamente
32 Costarella Gelateria
33 Key Largo Bar
34 Antica Pizzicheria al
   Palazzo della Chigiana
35 Pizzeria San Martino
36 Rosticceria Vitti
37 Consorzio Agrario
   Siena Grocery
38 Nannini Pastry Shop
39 Gelateria Grom
40 Un Tubo
41 Enoteca Italiana

SIENA

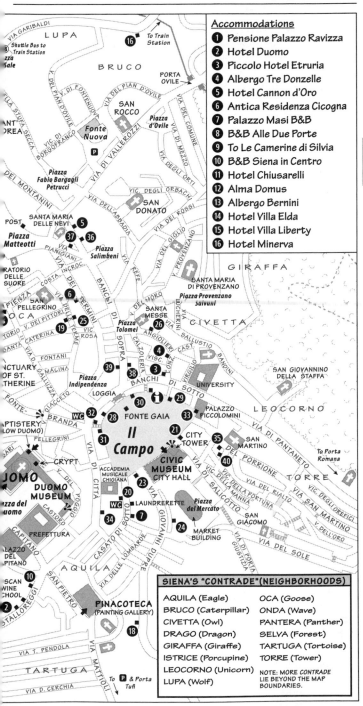

Accommodations
1 Pensione Palazzo Ravizza
2 Hotel Duomo
3 Piccolo Hotel Etruria
4 Albergo Tre Donzelle
5 Hotel Cannon d'Oro
6 Antica Residenza Cicogna
7 Palazzo Masi B&B
8 B&B Alle Due Porte
9 To Le Camerine di Silvia
10 B&B Siena in Centro
11 Hotel Chiusarelli
12 Alma Domus
13 Albergo Bernini
14 Hotel Villa Elda
15 Hotel Villa Liberty
16 Hotel Minerva

SIENA'S "CONTRADE" (NEIGHBORHOODS)

AQUILA (Eagle)
BRUCO (Caterpillar)
CIVETTA (Owl)
DRAGO (Dragon)
GIRAFFA (Giraffe)
ISTRICE (Porcupine)
LEOCORNO (Unicorn)
LUPA (Wolf)

OCA (Goose)
ONDA (Wave)
PANTERA (Panther)
SELVA (Forest)
TARTUGA (Tortoise)
TORRE (Tower)

NOTE: MORE CONTRADE
LIE BEYOND THE MAP
BOUNDARIES.

B&Bs in the Old Center

$$ Antica Residenza Cicogna is a seven-room guesthouse with a homey elegance and an ideal location. It's warmly run by the young and charming Elisa and her dad, Fabio, who set out biscotti, *vin santo,* and tea all day for their guests. With artfully frescoed walls and ceilings, this is remarkably genteel for the price (Db-€95, suite Db-€120, third bed-€15, air-con, free guest computer, free Wi-Fi, Via delle Terme 76, tel. 0577-285-613, mobile 347-007-2888, www.anticaresidenzacicogna.it, info@anticaresidenzacicogna.it).

$$ Palazzo Masi B&B, run by Alizzardo and Daniela, is just below Il Campo. They rent six pleasant, spacious, antique-furnished rooms with shared common areas on the second and third floors of an old building. While a bit pricey, the fine location and warm welcome are appreciated (D-€80, Db-€120 if you book direct, discounts for 4 or more nights, cash only, breakfast-€8, free Wi-Fi, discounted parking at nearby Il Campo lot-€25/24 hours; from City Hall, walk 50 yards down Via del Casato di Sotto to #29; mobile 349-600-9155, www.palazzomasi.com, info@palazzomasi.it). The place is sometimes unstaffed, so it's important to phone upon arrival.

$ B&B Alle Due Porte is a charming little establishment renting four big rooms with sweet furniture under big medieval beams. The shared breakfast room is delightful. The manager, Egisto, is a phone call and five-minute scooter ride away (Db-€85, windowless Db with small bed-€65, Tb-€110, air-con in two rooms, free Wi-Fi, Via di Stalloreggi 51, tel. 0577-287-670, mobile 368-352-3530, www.sienatur.it, soldatini@interfree.it).

$ Le Camerine di Silvia, a romantic hideaway perched near a sweeping, grassy olive grove, rents five simple but cozy rooms in a converted 16th-century building. A small breakfast terrace with fruit trees and a private hedged garden lends itself to contemplation (Db-€50-€80, rate depends on season, cash only, ask for a view room, fans, Wi-Fi, shared microwave and small fridge, nearby parking-€12, free parking a 10-minute walk away, Via Ettore Bastianini 1-3, just below recommended Pensione Palazzo Ravizza—see listing earlier, mobile 338-761-5052 or 339-123-7687, www.lecamerinedisilvia.com, info@lecamerinedisilvia.com, Conti family).

$ B&B Siena in Centro is a clearinghouse managing five good and centrally located private apartments. Their handy office functions as a reception renting out a total of about 20 rooms; stop by here to pick up your key and be escorted to your apartment. The rooms are generally spacious, quiet, and comfortable, but with no air-conditioning or Wi-Fi. Their website lets you visualize your options (Sb-€45-60, Db-€70-90, Tb-€90-120, reception open 9:00-13:30 & 15:00-19:00, later in high season, other times by phone request, OK to leave bags at reception, Via di Stalloreggi 14, tel. 0577-43041, mobile 331-281-0136 or 347-465-9753, www.bbsienaincentro.com, info@bbsienaincentro.com, Gioia or Michela).

Near San Domenico Church

These hotels are within a 10-minute walk northwest of Il Campo. Both Albergo Bernini and Alma Domus offer fine panoramas of the old town for reasonable prices.

$$$ Hotel Chiusarelli, with 48 classy rooms in a beautiful Neoclassical villa, has a handy location but is on a very busy street. Expect traffic noise at night—ask for a quieter room in the back (can be guaranteed with reservation). The bells of San Domenico are your 7:00 wake-up call (Sb-€105, Db-€150, Tb-€190, ask for 10 percent Rick Steves discount when you book, air-con, free Wi-Fi with this book, across from San Domenico at Viale Curtatone 15, tel. 0577-280-562, www.chiusarelli.com, info@chiusarelli.com).

$ Alma Domus is a church-run hotel featuring 43 spartan rooms with quaint balconies, some fantastic views (ask for a room *con vista*), stately public rooms, and a pleasant atmosphere. However, the thin doors, echoey halls, and nearby church bells can be drawbacks; ask for a room with double-paned windows or bring earplugs. The 10:00 checkout time is strict, but they will store your luggage in their secure courtyard (Sb-€48, Db-€85, Tb-€110, air-con, elevator, pay guest computer, pay Wi-Fi; from San Domenico, walk downhill toward the view with the church on your right, turn left down Via Camporegio, make a U-turn down the brick steps to Via Camporegio 37; tel. 0577-44-177, www.hotelalmadomus.it, info@hotelalmadomus.it, Luigi).

$ Albergo Bernini makes you part of a Sienese family in a modest, clean home with 10 traditional rooms. Giovanni, charming wife Daniela, and their three daughters welcome you to their spectacular view terrace for breakfast and picnic lunches and dinners (S-€55, D-€65, Sb or small Db with view-€78, Db-€85, less in winter, optional breakfast-€3.50/small or €7.50/big, cash only, free Wi-Fi, on the main Il Campo-San Domenico drag at Via della Sapienza 15, tel. 0577-289-047, www.albergobernini.com, hbernin@tin.it).

Farther from the Center

These options, a 10- to 20-minute walk from the center, are great for drivers.

Near Porta Romana City Gate

These two fine spots are about 200 yards outside the Porta Romana. To get to downtown Siena from here, catch minibus line A uphill to Piazza al Mercato, just behind Il Campo (€1.10). To reach the bus and train stations, take bus #2 (which becomes #17 at Piazza del Sale; when arriving, catch #17 from the station). If driving, from the freeway, take the Siena Sud exit, continue in direction Romana, then at the first light turn left, following *Pta Romana/Centro* signs for about half a mile until you see the big city gate.

$$$ Hotel Santa Caterina is a three-star, 18th-century place renting 22 comfy rooms. It's professionally run with real attention to quality. While it's on a big city street, it has a delightful garden terrace with views over the countryside (Sb-€125, four small Db-€125, Db-€165, split-level Tb or Qb-€215, prices promised with this book through 2014, can be cheaper in low season, garden side is quieter, air-con, fridge in room, elevator, free Wi-Fi, parking-€15/day—request when you reserve, Via E.S. Piccolomini 7, tel. 0577-221-105, www.hscsiena.it, info@hscsiena.it, Lorenza and her crew).

$$ Hotel Porta Romana is at the edge of town, off a busy road. Some of its 15 rooms face the open countryside (request one of these), and breakfast is served in the garden (Sb-€90, Db-€110, extra person-€20, 10 percent Rick Steves discount if you book direct and pay cash, air-con in most rooms, free guest computer, free Wi-Fi, free parking, inviting sun terrace, outdoor hot tub-€10/person per stay, Via E.S. Piccolomini 35, tel. 0577-42299, www.hotelportaromana.com, info@hotelportaromana.com; Marco and Evelia).

In the Posh Neighborhood South of the Fortress

These two places are in a villa-studded residential neighborhood across a gully from San Domenico Church. They're about 5-10 minutes farther than the listings under "Near San Domenico Church," earlier, but the extra walking gets you to a swankier address.

$$$ Hotel Villa Elda rents 11 bright and light rooms in a recently renovated villa. It's classy, stately, pricey, and run with a feminine charm (Db-€140-170, about €20 more for view, extra person-€30, air-con, free Wi-Fi, garden and view terrace, Viale Ventiquattro Maggio 10, tel. 0577-247-927, www.villaeldasiena.it, info@villaeldasiena.it).

$$$ Hotel Villa Liberty, across a busy street from the fortress, is a former private mansion. It has 17 big, bright, comfortable rooms and some road noise (Sb-€80, Db-€150, Tb-€180, €10 more for superior room, air-con, elevator, free Wi-Fi, bar, courtyard, free and easy street parking, facing fortress at Viale Vittorio Veneto 11, tel. 0577-44-966, www.villaliberty.it, info@villaliberty.it).

Just Inside Porta Ovile, at the North End of Town

$$ Hotel Minerva is your big, professional, plain, efficient option.

It's the most impersonal of my listings, with zero personality but predictable comfort. While its 56 rooms are boring, they don't hide any unpleasant surprises. It works best for those with cars—parking is reasonable (€12/day), and it's only a 10-minute walk from the action (Sb-€76, Db-€122, Tb-€168, bigger suites available for more, ask for a view room, air-con, elevator, free guest computer, pay Wi-Fi, Via Garibaldi 72, tel. 0577-284-474, www.albergominerva.it, info@albergominerva.it).

East of Siena

$$$ Frances' Lodge Relais is a tranquil and delightfully managed farmhouse B&B a mile out of Siena. Each of its six rooms is bursting with character (all well-described on their website). Franca and Franco run this rustic-yet-elegant old place, which features a 19th-century orangery that's been made into a "better homes and palaces" living room, as well as a peaceful garden, eight acres of olive trees and vineyards, and great views of Siena and its countryside—even from the swimming pool (small Db-€170, Db-€190, Db suite-€220, Tb-€210-220, Tb suite-€280, Qb suite-€340, these prices promised to Rick Steves readers through 2014 if you book direct, possibly cheaper for longer stays, air-con, free guest computer, free Wi-Fi, free parking, Strada di Valdipugna 2, tel. 0577-42379, mobile 337-671-608, www.franceslodge.it). To the center, it's a five-minute bus ride (€1.10, they'll call to arrange) plus a five-minute walk, or €10 by taxi. Consider having an al fresco dinner in the gazebo, complete with view (make your own picnic, or have your hosts assemble a very fancy one for €20/person).

Outside Siena

The following accommodations are set in the lush, peaceful countryside surrounding Siena, and are best for those traveling by car.

$$$ Borgo Argenina has seven rooms in a well-maintained, pricey splurge of a B&B. Run by helpful Elena Nappa, it's 20 minutes north of Siena by car in the Chianti region (Db-€170, beautiful gardens, free Wi-Fi, mobile 345-353-7673, www.borgoargenina.it, info@borgoargenina.it).

$$ Il Canto del Sole is a restored 18th-century farmhouse turned family-friendly B&B located about six miles outside the Porta Romana city gate. Run by Laura, Luciano, and their son Marco, it features 10 bright and airy rooms and two apartments with original antique furnishings, a saltwater swimming pool, a game room, and bike rentals (Db-€120, Tb-€140, extra bed-€30, apartment-€180-220, air-con, free Wi-Fi, free parking, dinner cooked on request, Val di Villa Canina 1292, 53014 Loc. Cuna, tel. 0577-375-127, www.ilcantodelsole.com, info@ilcantodelsole.com).

Eating in Siena

Sienese restaurants are reasonable by Florentine and Venetian standards. You can enjoy ordering high on the menu here without going broke. For me, the best €5 you can spend in Siena is on a cocktail at Bar Il Palio, overlooking Il Campo. For pasta, a good option is *pici* (PEE-chee), a thick Sienese spaghetti that seems to be at the top of every menu.

Fine Dining in the Old Town

For only a few euros more, these four places deliver a more upscale ambience and generally better food than my later recommendations.

Antica Osteria Da Divo is *the* place for a dressy and atmospheric €45 meal. The kitchen is creative, the ambience is flowery and candlelit, some of the seating fills old Etruscan tombs, and the food is fresh, delicate, and top-notch. While the cuisine is flamboyant and almost over-the-top, Chef Pino and his wife Susanna serve up my favorite splurge dinner in town. Pino is a fanatic for fresh ingredients, enjoys giving traditional dishes his creative spin, and is understandably proud of his desserts. The wine is good, too—you can order it by the glass (€4-7) if you ask (€10-12 pastas, €20-26 *secondi*, €3 cover, Wed-Mon 12:00-14:30 & 19:00-22:30, closed Tue, reservations smart; facing Baptistery door, take the far right street and walk one long curving block to Via Franciosa 29; tel. 0577-284-381, www.osteriadadivo.it). Those dining here with this book can finish with a complimentary biscotti and *vin santo* or coffee (upon request).

Taverna San Giuseppe, a local favorite, offers modern Tuscan cuisine in a chic grotto atmosphere. While the vibe is high energy and casual, the food compares favorably with the slightly more upscale places listed here. The wine-and-cheese cellar in back is cut from an Etruscan tomb. Check the posters tacked around the entry for daily specials. Reserve or arrive early to get a table (€8-10 pastas, €15-20 *secondi*, Mon-Sat 12:00-14:30 & 19:00-22:00, closed Sun, air-con, 7-minute climb up street to the right of City Hall at Via Giovanni Dupre 132, tel. 0577-42-286, www.tavernasangiuseppe.it, Matteo).

Compagnia dei Vinattieri serves modern Tuscan dishes with a creative twist. In this elegantly unpretentious space, you can enjoy a quiet and romantic meal under graceful brick arches. The menu is small and accessible, and the young staff will help you match your meal with the right wine. Marco, the owner, is happy to take you down to the marvelous wine cellar (€9-12 pastas, €16-18 *secondi*, leave this book on the table for a complimentary *aperitivo* or dessert drink, daily 12:30-15:00 & 19:30-23:00, near Via dei Pittori at Via delle Terme 79, tel. 0577-236-568, www.vinattieri.net).

Hostaria Il Carroccio, artsy and convivial, seats guests in a tight, sea-foam-green dining room and serves elegantly presented, traditional "slow food" recipes with innovative flair at affordable prices (€8 pastas, €14-18 *secondi*, €30 tasting *menu*—minimum two people, cash only, reservations wise, Thu-Tue 12:30-15:00 & 19:30-22:00, closed Wed, Via del Casato di Sotto 32, tel. 0577-41-165, sweet Renata and Mauro).

Traditional and Rustic Places in the Old Town

Trattoria La Torre is a thriving, unfussy *casalinga* (home-cooking) eatery, popular for its homemade pasta, plates of which entice customers as they enter. The sound of its busy open kitchen adds to the conviviality. Ten tables are packed under one medieval brick arch. Service is brisk and casual, and despite its priceless position below the namesake tower, it feels more like a local hangout than a tourist trap. Study the menu in the window before entering; otherwise, the owner likes to just recite his long list of dishes (€7-8 pastas, €8-10 *secondi*, €2 cover, Fri-Wed 12:00-15:00 & 19:00-22:00, closed Thu, just steps below Il Campo at Via di Salicotto 7, tel. 0577-287-548, Alberto Boccini).

Osteria del Gatto is a classic little hole-in-the-wall, thriving with townspeople and powered by a passion for serving good Sienese cuisine. Marco Coradeschi and his engaged staff cook and serve daily specials with attitude. As it's so small and popular, it can get loud (€8-9 pastas, €8-10 *secondi*, Mon-Fri 12:30-15:00 & 19:30-22:00, Sat 19:30-22:00 only, closed Sun, 5-minute walk away from the center at Via San Marco 8, tel. 0577-287-133).

Ristorante Guidoriccio, just a few steps below Il Campo, feels warm and welcoming. You'll get smiling service from Ercole and Elisabetta. While mostly filled with tourists, the place has a charm—especially if you let gentle Ercole explore the menu with you, and follow his suggestions (€9 pastas, €13-15 *secondi*, Mon-Sat 12:30-14:30 & 19:00-22:30, closed Sun, air-con, Via Giovanni Dupre 2, tel. 0577-44-350).

Trattoria Papei is a Sienese favorite, featuring a casual, rollicking family atmosphere and friendly servers dishing out generous portions of rib-stickin' Tuscan specialties and grilled meats. This big, sprawling place under tents in a parking lot is in all the guidebooks and often jammed—so call to reserve (€7 pastas, €8-12 *secondi*, daily 12:00-15:00 & 19:00-22:30, on the market square directly behind City Hall at Piazza del Mercato 6, tel. 0577-280-894; for 50 years Signora Giuliana has ruled her kitchen, Amadeo and Eduardo speak English).

Osteria Trombicche takes you back to another age—cheap and small, with tight indoor seating and two tiny outdoor tables from which to watch the street scene. Alessandro serves fast, hearty food to a local crowd (€6.50 *ribollita*—bean-and-vegetable soup—in winter, €5 *panzanella*—bread salad with tomato and basil—in summer, €8-10 mixed-vegetable antipasto plates, hand-cut prosciutto, Mon-Sat 11:00-15:00 & 18:00-22:00, Sun 11:00-15:00, Via delle Terme 66, tel. 0577-288-089).

La Taverna Di Cecco is a simple, comfortable little eatery on an uncrowded back lane where earnest Luca and Gianni serve tasty salads and Sienese specialties made by their grandmother from fresh ingredients (€8-12 pastas, €10-20 *secondi*, daily 12:00-16:00 & 19:00-24:00, Via Cecco Angiolieri 19, tel. 0577-288-518).

Il Pomodorino is a lively restaurant with a great view of the Duomo from its outdoor terrace. Tasty €8 pizzas pair well with a beer from their wide selection. The more intimate interior has Italian proverbs on the walls (daily 12:30-24:00 or later, a few steps from the recommended Alma Domus hotel at Via Camporegio 13, tel. 0577-286-811, mobile 345-026-5865).

Places on Il Campo

If you choose to eat on perhaps the finest town square in Italy, you'll pay a premium, meet waiters who don't need to hustle, and get mediocre food. And yet I recommend it. The clamshell-shaped square is lined with venerable cafés, bars, restaurants, and pizzerias.

To experience Il Campo without paying for a full meal, consider having drinks or breakfast on the square. Some bars serve food. And if your hotel doesn't include breakfast or if you'd like something more memorable, Il Campo has plenty of options. A cappuccino and a *cornetto* (croissant) run about €5-6.

Dining and Drinks on the Square

Ristorante Alla Speranza has perhaps the best view in all of Italy. If you're looking to eat reasonably on Il Campo, this is your place (€8-10 pastas and pizzas, €13-15 *secondi*, €3 cover charge, daily 9:00-late, tel. 0577-280-190). It's smart to reserve the view table of your choice by phone—or simply stop by earlier in the day while you're sightseeing in the square.

Il Bandierino is another decent option with an angled view of City Hall (€8-12 salads, €11-12 pizzas, €13-15 pastas; no cover but a 20 percent service fee, daily 11:00-23:00, tel. 0577-282-217, Hugo).

Bar Il Palio is the best bar on Il Campo for a pre- or post-dinner drink: It has straightforward prices, no cover, decent waiters, and a fantastic perspective out over the square.

Dynamic little **Osteria Liberamente** (on the square, not above it) has a trendy vibe and is popular with young people (fine wine by the glass, €7 cocktails with good tapas, Wed-Mon 8:00 until late, closed Tue, Pino).

Nightlife in Siena

Evenings are a wonderful time to be out and about in Siena, after the tour groups have left for the day.

Join the evening *passeggiata* (peak strolling time is 19:00) along Via Banchi di Sopra with gelato in hand. I like **Gelateria Grom,** which serves "Gelato like it used to be." Its seasonal flavors and all-natural ingredients make it a popular stop for any Sienese in need of something cool and sweet to lick while strolling (a little pricier than the competition, daily 11:00-24:00, Banchi di Sopra 13).

A fun trend in Siena is the *aperitivo*. All over town, you'll find bars attracting an early-evening crowd by serving a free buffet of food with the purchase of a drink. For many, this can be a light dinner for the cost of a drink. Or consider starting or ending a meal with a drink or dessert on Il Campo. For suggestions, see "Places on Il Campo."

Un Tubo is a chic little bar tucked away in a mysterious alley just five minutes from Il Campo. It's perched on top of Etruscan caves, which are open to visitors and serve as a cellar for their many international wines. The scene—mainly local artsy types—is sometimes accompanied by live music or a DJ playing lounge music (daily 13:00 until late, light snacks available, Via del Luparello 2; from Il Campo, head down Via Porrione and turn right on Via del Luparello, just after San Martino church; tel. 0577-271-312). Giandomenico speaks English and will make you feel welcome.

Enoteca Italiana is a good wine bar in a cellar in the Fortezza, funded in part by the government to promote Italian wine production. They have about 15 different bottles open on any given day, and they offer tastings for €3-10. To get there, enter the Fortezza via the bridge, cross the running track, and—after passing a tree—go left down a ramp (Mon-Sat 12:00-24:00, closed Sun, snacks served when the bar's pricey restaurant is between mealtimes, outside terrace, tel. 0577-228-832).

Drinks or Snacks from Balconies
Overlooking Il Campo

Three places have skinny balconies with benches overlooking the main square for their customers. Sipping a coffee or nibbling a pastry here while marveling at the Il Campo scene is one of my favorite things to do in Europe. And it's very cheap. Survey these three places from Il Campo (with your back to the tower, they are at 10 o'clock, high noon, and 3 o'clock, respectively).

The little **Costarella Gelateria,** on the corner of Via di Città and Costa dei Barbieri, has good drinks and light snacks, such as cute little €3.50 sandwiches, though the gelato tastes artificial (daily 8:00-late, Via di Città 33). While the restaurant is for regular service, you're welcome to take anything from the bar out to the simple benches (just walk through the "table service only" section upstairs) and eat with a grand view overlooking Il Campo.

Bar Paninoteca San Paolo has a youthful pub ambience and a row of stools lining a skinny balcony overlooking the square. It serves big €7 salads and 50 kinds of €4 sandwiches, hot and cold—not authentic Italian, but quick and filling (order and pay at the counter, food served daily 12:00-2:00 in the morning, on Vicolo di San Paolo, tel. 0577-226-622).

Key Largo Bar has two long, second-story benches in the corner offering a wonderful secret perch. Buy your drink or snack at the bar (no cover and no extra charge to sit on balcony), climb upstairs, and slide the ancient bar to open the door. Enjoy stretching out, and try to imagine how, during the Palio, three layers of spectators cram into this space—note the iron railing used to plaster the top row of sardines up against the wall. Suddenly you're picturing Palio ponies zipping wildly around the corner (€4 cocktails, daily 7:00-24:00, on the corner of Via Rinaldini). If you can't get a seat on the outdoor benches, skip the otherwise nondescript, youthful interior.

Eating Cheaply in the Center

Antica Pizzicheria al Palazzo della Chigiana (look for the sign reading *Pizzicheria de Miccoli*) may be the official name, but I bet locals just call it Antonio's. For most of his life, frenzied Antonio has carved salami and cheese for the neighborhood. Most of the day, a hungry line spills onto the street as people wait for their sandwiches—meat and cheese sold by weight—with a good €10 bottle of Chianti (Italian law dictates that he must sell you a bottle of wine—cheap and good—and lend you the glasses). Antonio and his boys offer a big cheese-and-meat plate (about €18 gets you 30 minutes of eating) and pull out a tiny tabletop in the corner so you can munch or sip while standing and watching the ham-hock-y scene. Or just grab a €4-5 sandwich. Even if you don't eat here, pop in to inhale the commotion or peruse Antonio's gifty traditional edibles (daily 8:00-20:00, Via di Città 95, tel. 0577-289-164).

Ciao Cafeteria, at the bottom of Il Campo, offers good-value, self-service lunches, but no ambience or views (hearty €5-7 meals, daily 12:00-15:00). The crowded **Spizzico,** a pizza counter in the front half of Ciao, serves huge €4-5 quarter-pizzas. For both places, the food and ambience recall a cut-rate truck stop—but on sunny days, people take the pizza out on Il Campo for a memorable picnic (daily 11:00-21:00, to left of City Tower as you face it).

Pizza: Spizzico (listed above) is worth considering only if you're standing on Il Campo, desperate for pizza, and unashamedly lazy. Budget eaters look for *pizza al taglio* shops, scattered throughout Siena, selling better pizza by the slice. One good bet, **San Martino,** a couple blocks behind Il Campo, is a local-feeling spot with €2-3 slices and sandwiches (Mon-Sat 8:00-14:30 & 16:30-21:00, closed Sun, Via del Porrione 64).

Rosticcerie: For cheap take-out food, look for a *rosticceria.* One affordable, central option that feels at least partly untouristed is **Rosticceria Vitti,** near Piazza Gramsci's bus terminus (point to what you want in the glass case, figure €5 for a light meal, Sun-Fri 9:00-21:30, until 16:00 off-season, closed Sat, Via dei Montanini 14/16, tel. 0577-289-291).

Supermarket: You won't find many cheap grocery shops in the touristy center of Siena. But one handy (if fancy) option is **Consorzio Agrario Siena.** Ask them to make you up a *panino.* As this place specializes in artisanal Tuscan foods, both the quality and prices are high (Mon-Sat 8:00-19:00, sometimes open Sun from 9:30, a block off Piazza Matteotti, toward Il Campo at Via Pianigiani 5).

Desserts and Treats

For a special dessert or a sweet treat any time of day, stop by **Nannini**—considered the top-end pastry shop and *the* place to go for quality local specialties (Mon-Sat 7:30-21:00, Sun 8:00-21:00, *aperitivo* happy hour 18:00-21:00, Banchi di Sopra 24). Across the street is the wonderful **Gelateria Grom** (see "Nightlife in Siena" sidebar)—but you have my permission to sample every gelateria in town to pick your favorite.

Siena Connections

Siena has sparse train connections but is a great hub for buses to the hill towns, though frequency drops on Sundays and holidays. For most, Florence is the gateway to Siena. Even if you are a railpass-user, connect these two cities by bus—it's faster than the train, and Siena's bus station is more convenient and central than its train station. (Note: Many travelers mistake old signs for a former bus company, Tra-In, as signs for trains or the train station. Those buses have nothing to do with the railway.)

By Train

Siena's train station is at the edge of town.

From Siena by Train to: Florence (direct trains hourly, 1.5-2 hours, €8.50; bus is better), **Pisa** (2/hour, 1.75 hours, change at Empoli, €9.80), **Assisi** (8/day, 4-5 hours, most involve 2 changes, from €13, bus is faster), **Rome** (1-2/hour, 3-3.5 hours, change in Florence or Chiusi, €26-53), **Orvieto** (12/day, 2-2.5 hours, change in Chiusi, €15.80). For more information, visit www.trenitalia. com.

By Bus

The main bus companies are **Tiemme** (part of a larger company called Siena Mobilità and formerly called Tra-In; mostly handles buses to regional destinations, tel. 0577-204-246, www.sienamobilita.it) and **Sena** (for long-distance connections, tel. 0577-208-282, www.sena.it). On schedules, the fastest buses are marked *rapida*. I'd stick with these. Most buses depart Siena from Piazza Gramsci; others leave from the train station (confirm when you buy your ticket).

Tiemme/Siena Mobilità Buses to: Florence (roughly 2/hour, 1.25-hour *rapida/via superstrada* buses are faster than the train, avoid the 2-hour *ordinaria* buses unless you have time to enjoy the beautiful scenery en route, €7.80; if there are lines at bus-ticket office, tickets also available at tobacco shops/*tabacchi*; generally leaves from Piazza Gramsci as well as train station), **San Gimignano** (8/day direct, no direct service on Sun, 1.25 hours, €6, leaves from Piazza Gramsci), **Volterra** (4/day Mon-Sat, no buses on Sun, 2 hours, change in Colle Val d'Elsa, €6.15, leaves from Piazza Gramsci), **Montepulciano** (8/day, none on Sun, 1.25 hours, €6.60, leaves from train station), **Pienza** (6/day, none on Sun, 1.5 hours, €4.40, leaves from train station), **Montalcino** (6/day Mon-Sat, 4/day Sun, 1.25 hours, €4.90, leaves from train station or Piazza del Sale), and **Pisa's Galileo Galilei Airport** (3/day, 1.75 hours, €14, one direct, two via Poggibonsi).

Sena Buses to: Rome (9-10/day, 3 hours, €23, from Piazza Gramsci, arrives at Rome's Tiburtina station on Metro line B with easy connections to the central Termini train station), **Naples** (2/day, 6.5 hours, one at 17:00 and an overnight bus that departs at 23:59, €33), and **Milan** (6/day, 4 hours, €36, departs from Piazza Gramsci, arrives at Milan's Cadorna Station with Metro access and direct trains to Malpensa Airport).

To reach the town center of **Pisa,** the train is better (described earlier).

Tickets and Information: You can buy tickets in the underground passageway (called Sottopassaggio la Lizza) beneath Piazza Gramsci—look for stairwells in front of NH Excelsior Hotel. The larger office (marked *Siena Mobilità*) handles Tiemme/Siena Mobilità buses (Mon-Fri 6:30-19:30, Sat-Sun 7:00-19:30). The smaller one is for Sena buses (Mon-Sat 8:30-19:45; on Sun, when the Sena bus ticket office is closed, buy tickets next door at Tiemme/Siena

Mobilità office; Sena office also has a desk selling *Eurolines* tickets for bus connections to other countries). Both offices accept credit cards. You can also get tickets for both Tiemme/Siena Mobilità buses and Sena buses at the train station (look for bus-ticket kiosk just inside main door). If necessary, you can buy tickets from the driver, but it costs €3 extra.

Services: Sottopassaggio la Lizza also has luggage storage, posted bus schedules, TV monitors listing imminent departures for several bus companies, and WCs (€0.50).

ASSISI

Assisi is famous for its hometown boy, St. Francis, who made very good. While Francis the saint is interesting, Francesco Bernardone the man is even more so, and mementos of his days in Assisi are everywhere—where he was baptized, a shirt he wore, a hill he prayed on, and a church where a vision changed his life.

About the year 1200, this simple friar from Assisi countered the decadence of Church government and society in general with a powerful message of non-materialism and a "slow down and smell God's roses" lifestyle. Like Jesus, Francis taught by example, living without worldly goods and aiming to love all creation. A huge monastic order grew out of his teachings, which were gradually embraced (some would say co-opted) by the Church. Christianity's most popular saint and its purest example of simplicity is now glorified in beautiful churches, along with his female counterpart, St. Clare. In 1939, Italy made Francis one of its patron saints; in 2013, the newly elected pope took his name.

Francis' message of love, simplicity, and sensitivity to the environment has a broad and timeless appeal. But every pilgrimage site inevitably gets commercialized, and Francis' legacy is now Assisi's basic industry. In summer, this Umbrian town bursts with flash-in-the-pan Francis fans and Franciscan knickknacks. Those able to see past the glow-in-the-dark rosaries and bobblehead friars can actually have a "travel on purpose" experience. Even a block or two off the congested main drag, you'll find pockets of serenity that, it's easy to imagine, must have made Francis feel at peace.

Planning Your Time

Assisi is worth a day and a night. Its old town has a half-day of sightseeing and another half-day of wonder. The essential sight is the Basilica of St. Francis. For a good visit, take my self-guided "Welcome to Assisi" walk, ending at the Basilica of St. Francis. With more time, be sure to wander the back streets and linger on the main square, Piazza del Comune.

Most visitors are day-trippers. While the town's a zoo by day, it's a delight at night. Assisi after dark is closer to a place Francis could call home.

Orientation to Assisi

Crowned by a ruined castle, Assisi spills downhill to its famous Basilica of St. Francis. The town is beautifully preserved and rich in history. A 5.5-magnitude earthquake in 1997 did more damage to the tourist industry than to the town's buildings. Fortunately, tourists—whether art lovers, pilgrims, or both—have returned, drawn by Assisi's special allure.

The city stretches across a ridge that rises from a flat plain. The Basilica of St. Francis sits at the low end of town; Piazza Matteotti (bus stop and parking lot) is at the high end; and the main square, Piazza del Comune, lies in between. The main drag (called Via San Francesco for most of its course) runs from Piazza del Comune to the basilica. Capping the hill above the town is the ruined castle, called the Rocca Maggiore, and rising above that is Mount Subasio. The town is smaller than its fame might lead you to think: Walking uphill from the basilica to Piazza Matteotti takes 30 minutes, while the downhill journey takes about 15 minutes. Some Francis sights lie outside the city walls, in the valley beneath the ridge (the modern part of town, called Santa Maria degli Angeli) and in the hills above.

Tourist Information

The TI, which hands out free maps, is in the center of town on Piazza del Comune (Mon-Fri 8:00-14:00 & 15:00-18:00—until 18:30 July-early Oct, Sat-Sun 9:30-17:00—until 18:00 in April-Oct, tel. 075-813-8680). There's also a branch down in the valley, across the street from the big piazza in front of the Basilica of St. Mary of the Angels.

Arrival in Assisi

By Train: The train station is about two miles below Assisi, in Santa Maria degli Angeli. You can check bags at the station's newsstand (€3/12 hours, daily 6:30-13:00 & 14:30-19:00), but not in the old town.

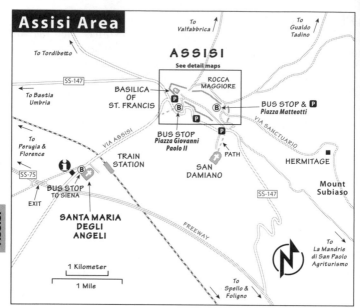

Orange city **buses** connect the station with the old town on the hilltop. Buses (line #C) usually leave at :16 and :46 past the hour from the bus stop immediately to your left as you exit the station (daily 5:30–23:00, 15 minutes; buy tickets at the newsstand inside the train station for €1, or on board the bus for €1.50—exact change only, valid for 70 minutes after being stamped, good for any bus within the old town). On the way up into town, buses stop at Piazza Giovanni Paolo II (near Basilica of St. Francis), then Largo Properzio (just outside the Porta Nuova city gate), and finally Piazza Matteotti (top of old town).

Going from the old town to the train station, the orange buses usually run from Piazza Matteotti at :10 and :40 past the hour (stopping outside Porta Nuova at Largo Properzio a couple of minutes later, and in Piazza Giovanni Paolo II a few minutes after that).

Taxis from the train station to the old town cost about €15. You can be charged extra for luggage, night service, additional people (four is customary)...and sometimes just for being a tourist. When departing the old town, you'll find taxi stands at Piazza Giovanni Paolo II, the Basilica of St. Francis, the Basilica of St. Clare, and Piazza del Comune (or have your hotel call for you, tel. 075-813-100). Expect to pay a minimum of €10 for any ride.

By Bus: Buses from Siena arrive at the stop next to the Basilica of St. Mary of the Angels, near the train station. Most other intercity buses arrive in the old town.

By Car: Drivers coming in for the day can follow the signs to several handy parking lots *(parcheggi)*. Piazza Matteotti's wonderful underground parking garage (#C) is at the top of the town and comes with bits of ancient Rome in the walls. Another big lot, Parcheggio Giovanni Paolo II (#A), is at the bottom end of town, 200 yards below the Basilica of St. Francis. Between them is the unlettered Parcheggio Mojano; although outside the town wall, this comes with an escalator that transports you near the Basilica of St. Clare. At Parcheggio Porta Nuova (#B), an elevator delivers you to Porta Nuova near St. Clare's. The lots vary in price (€1.30-1.60/hour, most €10-12/day but Matteotti costs €19/day). For day-trippers, the best plan is to park at Piazza Matteotti, follow my self-guided town walk, tour the basilica, and then either catch a bus back to Piazza Matteotti or simply wander back up through town to your car.

Helpful Hints

Best Shopping: Tacky knickknacks line the streets leading to the Basilica of St. Francis. For better shops (with local handicrafts), head to Via San Rufino and Corso Mazzini (both just off Piazza del Comune, shops described later in the "Welcome to Assisi" self-guided walk). A Saturday-morning market fills Via Borgo San Pietro (along the bottom edge of town).

Festivals: Assisi annually hosts several interesting festivals commemorating St. Francis and life in the Middle Ages. **Festa di Calendimaggio** is a springtime medieval festival featuring costume parades, concerts, and competitions among Assisi's rival neighborhoods (www.calendimaggiodiassisi.it). Rustic medieval "taverns" pop up around the center offering *porchetta* (roasted pig) and *vino* (starts the first Thu-Sat in May; if one of these days is already a public holiday, it's held the following week). The **Settimana Francescana** commemorates the beginning of the end of Francis' life, when he made his way for the last time to the Porziuncola Chapel (Sept 28). This week-long celebration culminates in the **Festa di San Francesco,** which marks his death with religious processions, special services, and an arts, crafts, and folklore fair. The TI has a monthly *Assisi Informa* leaflet with details on upcoming festivals and celebrations; see also the event listings at www.assisi.regioneumbria.eu.

Internet Access: Facing the Cathedral of San Rufino, **Caffè Duomo** has free Wi-Fi and Internet access for customers (daily 7:00-23:00, snacks, Piazza San Rufino 5, tel. 075-813-023).

Laundry: **3elleblu' Lavanderia** can do a load of laundry for you at a reasonable price on the same day, if they're not too busy (€5/

St. Francis of Assisi (1181-1226)

In 1202, young Francesco Bernardone donned armor and rode out to battle the Perugians (residents of Umbria's capital city). The battle went badly, and Francis was captured and imprisoned for a year. He returned a changed man. He avoided friends and his father's lucrative business and spent more and more time outside the city walls fasting, praying, and searching for something.

In 1206, a vision changed his life, culminating in a dramatic confrontation. He stripped naked before the town leaders, threw his clothes at his father—turning his back on the comfortable material life—and declared his loyalty to God alone.

Idealistic young men flocked to Francis, and they wandered Italy like troubadours, spreading the joy of the Gospel to rich and poor. Francis became a cult figure, attracting huge crowds. They'd never seen anything like it—sermons preached outdoors, in the local language (not Church Latin), making God accessible to all. Francis' new order of monks was also extremely unmaterialistic, extolling poverty and simplicity. Despite their radicalism, the order eventually gained the pope's approval and spread through the world. Francis, who died in Assisi at the age of 45, left a legacy of humanism, equality, and love of nature that would eventually flower in the Renaissance.

In Francis' Sandal-Steps

1. Baptized in Assisi's **Cathedral of San Rufino** (then called St. George's).
2. Raised in the family home just off Piazza del Comune (now the **Chiesa Nuova**).
3. Heard call to "rebuild church" in **San Damiano.** (The crucifix of the church is now in the **Basilica of St. Clare.**)
4. Settled and established his order of monks at the **Porziuncola Chapel** (inside today's St. Mary of the Angels Basilica).
5. Met Clare. (Her tomb and possessions are at the **Basilica of St. Clare.**)
6. Received the pope's blessing for his order (1223 document in the reliquary chapel at the **Basilica of St. Francis**).
7. Had many visions and was associated with miracles during his life (depicted in **Giotto's frescoes** in the Basilica of St. Francis' upper level).
8. Died at the **Porziuncola,** his body later interred beneath the **Basilica of St. Francis.**

ASSISI

wash, €4.50/dry, Mon-Fri 9:00-18:00, Sat 9:00-13:00, closed Sun, Via Borgo Aretino 6a, tel. 075-816-084).

Travel Agencies: You can purchase train and bus tickets at **Agenzia Viaggi Stoppini,** centrally located between Piazza del Comune and the Basilica of St. Clare. Manager Fabrizio is patient with tourists' needs (€1 surcharge for train tickets, Mon-Fri 9:00-12:30 & 15:30-19:00, Sat 9:00-12:30, closed Sun, Corso Mazzini 31, tel. 075-812-597). For more information, see "Assisi Connections," at the end of this chapter.

Local Guides: Giuseppe Karabotis is a good licensed guide (€130/2.5 hours, €260/6 hours, mobile 328-867-0567, iokarabot@libero.it). **Daniela Moretti** is a hardworking young guide from Perugia who knows both Assisi and all of Umbria (€120/half-day, €240/day, mobile 335-829-9984, www.danyguide.com, danyguide@hotmail.com). If they're busy, they can recommend other guides.

ASSISI

Getting Around Assisi

Most visitors need only their feet to get everywhere in Assisi, except to the train station and nearby Basilica of St. Mary of the Angels (via bus #C—see directions in "Arrival in Assisi").

Within the old town, pale-yellow minibuses #A and #B run every 20-40 minutes, linking the lower end (near the Basilica of St. Francis) with the middle (Piazza del Comune) and the top (Piazza Matteotti). While it's only a 15-minute stroll from the upper end to the lower, the climb back up can have you looking for a lift. Hop on a bus marked *Piazza Matteotti* if you're exhausted after your basilica visit and need a sweat-free five-minute return to the top of the old town (near many of my recommended hotels). Before boarding, confirm the destination (catch the bus below the Basilica of St. Francis at the Porta San Francisco).

You can buy a bus ticket (good on any city bus) at a newsstand or kiosk for €1, or get a ticket from the driver for €1.50 (exact change only). After you've stamped your ticket on board the bus, it's valid for 70 minutes.

Self-Guided Walk

▲▲Welcome to Assisi

There's much more to Assisi than just St. Francis and what the blitz tour groups see. This walk covers the town from top (Piazza Matteotti) to bottom (Basilica of St. Francis). To get to Piazza Matteotti, ride the bus from the train station (or from Piazza Giovanni Paolo II) to the last stop; drive up (and park in the underground lot); or hike five minutes uphill from Piazza del Comune.

• Start 50 yards beyond Piazza Matteotti (away from city center—see map).

❶ The Roman Amphitheater (Anfiteatro Romano)

A lane named Via Anfiteatro Romano skirts the cozy neighborhood built around a Roman amphitheater—a reminder that Assisi was once an important Roman town. Circle the amphitheater counterclockwise. Imagine how colorful the town laundry basin (on the right) must have been in previous generations, when the women of Assisi gathered here to do their wash. Just beyond the basin is a small rectangular pool; above it are the coats of arms of Assisi's leading families. A few steps farther, leave the amphitheater, hiking up the stairs on the right to the top of the hill, for an aerial view of the ancient oval. The Roman stones have long been absorbed into the medieval architecture. It was Roman tradition to locate the amphitheater outside of town, which this used to be. While the amphitheater dates from the first century A.D., the buildings filling it today were built in the 13th and 14th centuries.

• Continue on, enjoying the grand view of the fortress in the distance. The lane leads down to a city gate and an...

❷ Umbrian View

Step outside of Assisi at the Porta Perlici for a commanding view. Umbria, called the "green heart of Italy," is the country's geographical center and only landlocked region. Enjoy the various shades of green: silver green on the valley floor (olives), emerald green (grapevines), and deep green on the hillsides (evergreen oak trees). Also notice Rocca Maggiore ("big fortress"), which provided townsfolk a refuge in times of attack, and, behind you atop the nearer hill, Rocca Minore ("little fortress"), which gives the town's young lovers a little privacy. The quarry (under the Rocca Maggiore) was a handy source for Assisi's characteristic pink limestone.

• Go back through the gate and follow Via Porta Perlici—it's immediately on your right—downhill into town (toward Hotel La Rocca). Enjoy the higgledy-piggledy architecture (this neighborhood has some of the most photogenic back lanes in town). Keep an eye out for a wall containing an aqueduct (on the left, at the arch before #52) that goes back to Roman times. It still brings water from a

ASSISI

mountain spring into the city (push the brass tap for a taste). After another 50 yards, turn left through a medieval town gate (with Hotel La Rocca on your right). Just after the hotel, you'll pass a second gate dating from Roman times. Follow Via Porta Perlici downhill until you hit a fine square facing a big church.

❸ Cathedral of San Rufino (Cattedrale San Rufino)

Trick question: Who's Assisi's patron saint? While Francis is one of Italy's patron saints, Rufino (the town's first bishop, martyred and buried here in the third century) is Assisi's. The cathedral (seat of the local bishop) is 11th-century Romanesque with a Neoclassical interior. Although it has what is considered to be one of the best and purest Romanesque facades in all of Umbria, the big triangular top of it (just a decorative

wall) was added in Gothic times. Study the lions at the base of the facade, flanking each door. One is eating a Christian martyr, reminding worshippers of the courage of early Christians.

Enter the church. While the front of the church is an unremarkable mix of 17th- and 18th-century Baroque and Neoclassical, the rear (near where you enter) has several points of interest. Notice first the two fine statues: *St. Francis* and *St. Clare* (by Giovanni Dupré, 1888). To your right is an old baptismal font (in the corner with the semicircular black iron grate). In about 1181, a baby boy was baptized in this font. His parents were upwardly mobile Francophiles who called him Francesco ("Frenchy"). In 1194, a nobleman baptized his daughter Clare here. Eighteen years later, their paths crossed in this same church, when Clare attended a class and became mesmerized by the teacher—Francis. Traditionally, the children of Assisi are still baptized here.

The striking glass panels in the floor reveal foundations preserved from the ninth-century church that once stood here. You're walking on history. After the 1997 earthquake, structural inspectors checked the church from ceiling to floor. When they looked under the paving stones, they discovered graves (until Napoleon decreed otherwise, it was common practice to bury people in churches). Underneath that level, they found Roman foundations and some animal bones (suggesting the possibility of animal sacrifice). There might have been a Roman temple here; churches were often built upon temple ruins. Stand at the back of the church fac-

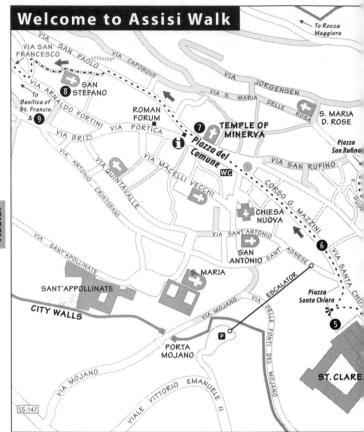

Welcome to Assisi Walk

ing the altar, and look left to the Roman cistern (inside the great stone archway, next to where you entered). Take the three steps down (to trigger the light) and marvel at the fine stonework and Roman engineering. In the Middle Ages, this was the town's emergency water source when under attack.

Underneath the church, incorporated into the Roman ruins, are the foundations of an earlier Church of San Rufino, now the crypt and **Diocesan museum.** When it's open, you can go below to see the saint's sarcophagus and the small museum featuring the cathedral's art from centuries past.

Cost and Hours: Cathedral—free, daily 7:30-19:00, Nov-mid-March closed Mon-Fri 12:30-14:30, tel. 075-812-283; crypt/museum—€3.50, mid-March-mid-Oct Thu-Tue 10:00-13:00 & 15:00-18:00, longer hours in Aug, shorter hours mid-Oct-mid-March, closed Wed except in Aug, tel. 075-812-712, www.assisi-museodiocesano.com.

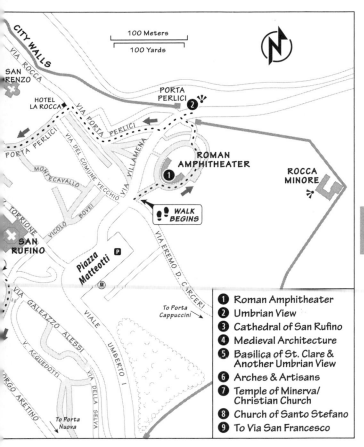

❶	Roman Amphitheater
❷	Umbrian View
❸	Cathedral of St. Rufino
❹	Medieval Architecture
❺	Basilica of St. Clare & Another Umbrian View
❻	Arches & Artisans
❼	Temple of Minerva/ Christian Church
❽	Church of Santo Stefano
❾	To Via San Francesco

• *Leaving the church, take a sharp left (at the pizza-by-the-slice joint, on Via Dono Doni). After 20 yards, take a right and go all the way down the stairway to see some...*

❹ Medieval Architecture

At the bottom of the stairs, notice the pink limestone pavement, part of the surviving medieval town. The arches built over doorways indicate that the buildings date from the 12th through the 14th centuries, when Assisi was booming. Italian cities such as Assisi—thriving on the north-south trade between northern Europe and Rome—were in the process of inventing free-market capitalism, dabbling in democratic self-rule, and creating the modern urban lifestyle. The vaults you see that turn lanes into tunnels are reminders of medieval urban expansion—creating more living space (mostly 15th century). While the population grew, people wanted to live within the town's protective walls.

St. Clare
(1194-1253)

The 18-year-old rich girl of Assisi fell in love with Francis' message, and made secret arrangements to meet him. The night of Palm Sunday, 1212, she slipped out of her father's mansion in town and escaped to the valley below. A procession of friars with torches met her and took her to (what is today) St. Mary of the Angels Basilica. There, Francis cut her hair, clothed her in a simple brown tunic, and welcomed her into a life of voluntary poverty. Clare's father begged, ordered, and physically threatened her to return, but she would not budge.

Clare was joined by other women who banded together as the Poor Clares. She spent the next 40 years of her life within the confines of the convent of San Damiano: barefoot, vegetarian, and largely silent. Her regimen of prayer, meditation, and simple manual labor—especially knitting—impressed commoners and popes, leading to her canonization almost immediately after her death. St. Clare is often depicted carrying a monstrance (a little temple holding the Eucharist wafer).

Medieval Assisi had several times the population density of modern Assisi.

Notice the blooming balconies; Assisi holds a flower competition each June.

• *From the bottom of the stairs, head to the left and continue downhill. When you arrive at a street, turn left, going slightly uphill for a long block, then take the low road (right) at the Y, and head down Via Sermei. Continue ahead, following the* S. Chiara *sign downhill to the big church. Cross the street and walk under the three massive buttresses to Piazza Santa Chiara and the front of the church.*

❺ Basilica of St. Clare (Basilica di Santa Chiara)

Dedicated to the founder of the Order of the Poor Clares, this Umbrian Gothic church is simple, in keeping with the nuns' dedication to a life of contemplation. In Clare's lifetime, the order was located in the humble Church of San Damiano, in the valley below, but after Clare's death, they needed a bigger and more glorious building. The church was built in 1265, and the huge buttresses were added in the next century.

The interior's fine frescoes were whitewashed in Baroque times. The battered remains of one on the left shows how the fresco surface was hacked up so whitewash would stick. Imagine all the pristine frescoes hiding behind the whitewash (here and all over Europe).

The Chapel of the Crucifix of San Damiano, on the right, has the wooden crucifix that changed Francis' life. In 1206, an emaciated, soul-searching, stark-raving Francis knelt before this crucifix (then located in the Church of San Damiano) and asked for guidance. The crucifix spoke: "Go and rebuild my Church, which you can see has fallen into ruin." Francis followed the call.

Stairs lead from the nave down to the tomb of St. Clare. Her tomb is at the far end (the image is wax; her bones lie underneath). As you circulate with the crowd of pilgrims, notice the paintings on the walls depicting spiritual lessons from Clare's life and death. At the opposite end of the crypt (back between the stairs, in a large glassed-in area) are important relics: the saint's robes, hair (in a silver box), and an enormous tunic she made—along with relics of St. Francis (including a blood-stained stocking he wore after receiving the stigmata). The attached cloistered community of the Poor Clares has flourished for 700 years.

Cost and Hours: Free, daily 6:30-12:00 & 14:00-19:00, until 18:00 in winter.

• *Leave the church and belly up to the viewpoint at the edge of the square for...*

Another Umbrian View: On the left is the convent of St. Clare (global headquarters of all the Poor Clares). Below you lies the olive grove of the Poor Clares, which has been there since the 13th century. In the distance is a grand Umbrian view. Assisi overlooks the richest and biggest valley in otherwise hilly and mountainous Umbria. The municipality of Assisi has a population of 25,000, but only 3,500 people live in the old town. The lower town, called Santa Maria degli Angeli, grew up with the coming of the railway in the 19th century. In the haze, the blue-domed church is St. Mary of the Angels (described later), the cradle of the Franciscan order. A popular pilgrimage site today, it marks the place where St. Francis lived and worked.

Spanish-speaking Franciscans settled in California. Three of their missions grew into major cities: Los Angeles (named after this church), San Francisco (named after St. Francis), and Santa Clara (named after St. Clare).

• *From the church square, step out into Via Santa Chiara.*

❻ Arches and Artisans

Notice the three medieval town gates (two behind the church, and one uphill toward the town center). The gate over the road behind the church dates from 1265. (Farther on, you can just see the crenellations of the 1316 Porta Nuova, which marks the final medieval expansion of Assisi.) Toward the city center (on Via Santa Chiara, the high road), an arch marks the site of the Roman wall. These three gates represent the town's three walls, illustrating how much the city has grown since ancient times.

ASSISI

Walk uphill along Via Santa Chiara (which becomes Corso Mazzini) to the city's main square. The street is lined with interesting shops selling traditional embroidery, religious souvenirs, and gifty local edibles. The shops on Corso Mazzini, on the stretch between the gate and the Piazza del Comune, show off many local crafts. As you browse, watch for the following shops: Galleria d'Arte Perna (on the left, #20) sells the medieval fantasy townscapes of Paolo Grimaldi, a local painter who runs this shop with his brother, Alessandro. A helpful travel agency is across the street and a few steps up (at #31, Agenzia Viaggi Stoppini; see "Helpful Hints," earlier).

Next, the shop L'Ulivo Sculture (on the left at #14D) sells olive-wood carvings, as does Poiesis, across the street at #23. It's said that St. Francis made the first nativity scene to help humanize and, therefore, teach the Christmas message. That's why you'll see so many crèches in Assisi. (Even today, nearby villages are enthusiastic about their "living" manger scenes, and Italians everywhere enjoy setting up elaborate crèches in churches for Christmas.) Adjacent to #14 is a bakery, Bar Sensi, selling the traditional raisin-and-apple strudel called *rocciata* (roh-CHAH-tah, €3.50 each). Farther along on the left (at #2) is Il Duomo, selling religious art, manger scenes, and crucifixion figurines. Across the street, on the right, is Centro Ricami, a respected embroidery shop. And on the square (at #34, opposite the flags), the recommended La Bottega dei Sapori is worth a visit for edible and drinkable souvenirs.

You've walked up what was, in ancient times, the main drag into town. Ahead of you, the six fluted Corinthian columns of the Temple of Minerva marked the forum (today's Piazza del Comune). Sit at the fountain on the piazza for a few minutes of people-watching—don't you just love Italy? Within a few hundred yards of this square, on either side, were the medieval walls. Imagine the commotion of 5,000 people confined within these walls. No wonder St. Francis needed an escape for some peace and quiet.

• *Now, head over to the temple on the square.*

❼ Temple of Minerva/Christian Church

Assisi has always been a spiritual center. The Romans went to great lengths to make this first-century B.C. Temple of Minerva a centerpiece of their city. Notice the columns that cut into the stairway. It was a tight fit here on the hilltop. In ancient times, the stairs went down—about twice as far as they do now—to the main drag, which has gradually been filled in over time. The Church of Santa Maria sopra ("over") Minerva was added in the ninth century. The bell tower is from the 13th century.

Pop inside the temple/church. Today's interior is 17th-century Baroque. Walk to the front. Flanking the altar are the original Roman temple floor stones. You can even see the drains for the bloody sacrifices that took place here. Behind the statues of Peter and Paul, the original Roman embankment peeks through.

Cost and Hours: Free, Mon-Sat 7:15-19:30, Sun 8:00-19:30, in winter closes at sunset and midday.

• *Across the square at #11, step into the 16th-century frescoed vaults of the...*

Old Market: Notice the Italian flair for design. Even this smelly market was once finely decorated. The art style is called "grotesque"—literally from a cave (grotto-esque), named for the fanciful Roman paintings found on the walls of Italian caves. This scene was indisputably painted after 1492. How do they know? Because it features turkeys—first seen in Europe after Columbus returned from the Americas with his bag of exotic souvenirs. The turkeys painted here may have been that bird's European debut.

• *From the main square, hike past the temple up the high road, Via San Paolo. After 200 yards (across from #24), a sign directs you down a stepped lane to the...*

❽ Church of Santo Stefano (Chiesa di Santo Stefano)

Surrounded by cypress, fig, and walnut trees, Santo Stefano—which used to be outside the town walls in the days of St. Francis—is a delightful bit of offbeat Assisi. Legend has it that Santo Stefano's bells miraculously rang on October 3, 1226, the day St. Francis died. Step inside. This is the typical rural Italian Romanesque church—no architect, just built by simple stonemasons who put together the most basic design. Hundreds of years later, it still stands.

Cost and Hours: Free, daily 8:30-21:30, Sept-May until 18:30.

• *The lane zigzags down to Via San Francesco. Turn right and walk under the arch toward the Basilica of St. Francis.*

❾ Via San Francesco

This main drag leads from the town to the basilica holding the body of St. Francis. Francis was a big deal even in his own day. He was made a saint in 1228—the same year that the basilica's foundations were laid—and his body was moved here by 1230. Assisi was a big-time pilgrimage center, and this street was its booming hub. The arch marks the end of what was Assisi in St. Francis' day.

Notice the fine medieval balcony immediately past the arch. About 30 yards farther down (on the left), cool yourself at the fountain, as medieval pilgrims might have. The hospice next door was built in 1237 to house pilgrims. Notice the three surviving faces of its fresco: Jesus, Francis, and Clare. Farther down, across from #12a (on the left), is the Oratorio dei Pellegrini, dating from the 1450s. A brotherhood ran a hostel here for travelers passing through to pay homage to St. Francis. The chapel offers a richly frescoed space in which to contemplate the saint's message.

• *Continuing on, you'll eventually reach Assisi's main sight, the Basilica of St. Francis. For the start of my self-guided tour, walk downhill to the basilica's lower courtyard.*

Self-Guided Tour

▲▲▲Basilica of St. Francis (Basilica di San Francesco)

The basilica is one of the artistic and religious highlights of Europe. It rises where, in 1226, St. Francis was buried (with the outcasts

he had stood by) outside of his town on the "Hill of the Damned"—now called the "Hill of Paradise." The basilica is frescoed from top to bottom with scenes by the leading artists of the day: Cimabue, Giotto, Simone Martini, and Pietro Lorenzetti. A 13th-century historian wrote, "No more exquisite monument to the Lord has been built."

From a distance, you see the huge arcades "supporting" the basilica. These were 15th-century quarters for the monks. The arcades that line the square and lead to the church housed medieval pilgrims.

Cost and Hours: Free entry; lower basilica daily 6:00-18:45, until 17:45 in Nov-March; reliquary chapel in lower basilica generally open Mon-Fri 9:00-18:00, often closed Sat-Sun and occasionally at other times for religious services; upper basilica daily 8:30-18:45, until 17:45 in Nov-March. Modest dress is required to enter the church—no sleeveless tops or shorts for men, women, or children.

Information: The church courtyard at the entrance of the lower basilica has an info office, often staffed by native English-speaking friars (Mon-Sat 9:15-12:00 & 14:15-17:30, closed Sun, tel. 075-819-0084, www.sanfrancescoassisi.org). Call or check the website to find out about upcoming concerts at the basilica.

Tours: Audioguides (boring and old-school) are available at the kiosk located outside the entrance of the upper basilica (€6 donation requested, €7/2 people, daily 9:00-17:00, 45 minutes). You can download a free Rick Steves audio version of this chapter's tour of the basilica. You can also take an English tour, offered daily except Sunday (€10 donation requested, call or email the information office to reserve, tel. 075-819-0084, www.sanfrancescoassisi.org, assisisanfrancesco@libero.it).

Bookstore: The church bookshop is in the inner courtyard behind the upper and lower basilica. It sells an excellent guidebook, *The Basilica of Saint Francis: A Spiritual Pilgrimage* (€3, by Goulet, McInally, and Wood; I used this book, and a tour with Brother Michael, as sources for this self-guided tour).

Services: Go before you enter, as there aren't any WCs inside. There are two different pay WCs within a half-block of the lower entrance—up the road in a squat building, and halfway down the big piazza on the left.

Attending Mass: To worship in the basilica, consider joining the Franciscan brothers in the lower basilica in the morning at 7:15 or 11:00, or experience a Mass sung by the basilica choir many Sundays at 10:30. On Sundays in summer (Easter-Oct), there's an English Mass in the upper basilica at 9:00. Additional English and sung Masses don't follow a set schedule. Call the basilica to find out when English-speaking pilgrimage groups or choirs have reserved Masses, and attend with them—although groups change their plans fairly often (tel. 075-819-0084).

Overview

The Basilica of St. Francis, a theological work of genius, can be difficult for the 21st-century tourist/pilgrim to appreciate.

Since the basilica is the reason that most people visit Assisi, and the message of St. Francis has even the least devout sightseers blessing the town Vespas, I've designed this self-guided tour with an emphasis on the place's theology (rather than art history).

A disclaimer before we start: Just as Francis used many biblical legends to help teach the Christian message, legends from the life of Francis were told in later ages to teach the same message. Are they true? In general, probably not. Are they in keeping with Francis' message? Yes. Do I share legends here as if they are historic? Sure.

The church has three parts: the upper basilica, the lower basilica, and the saint's tomb (below the lower basilica). To get oriented, stand at the lower entrance in the courtyard. While empty today, centuries ago this main plaza was cluttered with pilgrim services

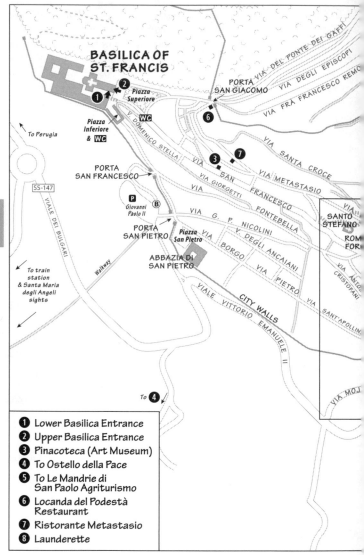

ASSISI

1 Lower Basilica Entrance
2 Upper Basilica Entrance
3 Pinacoteca (Art Museum)
4 To Ostello della Pace
5 To Le Mandrie di
San Paolo Agriturismo
6 Locanda del Podestà
Restaurant
7 Ristorante Metastasio
8 Launderette

and the medieval equivalent of souvenir shops. Opposite the entry to the lower basilica is the information center.

Enter through the grand doorway of the lower basilica. Just inside, decorating the top of the first arch, look up and see St. Francis, who greets you with a Latin inscription. Sounding a bit like John Wayne, he says the equivalent of, "Slow down and be joyful, pilgrim. You've reached the Hill of Paradise. And, if you're observant and thoughtful, this church will knock your spiritual socks off."

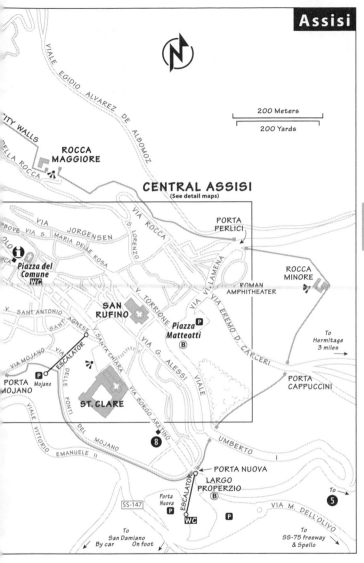

Assisi

ROCCA MAGGIORE

CENTRAL ASSISI
(See detail maps)

200 Meters
200 Yards

ASSISI

VIALE EGIDIO ALVAREZ DE ALBORNOZ

CITY WALLS

DELLA ROCCA

VIA ABOVE VIA S. MARIA DELLE ROSA

VIA JORGENSEN

S. LORENZO

VIA ROCCA

PORTA PERLICI

ROCCA MINORE

Piazza del Comune
WC

V. SANT'ANTONIO

SAN RUFINO

V. TORRIONE

Piazza Matteotti
B

VIA VILLAMENA

VIA EREMO D. CARCERI

ROMAN AMPHITHEATER

To Hermitage 3 miles →

VIA MOJANO

SANT'AGNESE

VIA SANTA CHIARA

ESCALATOR

VIA DELLE FONTI

PORTA MOJANO

Mojano P

ST. CLARE

VIA G. ALESSI

VIALE

PORTA CAPPUCCINI

VIA BORGO ARETINO

VIALE VITTORIO EMANUELE II

DEL MOJANO

8

UMBERTO I

PORTA NUOVA

LARGO PROPERZIO
B

To → 5

SS-147

Porta Nuova P

ESCALATOR

WC

P

VIA M. DELL'OLIVO

To San Damiano
By car   On foot

To SS-75 freeway & Spello →

• *Start with the tomb. To get there, turn left into the nave. Midway down, follow the signs and go right, to the tomb downstairs.*

The Tomb

The saint's remains are above the altar in the stone box with the iron ties. In medieval times, pilgrims came to Assisi because St. Francis was buried here. Holy relics were the "ruby slippers" of medieval Europe. Relics gave you power—they answered your prayers

The Franciscan Message

Francis' message caused a stir. Not only did he follow Christ's teachings, he followed Christ's lifestyle, living as a poor, wandering preacher. He traded a life of power and riches for one of obedience, poverty, and chastity. He was never ordained as a priest, but his influence on Christianity was monumental.

The Franciscan realm (Brother Sun, Sister Moon, and so on) is a space where God, man, and the natural world frolic harmoniously. Francis treated every creature—animal, peasant, pope—with equal respect. He and his "brothers" (*fratelli,* or friars) slept in fields, begged for food, and exuded the joy of non-materialism. Franciscan friars were known as the "Jugglers of God," modeling themselves on French troubadours (*jongleurs,* or jugglers) who roved the countryside singing, telling stories, and cracking jokes.

In an Italy torn by conflict between towns and families, Francis promoted peace and the restoration of order. (He set an example by reconstructing the crumbled San Damiano chapel.) While the Church was waging bloody Crusades, Francis pushed ecumenism and understanding. And the Franciscan message had an impact. In 1288, just 62 years after Francis died, a Franciscan became pope (Nicholas IV). Francis' message also led to Church reforms that many believe delayed the Protestant Reformation by a century.

This richly decorated basilica seems to contradict the teachings of the poor monk it honors, but it was built as an act of re-

and won your wars—and ultimately helped you get back to your eternal Kansas. Assisi made no bones about promoting the saint's relics, but hid his tomb for obvious reasons of security. His body was buried secretly while the basilica was under construction, and over the next 600 years, the exact location was forgotten. When the tomb was to be opened to the public in 1818, it took more than a month to find his actual remains.

Francis' four closest friends and first followers are memorialized in the corners of the room. Opposite the altar, up four steps between the entrance and exit, notice the small copper box behind the metal grill. This contains the remains of Francis' rich Roman patron, Jacopa dei Settesoli. She traveled to see him on his deathbed but was turned away because she was female. Francis waived the rule and welcomed "Brother Jacopa" to his side. These five tombs—in the Franciscan spirit of being with your friends—were added in the 19th century.

The candles you see are the only real candles in the church (others are electric). Pilgrims pay a coin, pick up a candle, and place it in the small box on the side. Franciscans will light it later.

• *Climb back up to the lower nave.*

ligious and civic pride to remember the hometown saint. It was also designed—and still functions—as a pilgrimage center and a splendid classroom. Though monks in robes may not give off an "easy-to-approach" vibe, the Franciscans of today are still God's jugglers (and many of them speak English).

Here is Francis' message, in his own words:

The Canticle of the Sun

Good Lord, all your creations bring praise to you!

Praise for Brother Sun, who brings the day. His radiance reminds us of you!

Praise for Sister Moon and the stars, precious and beautiful.

Praise for Brother Wind, and for clouds and storms and rain that sustain us.

Praise for Sister Water. She is useful and humble, precious and pure.

Praise for Brother Fire who cheers us at night.

Praise for our sister, Mother Earth, who feeds us and rules us.

Praise for all those who forgive because you have forgiven them.

Praise for our sister, Bodily Death, from whose embrace none can escape.

Praise and bless the Lord, and give thanks, and, with humility, serve him.

ASSISI

Lower Basilica

Appropriately Franciscan—subdued and Romanesque—this nave is frescoed with parallel scenes from the lives of Christ (right) and Francis (left), connected by a ceiling of stars. The Passion of Christ and the Compassion of Francis lead to the altar built over Francis' tomb. After the church was built and decorated, side chapels were erected to provide mausoleums for the rich families that patronized the work of the order. Unfortunately, in the process, huge arches were cut out of some frescoed scenes, but others survive. In the fresco directly above the entry to the tomb, Christ is being taken down from the cross (just the bottom half of his body can be seen, on the left), and it looks like the story is over. Defeat. But in the opposite fresco (above the tomb's exit), we see Francis preaching to the birds, reminding the faithful that the message of the Gospel survives.

These stories directed the attention of the medieval pilgrim to the altar, where he could meet God through the sacraments. The church was thought of as a community of believers sailing toward God. The prayers coming out of the nave (navis, or ship) fill the triangular sections of the ceiling—called vele, or sails—with spiritual

Basilica of St. Francis—Lower Level

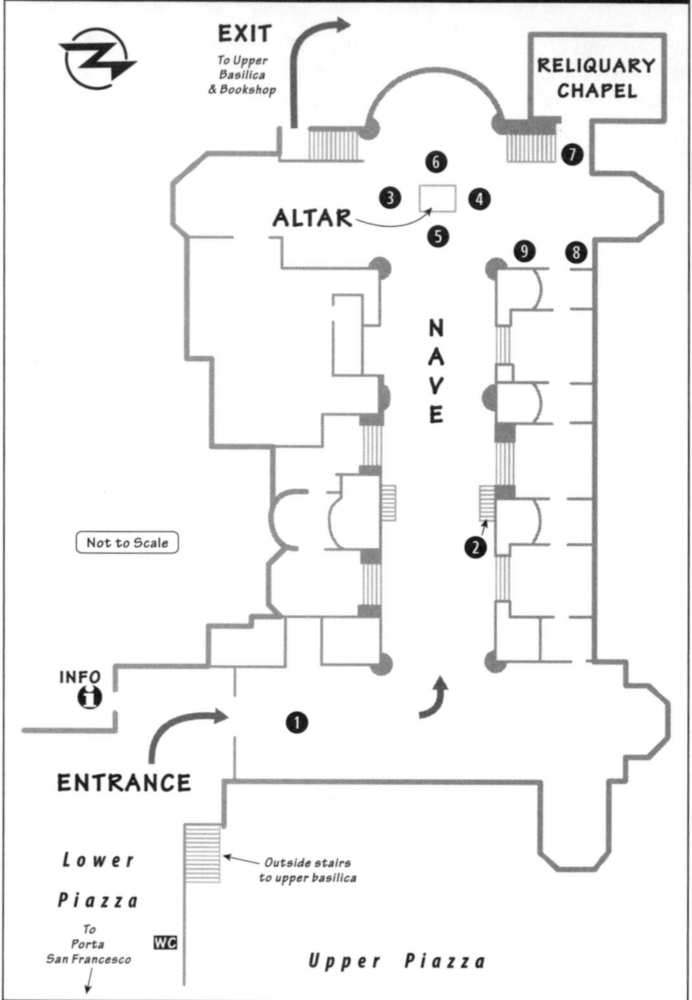

EXIT
To Upper
Basilica
& Bookshop

RELIQUARY CHAPEL

⑥

③ ④

ALTAR

⑤

⑦

⑨ ⑧

N A V E

Not to Scale

②

INFO

❶

ENTRANCE

Lower

Piazza

To
Porta
San Francesco

WC

Upper Piazza

Outside stairs
to upper basilica

ASSISI

❶ St. Francis (on ceiling)
❷ Stairs to Tomb
❸ Obedience (on ceiling)
❹ Chastity (on ceiling)
❺ Poverty (on ceiling)

❻ Francis on a Heavenly Throne
❼ Reliquary Chapel
❽ GIOTTO – Crucifixion
❾ CIMABUE – St. Francis

wind. With a priest for a navigator and the altar for a helm, faith propels the ship.

Stand behind the altar (toes to the bottom step, facing the entrance) and look up. The three scenes above you represent the creed of the Franciscans: Directly above the tomb of St. Francis, to the right, **Obedience** (Francis appears twice, wearing a rope harness and kneeling in front of Lady Obedience); to the left, **Chastity** (in her tower of purity held up by two angels); and straight ahead, **Poverty.** Here Jesus blesses the marriage as Francis slips a ring on Lady Poverty. In the foreground, two "self-sufficient" yet pint-size merchants (the new rich of a thriving northern Italy) are throwing sticks and stones at the bride. But Poverty, in her patched wedding dress, is fertile and strong, and even bare brambles blossom into a rosebush crown.

The three knots in the rope that ties the Franciscan robe symbolize the monks' vows of obedience, chastity, and poverty. St. Francis called money the "devil's dung." The jeweled belt of a rich person was all about material wealth. A bag of coins hung from it, as did a weapon to protect that person's wealth. Franciscans instead bound their tunics with a simple rope, its three knots a constant reminder of their vows.

Now put your heels to the altar and—bending back like a drum major—look up for a peek at the reward for a life of obedience, chastity, and poverty: **Francis on a heavenly throne** in a rich, golden robe. He traded a life of earthly simplicity for glory in heaven.

• *Turn to the right and march to the corner, where steps lead down into the...*

Reliquary Chapel

This chapel is filled with fascinating relics (which a €0.50 flier explains in detailed English; often closed Sat-Sun). Step in and circle the room clockwise. You'll see the silver chalice and plate that Francis used for the bread and wine of the Eucharist (in a small, dark, windowed case set into wall, marked *Calice e Patena*). Francis believed that his personal possessions should be simple, but the items used for worship should be made of the finest materials. Next, the Veli di Lino is a cloth Jacopa wiped her friend's brow with on his deathbed. In the corner display case is a small section of the itchy haircloth *(cilizio)*—not sheep's wool, but cloth made from scratchy horse or goat hair—worn by Francis as penance (the cloth he chose was the opposite of the fine fabric his father sold). In the next corner are the tunic and slippers that Francis donned during his last days. Next, find a prayer (in a fancy silver stand) that St. Francis wrote for Brother Leo and signed with a T-shaped character—his tau cross. The last letter in the Hebrew alphabet, tav ("tau" in Greek) is symbolic of faithfulness to the end, and Francis adopted it for his signature. Next is a papal document (1223) legitimizing the Franciscan order and assuring his followers that they were not risking a (deadly) heresy charge. Finally, just past the altar, see the tunic that was lovingly patched and stitched by followers of the five-foot, four-inch-tall St. Francis.

Before leaving the chapel, notice the modern paintings done in the last year or so by local artists. Over the entrance, Francis is shown being born in a stable like Jesus (by Capitini). Scenes from the life of Clare and Padre Pio (a Capuchin priest, very popular in Italy, who was sainted in 2002) were painted by Stefanelli and Antonio.

• *Return up the stairs, stepping into the...*

Lower Basilica's Transept

The decoration of this church brought together the greatest Sienese (Lorenzetti and Simone Martini) and Florentine (Cimabue and Giotto) artists of the day. Look around at the painted scenes. In 1300, this was radical art—believable homespun scenes, landscapes, trees, real people. Directly opposite the reliquary chapel, study **Giotto's painting of the Crucifixion,** with the eight sparrow-like angels. For the first time, holy people are expressing emotion: One angel turns her head sadly at the sight of Jesus, and another scratches her hands down her cheeks, drawing blood. Mary (lower left), previously in control, has fainted in despair. The Franciscans, with their goal of bringing God to the people, found a natural partner in Europe's first naturalist (and therefore modern) painter, Giotto.

To grasp Giotto's artistic leap, compare his work with the painting to the right, by Cimabue. It's Gothic, without the 3-D architecture, natural backdrop, and slice-of-life reality of Giotto's work. **Cimabue's St. Francis** (far right) shows the saint with the stigmata—Christ's marks of the Crucifixion. Contemporaries described Francis as being short, with a graceful build, dark hair, and sparse beard. (This is considered the most accurate portrait of Francis—done according to the description of one who knew him.) The sunroof haircut (tonsure) was  standard for monks of the day. According to legend, the brown robe and rope belt were inventions of necessity. When Francis stripped naked and ran away from Assisi, he grabbed the first clothes he could, a rough wool peasant's tunic and a piece of rope, which became the uniform of the Franciscan order. To the left, at eye level under the sparrow-like angels, are paintings of saints and their exquisite halos (by Simone Martini or his school). To the right of the door at the same level, see five of Francis' closest followers—clearly just simple folk.

Francis' friend, "Sister Bodily Death," was really not all that terrible. In fact, Francis would like to introduce you to her now (above and to the right of the door leading into the reliquary chapel). Go ahead, block the light from the door with this book and meet her. Before his death, Francis added a line to *The Canticle of the Sun:* "Praise for our sister, Bodily Death, from whose embrace none can escape."

• *Now cross the transept to the other side of the altar (enjoying some of the oldest surviving bits of the inlaid local-limestone flooring—c. 13th century), and find the staircase going up. Immediately above the stairs is Pietro Lorenzetti's* Francis Receiving the Stigmata. *(Francis is considered the first person ever to earn the marks of the cross through his great faith and love of the Church.) Make your way to the...*

ASSISI

Courtyard

The courtyard overlooks the 15th-century cloister, the heart of this monastic complex. Pope Sixtus IV (of Sistine Chapel fame) had it built as a secure retreat for himself. Balanced and peaceful by design, the courtyard also functioned as a cistern to collect rainwater, supplying enough for 200 monks (today, there are about 40). The Franciscan order emphasizes teaching. This place functioned as a kind of theological center of higher learning, which rotated monks in for a six-month stint, then sent them back home more prepared and better inspired to preach effectively. That explains the complex narrative of the frescoes wallpapering the walls and halls here.

The **treasury** *(Museo del Tesoro)* to the left of the bookstore features ornately decorated chalices, reliquaries, vestments, and altarpieces (free but donation requested, April-Oct Mon-Sat 10:30-13:00 & 14:00-17:30, Sun 10:00-17:30, closed Nov-March).

• *From the courtyard, climb the stairs (next to the bookshop) to the...*

Upper Basilica

Built later than its counterpart below, the brighter upper basilica is considered the first Gothic church in Italy (started in 1228). You've followed the intended pilgrims' route, entering the lower church and finishing here. Notice how the pulpit (embedded in the corner pillar) can be seen and heard from every spot in the packed church. The spirit of the order was to fill the church and preach. See also the design in the round window in the west end (high above the

Basilica of St. Francis—Upper Level

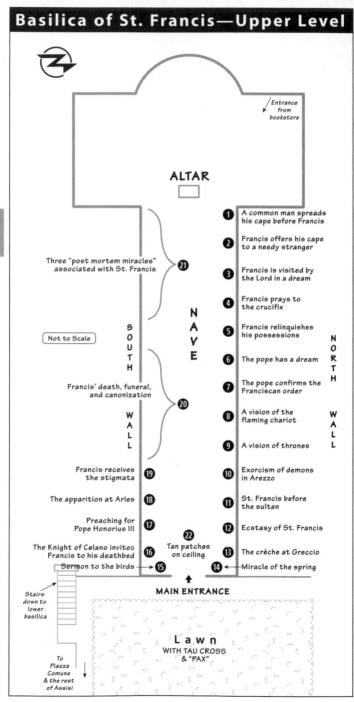

ASSISI

ALTAR

Entrance from bookstore

21 Three "post mortem miracles" associated with St. Francis

Not to Scale

S O U T H

N A V E

20 Francis' death, funeral, and canonization

W A L L

19 Francis receives the stigmata

18 The apparition at Arles

17 Preaching for Pope Honorius III

16 The Knight of Celano invites Francis to his deathbed

15 Sermon to the birds →

22 Tan patches on ceiling

Stairs down to lower basilica

To Piazza Comune & the rest of Assisi

MAIN ENTRANCE

1 A common man spreads his cape before Francis

2 Francis offers his cape to a needy stranger

3 Francis is visited by the Lord in a dream

4 Francis prays to the crucifix

5 Francis relinquishes his possessions

6 The pope has a dream

7 The pope confirms the Franciscan order

8 A vision of the flaming chariot

9 A vision of thrones

10 Exorcism of demons in Arezzo

11 St. Francis before the sultan

12 Ecstasy of St. Francis

13 The crèche at Greccio

14 ← Miracle of the spring

N O R T H

W A L L

L a w n
WITH TAU CROSS & "PAX"

entry). The tiny centerpiece reads "IHS" (the first three letters of Jesus' name in Greek). And, as you can see, this trippy kaleidoscope seems to declare that all light radiates from Jesus. The windows here are treasures from the 13th and 14th centuries. Those behind the apse are among the oldest and most precious in Italy. Imagine illiterate medieval peasants entranced by these windows, so full of meaning that they were nicknamed "Bibles of the Poor." But for art lovers, the basilica's draw is that Giotto and his assistants practically wallpapered it circa 1297-1300. Or perhaps the job was subcontracted to other artists—scholars debate it. Whatever the case, the anatomy, architectural depth, and drama of these frescoes helped to kick off the Renaissance. The gallery of frescoes shows 28 scenes from the life of St. Francis. The events are a mix of documented history and folk legend.

• *Working clockwise, start on the north wall (to the left, if you just climbed the stairs from the bookstore) and follow along with the help of the numbered map key. The subtitles in the black strip below the frescoes describe each scene in clear Latin—and affirm my interpretation.*

❶ **A common man spreads his cape before Francis** in front of the Temple of Minerva on Piazza del Comune. Before his conversion, young Francis was the model of Assisian manhood—handsome, intelligent, and well dressed, befitting the son of a wealthy cloth dealer. Above all, he was liked by everyone, a natural charmer who led his fellow teens in nights of wine, women, and song. Medieval pilgrims understood the deeper meaning of this scene: The "eye" of God (symbolized by the rose window in the Temple of Minerva) looks over the young Francis, a dandy "imprisoned" in his own selfishness (the Temple—with barred windows—was once a prison).

❷ **Francis offers his cape to a needy stranger.** Francis was always generous of spirit. He became more so after being captured in battle and held for a year as a prisoner of war, then suffering from illness. Charity was a Franciscan forte.

❸ **Francis is visited by the Lord in a dream.** Still unsure of his calling, Francis rode off to the Crusades. One night, he dreams of a palace filled with armor marked with crosses. Christ tells him to leave the army—to become what you might consider the first "conscientious objector"—and go home to wait for a non-military assignment in a new kind of knighthood. He returned to Assisi and, though reviled as a coward, would end up fighting for spiritual wealth, not earthly power and riches.

❹ **Francis prays to the crucifix** in the Church of San Damiano. After months of living in a cave, fasting, and meditating, Francis kneels in the run-down church and prays. The crucifix speaks, telling him: "Go and rebuild my Church, which you can see has fallen into ruin." Francis hurried home and sold his father's cloth to pay for God's work. His furious father dragged him before the bishop.

❺ **Francis relinquishes his possessions.** In front of the bishop and the whole town, Francis strips naked and gives his dad his clothes, credit cards, and time-share on Capri. Francis raises his hand and says, "Until now, I called you father. From now on, my only father is my Father in Heaven." Notice God's hand blessing the action from above. Francis then ran off into the hills, naked and singing. In this version, Francis is covered by the bishop, symbolizing his transition from a man of the world to a man of the Church. Notice the disbelief and concern on the bishop's advisors' faces; subtle expressions like these wouldn't have made it into other medieval frescoes of the day.

❻ **The pope has a dream.** Francis headed to Rome, seeking the pope's blessing on his fledgling movement. Initially rebuffing Francis, the pope then dreams of a simple, barefooted man propping up his teetering Church, and then...

❼ **The pope confirms the Franciscan order,** handing Francis and his gang the document now displayed in the reliquary chapel.

Francis' life was peppered with visions and miracles, shown in three panels in a row: ❽ **vision of the flaming chariot,** ❾ **vision of thrones,** and ❿ **exorcism of demons in Arezzo.**
• *Next see...*

⓫ **St. Francis before the sultan.** Francis' wandering ministry took him to Egypt during the Crusades (1219). He walked unarmed into the Muslim army camp. They captured him, but the sultan was impressed with Francis' manner and let him go, reportedly whispering, "I'd convert to your faith, but they'd kill us both." Here the sultan gestures from his throne.

⓬ **Ecstasy of St. Francis.** This oft-painted scene shows the mystic communing with Christ.

⓭ **The crèche at Greccio.** A creative teacher, Francis invents the tradition of manger scenes.
• *Around the corner, see the...*

⓮ **Miracle of the spring.** Shown here getting water out of a rock to quench a stranger's thirst, Francis felt closest to God when in the hills around Assisi, seeing the Creator in the creation.
• *Cross over to the far side of the entrance door.*

⓯ Sermon to the birds. In his best-known miracle, Francis is surrounded by birds as they listen to him teach. Francis embraces all levels of creation. One interpretation of this scene is that the birds, which are of different species, represent the diverse flock of humanity and nature, all created and beloved by God and worthy of one another's love.

This image of well-fed birds is an appropriate one to take with you. It's designed to remind pilgrims that, like the birds, God gave us life, plenty of food, feathers, wings, and a world to fly around in. Francis, patron saint of the environment and animals, taught his followers to count their blessings. A monk here reminded me that even a student backpacker today eats as well as the wealthiest nobleman in the days of Francis.

• Continue to the south wall for the rest of the panels.

Despite the hierarchical society of his day, Francis was welcomed by all classes, shown in these three panels: **⓰ the knight of Celano invites Francis to his deathbed; ⓱ preaching for Pope Honorius III,** who listens intently; and **⓲ the apparition at Arles,** which illustrates how Francis could be in two places at once (something only Jesus and saints can pull off). The proponents of Francis, who believed he was destined for sainthood, show him performing the necessary miracles.

⓳ Francis receives the stigmata. It's September 17, 1224, and Francis is fasting and praying on nearby Mount Alverna when a six-winged angel (called a seraph) appears with holy laser-like powers to burn in the marks of the Crucifixion, the stigmata. For the strength of his faith, Francis is given the marks of his master, the "battle scars of love." These five wounds suffered by Christ (nails in palms and feet, lance in side) marked Francis' body for the rest of his life.

The next panels deal with **⓴ Francis' death, funeral, and canonization.** The last panels show **㉑ miracles** associated with the saint after his death, proving that he's in heaven and bolstering his eligibility for sainthood.

Francis died thanking God and singing his *Canticle of the Sun.* Just as he referred to the sun as his brother and the moon as his sister, Francis called his body "brother." On his deathbed he conceded, "Maybe I was a bit tough on brother ass." Ravaged by an asceticism extreme enough to earn him the stigmata and tuberculosis, Francis died in 1226.

Before leaving through the front entrance, look up at the ceiling and the walls near the rose window to see **㉒ large tan patches.** In 1997, when a 5.5-magnitude quake hit Assisi, it shattered the upper basilica's frescoes into 300,000 fragments. Shortly after the quake, an aftershock shook the ceiling frescoes down, killing two monks and two art scholars standing here. Later, the fragments were meticulously picked up and pieced back together.

Outside, on the lawn, the Latin word *pax* (peace) and the Franciscan tau cross are sculpted from shrubbery. For a drink or snack, the Bar San Francesco (facing the upper basilica) is handy. For *pax,* take the high lane back to town, up to the castle, or into the countryside.

More Sights in Assisi

▲Roman Forum (Foro Romano)
For a look at Assisi's Roman roots, tour the Roman Forum, which is underneath Piazza del Comune. The floor plan is clearly explained in English, as are the surviving odd bits and obscure pieces. During your visit, you'll walk on an ancient Roman road.

Cost and Hours: €4, included in €8 combo-ticket that also covers next two sights daily March-Oct 10:00-13:00 & 14:30-18:00—until 19:00 in June-Aug, Nov-Feb 10:30-13:00 & 14:00-17:00; from Piazza del Comune, go a half-block down Via Portica—it's on your right; tel. 075-815-5077.

Pinacoteca
This small, unexciting museum attractively displays its 13th- to 17th-century art (mainly frescoes), with general English information in nearly every room. There's a damaged Giotto Madonna and a rare secular fresco (to the right of the Giotto art), but it's mainly a peaceful walk through a pastel world—best for art lovers.

Cost and Hours: €3, included in €8 combo-ticket, same hours as Roman Forum, Via San Francesco, across from #13C—look for banner above entryway, on main drag between Piazza del Comune and Basilica of St. Francis, tel. 075-815-5077.

▲Rocca Maggiore
The "big castle" offers a good look at a 14th-century fortification and a fine view of Assisi and the Umbrian countryside. If you're pinching your euros, skip it—the view is just as good from outside the castle. There's talk of restoring some rooms in their original medieval style, possibly in time for your visit.

Cost and Hours: €5, included in €8 combo-ticket, daily from 10:00 until an hour before sunset—about 19:15 in summer, tel. 075-815-5077.

Church of San Damiano (Chiesa di San Damiano)
Located on the slope steeply below the Basilica of St. Clare, this church and convent was where Francis received his call and where Clare spent her days as mother superior of the Poor Clares. Today, there's not much to see, but it's a relatively peaceful escape from touristy Assisi. Drivers can zip right there (watch for the turnoff on

the road up to Piazza Matteotti), while walkers descend pleasantly from Assisi for 15 minutes through an olive grove.

In 1206, Francis was inside the church when he heard the wooden crucifix order him to rebuild the church. (The crucifix in San Damiano is a copy; the original is now displayed in the Basilica of St. Clare.) Francis initially interpreted these miraculous words as a call to rebuild crumbling San Damiano. He sold his father's cloth for money to fix the church. (The church we see today, however, was rebuilt later by others.) Eventually, Francis realized his charge was to revitalize the Christian Church at large.

As he approached the end of his life, Francis came to San Damiano to visit his old friend Clare. She set him up in a simple reed hut in the olive grove, where he was inspired to write his poem *The Canticle of the Sun.*

Cost and Hours: Free, daily, convent open 10:00-12:00 & 14:00-18:00, closes at 16:30 in winter, church opens at 6:15, start walking from the Porta Nuova parking lot at the south end of Assisi and follow the signs, tel. 075-812-273, www.assisiofm.it.

Commune with Nature

For a picnic with the same birdsong and views that inspired St. Francis, leave the tourists behind and hike to the Rocca Minore (small private castle, not tourable) above Piazza Matteotti.

In Santa Maria degli Angeli

This modern part of Assisi sits in the flat valley below the hill town (see "Assisi Area" map, earlier). Whether you're arriving by car or by train, it's practical to visit these sights on the way into or out of Assisi (they're an easy walk from the train station—which has baggage storage—and there's ample, well-marked parking).

▲▲Basilica of St. Mary of the Angels
(Basilica di Santa Maria degli Angeli)

This huge basilica, towering above the buildings below Assisi, marks the spot where Francis lived, worked, and died. It's a grandi-

ose church built around a humble chapel—reflecting the monumental impact of this simple saint on his town and the world.

Cost and Hours: The basilica is free to enter and open Mon-Sat 6:15-12:50 & 14:30-19:30, Sun 6:45-12:50 & 14:30-19:30 (tel. 075-805-11). A little TI kiosk is across the street from the souvenir stands (generally daily 10:00-13:00 & 15:30-18:30 but hours a bit erratic, tel. 075-

804-4554). As you face the church, the best WC is on your right (€0.50).

Getting There: From Assisi's train station, it's a five-minute walk to the basilica (exit station left, after 50 yards take the underground pedestrian walkway—*sottopassaggio*—on your left, then walk straight ahead, passing several handy eateries).

From the old town, you can reach the basilica on the same orange bus (line #C) that runs down to the train station (stay on one more stop to reach the basilica). In the opposite direction, buses from the basilica up to the old town run twice hourly, usually at :14 and :44 after the hour. Leaving the church, the stop is on your right, by the side of the building. For information on tickets, see "Getting Around Assisi," earlier.

Visiting the Basilica: This grand church was built in the 16th century around the tiny but historic **Porziuncola Chapel** (now di-

rectly under the dome), after the chapel became too small to accommodate the many pilgrims wanting to pay homage to St. Francis. Some local monks had given Francis this *porziuncola*, or "small portion," after his conversion—a little land with a fixer-upper chapel. Francis lived here after he founded the Franciscan Order, and this was where he consecrated St. Clare as a Bride of Christ. What would humble Francis think of the huge church—Christianity's 10th largest—built over his tiny chapel?

Behind the Porziuncola Chapel on the right, find the **Cappella del Transito,** which marks the site of Francis' death on October 3, 1226. Francis died as he'd lived—simply, in a small hut located here. On his last night on earth, he invited some friars to join him in a Last Supper-style breaking of bread. Then he undressed, lay down on the bare ground, and began to recite Psalm 141: "Lord, I cry unto thee." He spoke the last line, "Let the wicked fall into their own traps, while I escape"...and he passed on.

From the right transept, follow *Roseto* signs to the rose garden. You'll walk down a passage with gardens on either side (viewable through the windows)—on the left, a tranquil park with a statue of Francis petting a sheep, and on the right, the **rose garden.** Francis, fighting a temptation that he never named, once threw himself onto the roses. As the story goes, the thorns immediately dropped off. Thornless roses have grown here ever since.

Exiting the passage, turn right to find the **Rose Chapel** (Cappella delle Rose), built over the place where Francis lived.

In the autumn, a room in the next **hallway** displays a giant animated nativity scene (a reminder to pilgrims that Francis first established the tradition of manger scenes as a teaching aid). You'll pass a room with a free 10-minute video about the church (ask for English, daily 10:00-12:30 & 16:00-18:00). The bookshop has some works in English and an "old pharmacy" selling herbal cures.

Continuing on, you'll pass the **Porziuncola Museum,** featuring early depictions of St. Francis by 13th-century artists, a model of Assisi during Francis' lifetime, and religious art and objects from the basilica. On the museum's upper floor are some monks' cells, which provide intriguing insight into the spartan lifestyles of the pious and tonsured (€4 to see both floors, ask for English brochure, museum open April-Oct Tue-Sun 9:30-12:30 & 15:30-19:00, Nov-March until 18:00, closed Mon, tel. 075-805-1419, www. porziuncola.org).

Museo Pericle Fazzini

This small museum, housed in the arcaded building across the street from the basilica, features works by the contemporary Italian sculptor Pericle Fazzini. His works feature elongated, wildly distorted, and very expressive figures. The permanent collection, on the first floor, includes bronzes, wooden sculptures (including one of St. Francis), and the original bronze casting of *The Risen Christ*—a miniature of Fazzini's famous bronze of Jesus rising from a nuclear-bomb crater, commissioned by the pope for the Sala Nervi audience hall of the Vatican. Biographical information on the sculptor is provided in English. Upstairs on the second floor are temporary exhibits.

Cost and Hours: €5, Tue-Sun 10:00-13:00 & 16:00-19:00, closed Mon, tel. 075-804-4586, www.museo.periclefazzini.it.

Outside of Assisi

Hermitage (Eremo delle Carceri)

If you want to follow further in St. Francis' footsteps, take a trip up the rugged slopes of nearby Mount Subasio to the humble hermitage where Francis and his followers retreated for solitude. Today the spot is marked by a 14th-century convent. The highlight is a look at the tiny, dank cave where Francis would retire for private prayer.

Cost and Hours: Free, daily 6:30-19:00, until 18:00 in winter, last entry 30 minutes before closing, tel. 075-812-301, www. eremocarceri.it.

Getting There: There is no public transportation; either drive, take a taxi, or hike. Starting from Assisi's Porta Cappuccini gate, it's a stiff 3-mile, 1.5-hour hike with an elevation gain of about 1,000 feet. You'll walk along a narrow, switchbacked, paved road enjoying brisk air and sporadic views. A souvenir kiosk at the entrance sells drinks and sandwiches.

ASSISI

Sleep Code

(€1 = about $1.30, country code: 39)
S = Single, **D** = Double/Twin, **T** = Triple, **Q** = Quad, **b** = bathroom, **s** = shower only. Unless otherwise noted, credit cards are accepted, English is spoken, and breakfast is included. Many cities in Italy levy a hotel tax of €2 per person, per night, which must be paid in cash (not included in the rates I've quoted).

To help you sort easily through these listings, I've divided the accommodations into three categories based on the price for a standard double room with bath:

$$$ **Higher Priced**—Most rooms €100 or more.
 $$ **Moderately Priced**—Most rooms between €55-100.
  $ **Lower Priced**—Most rooms €55 or less.

Prices can change without notice; verify the hotel's current rates online or by email. For the best prices, always book direct.

Sleeping in Assisi

Assisi accommodates large numbers of pilgrims on religious holidays. Finding a room at any other time should be easy. I've listed prices for spring (April-mid-June) and fall (mid-Aug-Oct). At most places, expect slightly lower rates in midsummer and winter. Breakfast is often included in the room rate—I've noted where it costs extra.

Few hotels are air-conditioned. Locals suggest that you keep your windows closed through the middle of the day so that your room will be as cool as possible in the evening.

Hotels and Rooms

$$$ Hotel Umbra, a quiet villa in the middle of town, has 24 spacious but overpriced rooms with great views, thinning carpets, and older decor (Sb-€75, standard Db-€110, bigger "superior" Db with better views-€125, Tb-€155, 10 percent discount with this book if you pay cash and stay for 2 or more nights, air-con, elevator, free Wi-Fi, peaceful garden and view sun terrace, most rooms have views—request when you reserve, closed Dec-March, just off Piazza del Comune under the arch at Via degli Archi 6, tel. 075-812-240, www.hotelumbra.it, info@hotelumbra.it, family Laudenzi).

$$ Hotel Ideale, on a ridge overlooking the valley, offers 14 airy rooms with simple modern furnishings (most with views and balconies), a tranquil garden setting, and free parking (Sb without view-€50, nicer Sb-€65, Db-€85, Tb-€100, prices good with this book through 2014, 10 percent discount for stays of 3 or more nights, air-con, free Wi-Fi, confirm your arrival time—especially if it's after 17:00, Piazza Matteotti 1, tel. 075-813-570, www.hotelideale.it, info@hotelideale.it, friendly sisters Lara and Ilaria and their monolingual family). The hotel is across the street from the bus stop (and parking lot) at Piazza Matteotti, at the top end of town.

$$ Hotel Belvedere, a great value, is a modern building with 12 spacious, classic-feeling rooms; eight come with sweeping views (Sb-€50, Db-€70, Tb-€85, Qb-€100, breakfast-€5, elevator, free Wi-Fi, large communal view terrace, 2 blocks past Basilica of St. Clare at Via Borgo Aretino 13, tel. 075-812-460, www.assisihotelbelvedere.com, hotelbelvedereassisi@yahoo.it, thoughtful Enrico speaks fluent New Jerseyan). Coming by bus from the train station, get off at Porta Nuova; the hotel is steps away.

$$ La Pallotta offers seven fresh, bright, small rooms and a shared top-floor lounge with view. They provide guests with a loaner Assisi guidebook, map, and audioguide, as well as a bus ticket and English helpline number (Sb-€45, Db-€79, free guest computer and Wi-Fi, free use of washer and drying rack, free hot drinks and cake at teatime; a block off Piazza del Comune at Via San Rufino 6—go up a short flight of stairs outside building, above the arch, to reach entrance; tel. 075-812-307, www.pallottaassisi.it, pallotta@pallottaassisi.it; helpful Stefano, Serena, and family). If you're driving, head to Piazza San Rufino, where they'll meet you (call ahead). They also have a good restaurant (see "Eating in Assisi," later).

$$ Hotel San Rufino offers a great locale, solid stone quality, and 11 comfortable rooms (Sb-€46, Db-€58, Tb-€78, Qb-€92, breakfast-€5, elevator, free Wi-Fi; from Cathedral of San Rufino, follow sign to Via Porta Perlici 7; tel. 075-812-803, www.hotelsanrufino.it, info@hotelsanrufino.it). Their nine-room annex, Albergo Il Duomo (listed later), saves you about €5 a night for a double with no loss in comfort.

$$ Hotel La Rocca, on the peaceful top end of town, has 32 solid and modern rooms in a medieval shell (Sb-€46, Db-€59, Tb-€79, breakfast-€5, air-con, elevator, pay Wi-Fi, parking-€7, sunny rooftop terrace, decent restaurant upstairs, 3-minute walk from Piazza Matteotti at Via Porta Perlici 27, tel. 075-812-284, www.hotelarocca.it, info@hotelarocca.it, Carlo).

$$ Hotel Sole, renting 38 rooms in a 15th-century building, is well-worn and forgettable, but the location is central. Half of its rooms are in a newer annex across the street (Sb-€50, Db-€70, Tb-€90, ask for a discount, breakfast-€5, air-con-€5 extra, free Wi-Fi in common areas, public parking nearby, 100 yards before Basilica of St. Clare at Corso Mazzini 35, tel. 075-812-373, www.assisihotelsole.com, info@assisihotelsole.com).

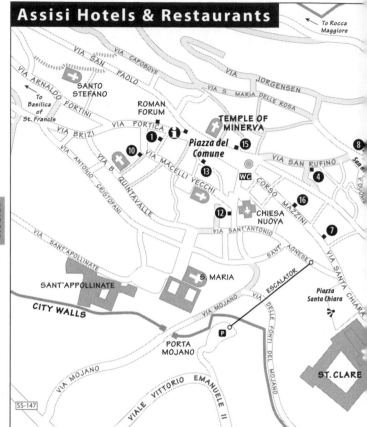

$ Camere Carli has six shiny, spacious, new rooms in a solid, minimalist place above a shop (Sb-€35, Db-€48, Tb-€60, Qb-€70, no breakfast, show this book to get these prices, family lofts, lots of stairs and no elevator, free Wi-Fi, free parking 150 yards away, facing the Duomo at Via Porta Perlici 1, tel. 075-812-490, mobile 339-531-1366, www.camerecarli.it, carliarte@live.it, pleasant Carli speaks limited English).

$ Albergo Il Duomo's nine rooms are tidy and *tranquillo*. Located on a stair-stepped lane one block up from Hotel San Rufino, it's more atmospheric and has nicer bathrooms than its parent hotel (Sb-€43, Db-€55, Tb-€68, breakfast-€5, free Wi-Fi in Hotel San Rufino lobby, Vicolo San Lorenzo 2 but check in at Hotel San Rufino—see earlier, tel. 075-812-742, www.hotelsanrufino.it, info@hotelsanrufino.it).

$ Camere Annalisa Martini is a cheery home amid vines and roses in the town's medieval core. This is a good budget choice—

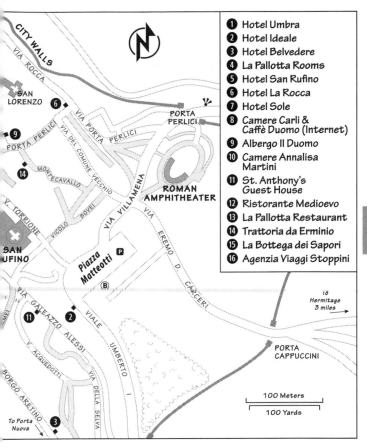

1. Hotel Umbra
2. Hotel Ideale
3. Hotel Belvedere
4. La Pallotta Rooms
5. Hotel San Rufino
6. Hotel La Rocca
7. Hotel Sole
8. Camere Carli & Caffè Duomo (Internet)
9. Albergo Il Duomo
10. Camere Annalisa Martini
11. St. Anthony's Guest House
12. Ristorante Medioevo
13. La Pallotta Restaurant
14. Trattoria da Erminio
15. La Bottega dei Sapori
16. Agenzia Viaggi Stoppini

Annalisa enthusiastically accommodates her guests with a picnic garden, a washing machine (€7/small load, includes line drying), a communal refrigerator, and six homey rooms (S-€27, Sb-€30, D-€40, Db-€42, Tb-€58, Qb-€68, rates soft for last-minute bookings, cash only, 3 rooms share 2 bathrooms, no breakfast, free Wi-Fi; 1 block from Piazza del Comune—go downhill toward basilica, turn left on Via San Gregorio to #6; tel. 075-813-536, cameremartini@libero.it, Mamma Rosignoli—"roh-sin-YOH-lee"—doesn't speak English, but Annalisa does).

Hostel: Francis probably would have bunked with the peasants in Assisi's 65-bed **$ Ostello della Pace** (€17 beds in 4- to 8-bed rooms, €20-22/person in private 2- to 4-person rooms with bath, dinner-€10.50, laundry service-€4, pay guest computer, free Wi-Fi, free parking, lockout 10:00-16:00, midnight curfew, closed Nov-Feb; take orange shuttle bus from station to Piazza Giovanni Paolo II, then walk 15 minutes downhill on via Marconi, then left at bend on Via di Valecchie to #4; tel. 075-816-767, www.assisihostel.com, info@assisihostel.com).

Sweet Dreams in a Convent

Assisi is filled with convents, most of which rent rooms to pilgrims and travelers. While you don't need to be a pilgrim or even a Christian to be welcome, it's just common sense to stay in a convent *only* if you're approaching Assisi with a contemplative mindset. Convents feel institutional, house many groups, and are not particularly cheap—but they come with all the facilities you might need to enjoy a spirit-filled visit to Assisi.

$$ St. Anthony's Guest House is where the Franciscan Sisters of the Atonement (including several Americans and Canadians) offer a very warm and tranquil welcome. Their oasis of peace is just above the Basilica of St. Clare. With only 35 beds in 19 rooms (some with great views—request when you reserve) at a reasonable price, they book up literally months in advance (Sb-€45, Db-€65, Tb-€85, 2-night minimum, cash only for short stays, no problem if couples want to share a bed, elevator, no air-con but fans, free Wi-Fi in common areas, 23:00 curfew, closed mid-Nov-Feb, library, views, picnic garden, parking-€3 donation, just below Piazza Matteotti at Via Galeazzo Alessi 10, tel. 075-812-542, atoneassisi@tiscali.it).

Agriturismo near Assisi

$$ Le Mandrie di San Paolo ("The Herd of St. Paul") is a meticulously restored 1,000-year-old stone house renting 13 rustic but comfortable rooms. Soulful Alex and the Damiani family are justifiably proud of their fine craftsmanship, passion for hospitality, and connection to the land. They have an olive grove (ask Alex if he'll give you a tour of their modern mill in the valley), lots of animals, a beautiful swimming pool, sauna/steam room, fine restaurant, and spectacular views over Assisi and the valleys of Umbria (Db-€90; 2-bedroom apartments: Db-€105, Qb-€130; family deals, 3-night minimum in June-mid-Sept, free Wi-Fi, mobile 349-821-7867, tel. 075-806-4070, www.agriturismomandriesanpaolo.it, mandrie10@gmail.com). Their restaurant is a great choice, and worth considering for non-guests who just want to get out of town—they produce their own olive oil and flour, and fire their bread ovens with their own wood (€25-30 for four-course meal, daily 19:30-22:00, in winter on request, reservations preferred). It's about a 10-minute drive from Assisi, on the hill high above the village of Viole (a.k.a. San Vitale). Just head southeast of Assisi following signs for *Viole*; when you enter town, before you reach the arch, turn left and follow signs up the hill.

Eating in Assisi

I've listed decent, central, good-value restaurants. Assisi's food is heavy and rustic. Locals brag about their sausage and love to grate truffles on pasta. Many restaurants in town offer a fixed-price *menù turistico* for €18—for the best value, find one that includes dessert and something to drink, such as at La Pallotta.

To bump up any meal, consider a glass or bottle of the favorite homegrown red wine, Sagrantino de Montefalco. Sagrantino is Umbria's answer to Brunello (although many wine lovers around here would say that it's vice versa). Before or after dinner, enjoy a drink on the main square facing the Roman temple...or hang out with the local teens with a take-away beer under the temple's columns.

Fine Dining

Ristorante Medioevo is my vote for your best splurge. With heavy but spacious cellar vaults, William Ventura's restaurant is an elegant, accessible playground of gastronomy. Maître d' Massimo will guide you to the best of Umbrian cuisine. He features traditional cuisine with a modern twist, dictated by what's in season. While his first passion is cooking, his second is music—mellow jazz and bossa nova give a twinkle to the medieval atmosphere. Dishes are well-presented; beef and game dishes are the specialties, and the wonderful Sagrantino wine is served by the glass. As a special treat for readers of this book, when you order a glass of Sagrantino, you'll receive a small slice of just the right strong pecorino cheese—to better understand the Italian fascination with "a good marriage" between food and wine (€9-13 pastas, €12-16 *secondi*, Tue-Sun 12:30-15:00 & 19:30-22:45, closed Mon, in winter open weekends only; from the fountain on Piazza del Comune, hike downhill two blocks to Via Arco dei Priori 4; tel. 075-813-068).

Casual Eateries

La Pallotta, a local favorite run by a friendly and hardworking family—with Margarita in charge of the kitchen—offers delicious, well-presented regional specialties, such as *piccione* (squab, a.k.a. pigeon) and *coniglio* (rabbit). And they like to serve split courses *(bis)* featuring the two local pastas. Reservations are smart (€5-9 pastas, €8-15 *secondi*, €18 fixed-price meal includes dessert and wine or water, better €27 fixed-price meal showcases local specialties, Wed-Mon 12:15-14:30 & 19:00-23:00, last orders at 21:30, closed Tue, vegetarian options, a few steps off Piazza del Comune across from temple/church at Vicolo della Volta Pinta 2, tel. 075-812-649).

At **Locanda del Podestà,** chef Stelvio cooks up tasty grilled Umbrian sausages, *gnocchi alla locanda,* and all manner of truffles, while Romina graciously serves happy diners who know a good value. Try the tasty *scottaditto* ("scorch your fingers") lamb chops (€5-9 pastas, €7-16 *secondi*, €18 fixed-price meal includes coffee, Thu-Tue 12:00-14:30 & 19:00-21:30, closed Wed and Feb, 5-minute walk uphill along Via Cardinale Merry del Val from basilica, Via San Giacomo 6c, tel. 075-816-553).

Ristorante Metastasio, just up the street from Podestà, offers a pricey, traditional menu and Assisi's best view terrace for dining (€9-13 pastas, €10-18 *secondi*, Thu-Tue 12:00-14:30 & 19:00-21:30, closed Wed, terrace closed in bad weather, Via Metastasio 9, tel. 075-816-525).

Trattoria da Erminio has peaceful tables on a tiny square, and indoor seating under a big, medieval (but air-conditioned) brick vault. Run by Federico and his family for three generations, it specializes in local meat cooked on an open-fire grill. They have good Umbrian wines—before you order, ask Federico or Giuliana for a taste of the Petranera wine (€8-11 pastas, €9-14 grilled meats, €18 fixed-price meal changes weekly, Fri-Wed 12:00-14:30 & 19:00-21:00, closed Thu; from Piazza San Rufino, go a block up Via Porta Perlici and turn right to Via Montacavallo 19; tel. 075-812-506).

Picnic on the Main Square

There are many little grocery stores *(alimentari)* near Piazza del Comune (one is a block uphill from the main square, at Via San Rufino 19), plus bakeries selling pizza by the slice. But try **La Bottega dei Sapori** to assemble a picnic of Umbrian treats: good prosciutto sandwiches and specialty items, including truffle paste and olive oil. Friendly Fabrizio, who is a slow-food enthusiast, may give you a taste. He also stocks the best Umbrian wines at good-to-go prices—nice if you have an appointment with your terrace for sunset (€3-4 sandwiches, daily 9:30-20:00, until 21:00 in summer, closed Jan-Feb, Piazza del Comune 34, tel. 075-812-294).

Assisi Connections

From Assisi by Train to: Rome (nearly hourly, 2-3.5 hours, 5 direct, most others change in Foligno; train timetables change frequently—double-check details), **Florence** (8/day direct, 2-3 hours), **Orvieto** (roughly hourly, 3 hours, with transfer in Terantola or Orte), **Siena** (hourly, 3.25-4.25 hours, most involve 2 transfers; bus is faster), **Cortona** (every 2 hours, 70 minutes to Camucia-Cortona station). The train station's ticket office is often open only Mon-Fri 12:00-20:00, closed Sat-Sun; when the office is closed, use the ticket machine (may only accept credit cards; newsstands sell only regional tickets and accept cash). Up in Assisi's old town, you can get train information and tickets from Agenzia Viaggi Stoppini. Also try online, at www.trenitalia.com.

By Bus: Service to **Rome** is operated by the Sulga bus company (2/day, 3 hours, pay driver, departs from Piazza San Pietro, arrives at Rome's Tiburtina station, where you can connect with the train to Fiumicino airport, tel. 800-099-661, www.sulga.it). A bus for **Siena** (1/day at 10:20, 2 hours, www.sena.it) departs from the stop next to the Basilica of St. Mary of the Angels, near the train station; you can't buy Siena tickets from the driver—buy them at Assisi's Agenzia Viaggi Stoppini.

Don't take the bus to **Florence;** the train is better. To see either **Gubbio** or **Todi** as a side-trip from Assisi, you'll need a car—bus schedules don't accommodate day-trippers. Day trips to **Spello** and **Lake Trasimeno** work by train, but not by bus. A day trip to **Perugia** is possible with buses operated by Umbria Mobilità (www.umbriamobilita.it). For nearby day-trip options like these, you could also consider taking a tour; the recommended Agenzia Viaggi Stoppini offers several (www.viaggistoppiniassisi.it).

By Plane: Perugia/Assisi Airport, about 10 miles from Assisi, has daily connections to London Stansted and Brussels (on Ryanair), and to a few Mediterranean destinations (airport code: PEG, tel. 075-592-141, www.airport.umbria.it). Bus service between Assisi and the airport is so sporadic (just a few times a day—see www.umbriamobilita.it) that you should plan on taking a taxi (about €30).

ORVIETO AND CIVITA

While Tuscany is justifiably famous for its many fine hill towns, Umbria, just to the south, has some stellar offerings of its own. Assisi (covered in its own chapter) is a must for nature lovers and Franciscan pilgrims. But if you're after views, wine, and charming villages, you'll find Umbria's best in Orvieto and in Civita di Bagnoregio (which is technically just across the border in Lazio, the same region as Rome). About a 30-minute drive apart, these hill towns—one big, one small—perch high above scenic plains. Pleasant Orvieto is best known for its colorful-inside-and-out cathedral and its fine Orvieto Classico wine. Tiny Civita di Bagnoregio, my favorite hill town, is an improbable pinnacle of traditional Italian village culture, just accessible enough that modern tourists are keeping it going. Taken together, Orvieto and Civita make a perfect duet for experiencing what all the hill-town fuss is about.

Planning Your Time

The town of Orvieto and the village of Civita deserve at least an overnight, although even a few hours in each is enough to sample what they have to offer. Both are also great places to slow down and relax. Stay in one, and side-trip to the other (Orvieto has more restaurants and other amenities and is easier to reach, while Civita really lets you get away from it all). The two towns are connected by a 30-minute drive or a 45-minute bus ride, and Orvieto is conveniently close to Rome (about an hour away by train or expressway).

Orvieto

Just off the freeway and the main train line, Umbria's grand hill town entices those heading to and from Rome. While no secret, it's well worth a visit. The town sits majestically on its *tufo* throne a thousand feet above the valley floor. Orvieto became a regional power in the Middle Ages, and even earlier, a few centuries before Christ, it was one of a dozen major Etruscan cities. Some historians believe Orvieto may have been a religious center—a kind of Etruscan Mecca (locals are looking for archaeological proof—the town and surrounding countryside are dotted with Etruscan ruins).

Orvieto has three popular claims to fame: cathedral, Classico wine, and ceramics. Drinking a shot of the local white wine in a ceramic cup as you gaze up at the cathedral lets you experience Orvieto's three C's all at once. (Is the cathedral best in the afternoon, when the facade basks in golden light, or early in the morning, when it rises above the hilltop mist? You decide.) Though loaded with tourists by day, Orvieto is quiet by night, and a visit here comes with a wonderful bonus: close proximity to the unforgettable Civita di Bagnoregio (covered later in this chapter).

Orientation to Orvieto

Orvieto has two distinct parts: the old-town hilltop and the dreary new town below (called Orvieto Scalo). Whether coming by train or car, you first arrive in the nondescript, modern lower part of town. From there you can drive or take the funicular, elevator, or escalator up to the medieval upper town, an atmospheric labyrinth of streets and squares where all the sightseeing action is.

Tourist Information

The TI is on the cathedral square at Piazza del Duomo 24 (Mon-Fri 8:15-13:50 & 16:00-19:00, Sat-Sun 10:00-13:00 & 15:00-18:00, tel. 0763-341-772). Pick up the free city map and their green city guide, and ask about train and bus schedules. The ticket office next to the main TI sells combo-tickets and books reservations for the underground tours (tel. 0763-340-688). Depending on funding, the town may also have a branch TI at Piazza Cahen (at the top of the funicular) during summer.

Combo-Ticket: The €18 **Carta Unica** combo-ticket covers Orvieto's top sights (virtually every sight recommended here, including Underground Orvieto Tours) and includes one round-trip on the bus and/or funicular (www.cartaunica.it). To cover your funicular ride, you can buy the combo-ticket on your arrival in the

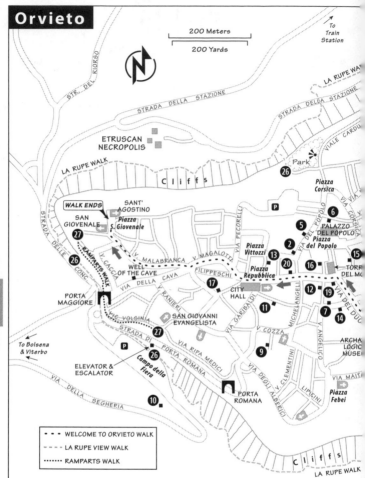

Orvieto

200 Meters
200 Yards

To Train Station

LA RUPE WALK

STRADA DELLA STAZIONE

STR. DEL RIORSO

STRADA DELLA STAZIONE

VIALE CARDU

ETRUSCAN NECROPOLIS

LA RUPE WALK

Park

Cliffs

Piazza Corsica

WALK ENDS

SANT' AGOSTINO

SAN GIOVENALE

Piazza S. Giovenale

PALAZZO DEL POPOLO

Piazza del Popolo

V. PECORELLI

V. MALABRANCA   V. MAGALOTTI

Piazza Vittozzi

WELL OF THE CAVE

Piazza Repubblica

TORRE DEL MO

FILIPPESCHI

STRADA DELLE CONC

RAMPARTS WALK

V. CACCIA

VIA DELLA CAVA

RANIERI

CITY HALL

VIA DEL DUO

PORTA MAGGIORE

SAN GIOVANNI EVANGELISTA

VIC. VOLSINIA

VIA GARIBALDI

MICHELANGELI

To Bolsena & Viterbo

V. COZZA

ARCHA LOGIC MUSE

STRADA DI PORTA ROMANA

VIA RIPA MEDICI

V. ANGELICO

ELEVATOR & ESCALATOR

Campo della Fiera

VIA DEGLI ALBERICI

CLEMENTINI

LIPCINI

VIA MALT

Piazza Febei

VIA DELLA SEGHERIA

PORTA ROMANA

Cliffs

LA RUPE WALK

- - - WELCOME TO ORVIETO WALK
- - - LA RUPE VIEW WALK
······ RAMPARTS WALK

ORVIETO & CIVITA

1 Hotel Duomo
2 Grand Hotel Italia
3 Hotel Corso
4 Villa Mercede
5 Istituto S.S. Salvatore
6 Affitacamere Valentina
7 Hotel Posta
8 La Magnolia B&B
9 B&B Michelangeli
10 Casa Sèlita B&B
11 La Palomba Restaurant
12 Trattoria Antico Bucchero
13 L'Antica Trattoria dell'Orso
14 Trattoria la Grotta & Despar Supermarket

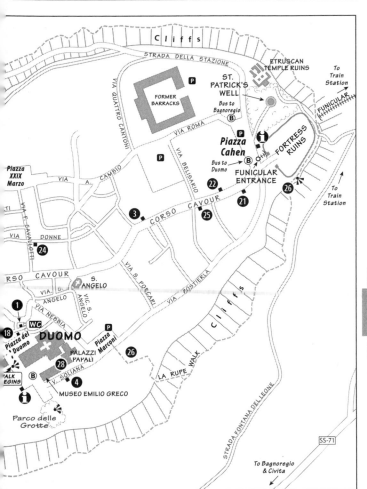

- ⑮ Trattoria del Moro Aronne
- ⑯ Trattoria da Carlo
- ⑰ Pizzeria & Rest. Charlie
- ⑱ Enoteca al Duomo &
  Pasqualetti Gelateria
- ⑲ L'Oste del Re
- ⑳ Caffè Montanucci
- ㉑ Idea Pizza
- ㉒ Peng Cheng Restaurant
- ㉓ Metà Supermarket
- ㉔ Internet Café
- ㉕ Tobacco Shop (Bus Tickets)
- ㉖ La Rupe View Walk Access (5)
- ㉗ Romantic Rampart Stroll
- ㉘ MoDo Art Galleries &
  National Arch. Museum

ORVIETO & CIVITA

lower town—either at the bar at the train station (if they haven't run out), or at a seasonal ticket office in the parking lot (below the station, Easter-Sept daily 9:00-16:00, closed Oct-Easter, tel. 0763-302-378). The combo-ticket is also available at the ticket office next to the TI on Piazza del Duomo, as well as at most of the sights it covers.

Arrival in Orvieto

By Train: The train station is at the foot of the hill the old town sits on. There's no baggage storage at the train station, but Hotel Picchio, 300 yards from the station at Via G. Salvatori 17, stores day-trippers' luggage for €5 per bag (leaving the station, go left, then right up Via G. Salvatori, tel. 0763-301-144).

The easiest way to the top of town (including the cathedral and my recommended hotels) is by **funicular:** Buy your ticket at the entrance to the *funiculare;* look for the *biglietteria* sign (€1, €0.80 with same-day train ticket, good for 70 minutes, includes minibus from Piazza Cahen to Piazza del Duomo, Mon-Sat 7:20-20:30, Sun 8:00-20:30, about every 10 minutes). Or buy a Carta Unica combo-ticket (described earlier) to cover your funicular ride.

As you exit the funicular at the top, you're in Piazza Cahen, located at the east end of the upper town. To your left is a ruined fortress with a garden and a commanding view. To your right, down a steep path, is St. Patrick's Well. Farther to the right is a park with Etruscan ruins and another sweeping view.

Just in front of you is the orange **shuttle bus,** waiting to take you to Piazza del Duomo at no extra charge (included in your funicular ticket). The bus fills up fast, but the views from the ruined fortress are worth pausing for—if you miss the bus, you can wait for the next one, or just walk to the cathedral (head uphill on Corso Cavour; after about 10 minutes, take a left onto Via del Duomo). The bus drops you in Piazza del Duomo, just steps from the main TI and within easy walking distance of most of my recommended sights and hotels. If you forgot to check at the station for the train schedule to your next destination, no problem—the schedule is posted at the top of the funicular and is also available at the TI.

If you arrive outside the funicular's operating hours, you can reach the upper part of town by **taxi** (figure about €12—see later) or **bus** to Piazza della Repubblica (buses run roughly 2/hour until midnight, buy €1.50 ticket from driver).

By Car: For free parking, use the huge lot below the train station (5 minutes off the autostrada; follow the *P funiculare* signs). Walk through the station and ride the funicular up the hill (see "By Train," above).

It's also possible to park in the old town. Some free parking is available in the north half (white lines) of Piazza Cahen (at the top end of the funicular). There are also several pay options: the small lot in Piazza Marconi, near Orvieto's cathedral (€1.50 for first hour, €1/hour thereafter); the south half (blue lines) of Piazza Cahen (€1.20/hour); and the Campo della Fiera lot just below the west end of town (€1/hour; from top level of lot, walk up into town or take escalator—7:00-21:00—or elevator—7:00-24:00; both free). Generally, white lines indicate free parking, and blue lines require you to buy a "pay and display" slip from a nearby machine.

While you can drive up Via Postierla and Via Roma to get to central parking lots, Corso Cavour and other streets in the old center are closed to traffic and monitored by cameras (look for red lights, and avoid streets marked by a red circle).

By Taxi: Taxis line up in front of the train station and charge about €12 for a ride to the cathedral (a ridiculous price considering the ease and pleasure of the €1 funicular/shuttle-bus ride to the cathedral square; mobile 360-433-057).

Helpful Hints

Market Days and Festivals: On Thursday and Saturday mornings, Piazza del Popolo becomes a busy farmers' market. The same square hosts an arts-and-crafts market some Sundays. Orvieto is also busy during the Umbria Jazz festival that takes place for a few days before New Year's (www.umbriajazz.com).

Internet Access: Caffè Montanucci has four terminals (€2.50/30 minutes, free if you buy food, daily 7:00-24:00, Corso Cavour 21), and **Copisteria ESPA** has two (€3/30 minutes, Mon-Fri 9:00-13:00 & 16:00-19:40, Sat 9:00-13:00, closed Sun, Via Felice Cavallotti 9).

Laundry: There's a coin launderette in the lower town, a 10-minute walk from the train station, in the complex on top of the big Co-op supermarket. It's a bit of a haul from central hotels, and instructions are in Italian only, but it's workable if you're desperate (daily 7:00-22:00, Piazza del Comercio, off via Monte Nibbio, mobile 393-758-6120).

Car/Minibus Service: Giuliotaxi is run by charming, English-speaking Giulio and his sister, Maria Serena. They have a car (for up to 4) and a minibus (for up to 8). I've organized two special excursions with them that offer great efficiency and value for couples and small groups going from Orvieto to Civita: Rather than hassle with a bus and long walks, book Giulo for the drive to Civita, a two-hour wait, and the return to Orvieto (€80/car, €100/minibus). For a longer trip, book a drive to Civita, visit for two hours, explore around Lake Bolsena for a couple more hours, and then head back to Orvieto (5 hours total, €150/car, €180/minibus). If you assemble a small group at your hotel and split the cost, this service becomes an even better deal. They can take you to other destinations, as well (mobile 360-433-057, www.italy-driver.com, giuliotaxi@libero.it).

Local Guide: Manuela del Turco is good (€120/2.5-hour tour, mobile 333-221-9879, manueladel@virgilio.it).

After Dark: In the evening, there's little going on other than strolling and eating. The big *passeggiata* scene is down Via del Duomo and Corso Cavour.

Self-Guided Walk

Welcome to Orvieto

This quickie L-shaped walk takes you from the Duomo through Orvieto's historic center. Each evening, this route is the scene of the local *passeggiata*.

Facing the cathedral, head left. Stroll past the clock tower (first put here in 1347 for the workers building the cathedral), which marks the start of Via del Duomo, lined with shops selling ceramics. **Via dei Magoni** (second left) has several artisan shops and the crazy little Il Mago di Oz ("Wizard of Oz") shop, a wondrous toyland created by eccentric Giuseppe Rosella (Via dei Magoni 3, tel. 0763-342-063). Have Giuseppe push a few buttons, and you're far from Kansas (no photos allowed).

Via del Duomo continues to Orvieto's main intersection, where it meets Corso Cavour and a tall, stark tower—the **Torre del Moro.** The tower marks the center of town, serves as a handy orientation tool, and is decorated by the coats of arms of past governors. The elevator leaves you with 173 steps still to go to earn a commanding view (€3, daily March-Oct 10:00-19:00, May-Aug until 20:00, Nov-Feb 10:30-17:00).

This crossroads divides the town into **four quarters** (notice the *Quartiere* signs on the corners). In the past, residents of these four districts competed in a lively equestrian competition on Piazza del Popolo during the annual Corpus Christi celebration. Historically, the four streets led from here to the market and the fine palazzo on Piazza del Popolo, the well, the Duomo, and City Hall.

Before heading left down Corso Cavour, side-trip a block farther ahead, behind the tower, for a look at the striking **Palazzo del Popolo.** Built of local *tufo,* this is a textbook example of a fortified medieval public palace: a fortress designed to house the city's leadership and military, with a market at its base, fancy meeting rooms upstairs, and aristocratic living quarters on the top level.

Return to the tower and head down Corso Cavour (turning right) past classic storefronts to **Piazza della Repubblica** and City Hall. The original vision—though it never came to fruition—was for City Hall to have five arches flanking the main central arch (marked by the flags today). The Church of Sant'Andrea (left of City Hall) sits atop an Etruscan temple that was likely the birthplace of Orvieto centuries before Christ. Inside is an interesting architectural progression: Romanesque (with few frescoes surviving), Gothic (the pointy vaults over the altar), and a Renaissance barrel vault in the apse (behind the altar)—all lit by fine alabaster windows.

From City Hall, you can continue to the far end of town to the **Church of Sant'Agostino,** where you can see the statues of the apostles that once stood in the Duomo (included in the MoDo ticket). From here you can take a left and walk the cliffside ramparts (see "View Walks," later).

Sights in Orvieto

▲▲▲Duomo

Oriveto's cathedral has Italy's liveliest facade. This colorful, prickly Gothic facade, divided by four pillars, has been compared to a me-

dieval altarpiece. The optical-illusion interior features some fine art, including Luca Signorelli's lavishly frescoed Chapel of San Brizio.

Cost and Hours: €3; April-Sept Mon-Sat 9:30-19:00, Sun 13:00-17:30 or until 18:30 July-Sept; March and Oct Mon-Sat 9:30-18:00, Sun 13:00-17:30; Nov-Feb Mon-Sat 9:30-13:00 & 14:30-17:00, Sun 14:30-17:30; last entry 30 minutes before closing. A €5 combo-ticket includes the Duomo, the chapel, and the Museo dell'Opera del Duomo, called the "MoDo" (available at the chapel; MoDo alone costs €4). Admission is also covered by the €18 Carta Unica combo-ticket.

○ Self-Guided Tour: Begin by viewing the **exterior facade.** Study this gleaming mass of mosaics, stained glass, and sculpture (c. 1300, by Lorenzo Maitani and others).

At the base of the cathedral, the four broad **marble pillars** carved with biblical scenes tell the history of the world in four acts, from left to right. The relief on the far left shows the Creation (see God creating Eve from Adam's rib, and the snake tempting Eve). Next is the Tree of Jesse (Jesus' family tree—with Mary, then Jesus on top) flanked by Old Testament stories, then the New Testament (look for the unique manger scene, and other events from the life of Christ). On the far right is the Last Judgment (Christ judging on top, with a commotion of sarcophagi popping open and all hell breaking loose at the bottom).

Each pillar is topped by a bronze symbol of one of the Evangelists: angel (Matthew), lion (Mark), eagle (John), and ox (Luke). The bronze doors are modern, by the Sicilian sculptor Emilio Greco. (A gallery devoted to Greco's work is to the immediate right of the church.) In the mosaic below the rose window, Mary is transported to heaven. In the uppermost mosaic, Mary is crowned.

• *Now step inside.*

The **nave** feels spacious and less cluttered than most Italian churches. Until 1877, it was much busier, with statues of the apostles at each column and fancy chapels. Then the people decided they wanted to "un-Baroque" their church. (The original statues are now on display in the Church of Sant'Agostino, at the west end of town.)

The interior is warmly lit by **alabaster windows,** highlighting the black-and-white striped stonework. Why such a big and impressive church in such a little town? First of all, it's not as big as it looks. The architect created an illusion—with the nave wider at the back and narrower at the altar, the space seems longer than it is. Still, it's a big and rich cathedral—the seat of a bishop. Its historic importance and wealth is thanks to a miracle that happened nearby in 1263. According to the story, a skeptical priest named Peter of Prague passed through Bolsena (12 miles from Orvieto) while on a pilgrimage to Rome. He had doubts that the bread used in communion could really be transformed into the body of Christ. But during Mass, as he held the host aloft and blessed it, the bread began to bleed, running down his arms and dripping onto a linen cloth (a "corporal") on the altar. That miraculously blood-stained cloth is now kept here, in the Chapel of the Corporal.

• *We'll tour the church's interior. First, find the chapel in the north transept, left of the altar. (You'll see lots of pilgrims here celebrating the 750th anniversary of the Miracle of Bolsena. There's likely a black metal railing where pilgrims come in from outside without a ticket. Cross into this zone, then return to the rest of the church by showing your ticket.)*

Chapel of the Corporal: The bloody cloth from the miracle is displayed in the turquoise frame atop the chapel's altar. It was brought from Bolsena to Orvieto, where Pope Urban IV happened to be visiting. The amazed pope proclaimed a new holiday, Corpus Christi (Body of Christ), and the Orvieto cathedral was built (begun in 1290) to display the miraculous relic. Find the fine reliquary in a glass case on the left. Until the 1970s, this silver-and-blue enamel reliquary—made in the early 1300s, and considered one of the finest medieval jewels in Italy—held the linen relic as if in a frame. Notice how it evokes the facade of this cathedral. For centuries, the precious linen was paraded through the streets of Orvieto in this ornate reliquary.

Orvieto's Duomo

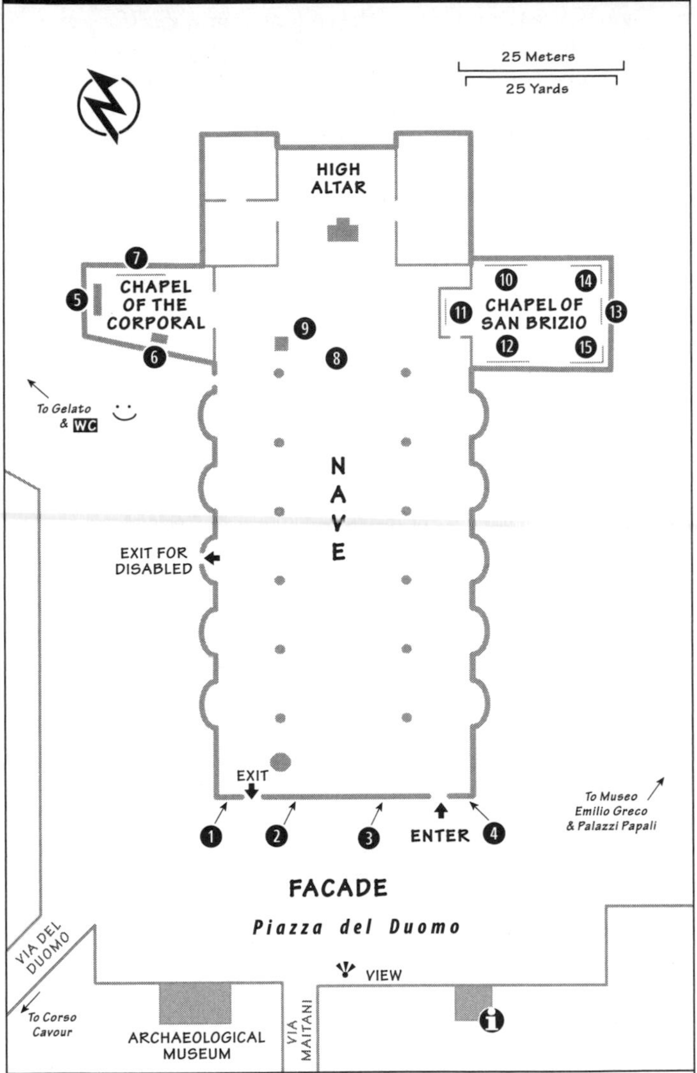

25 Meters
25 Yards

HIGH ALTAR

CHAPEL OF THE CORPORAL

CHAPEL OF SAN BRIZIO

N A V E

To Gelato & WC

EXIT FOR DISABLED

EXIT

ENTER

To Museo Emilio Greco & Palazzi Papali

FACADE

Piazza del Duomo

VIA DEL DUOMO

To Corso Cavour

ARCHAEOLOGICAL MUSEUM

VIA MAITANI

VIEW

1 Creation
2 Tree of Jesse & Old Testament Stories
3 New Testament Stories
4 Last Judgment
5 "Corporal" (Linen Cloth)
6 Reliquary
7 Miracle of Bolsena Fresco
8 Marble Floor Patch
9 Pietà
10 Sermon of the Antichrist
11 End of the World (above doorway)
12 Resurrection of the Bodies
13 Last Judgment
14 Elect in Heaven
15 Damned in Hell

The room was frescoed in the 14th century with scenes attesting to Christ's presence in the communion wafer (for example, the panel above the glass case to the left illustrates how the wafer bleeds if you cook it). You can see the Miracle of Bolsena depicted in the fresco on the chapel's right wall.

• *Leave the Chapel of the Corporal and walk to the middle front of the church, where you'll see a...*

Patch in the Marble Floor Before the High Altar: Stand on the patch, which is a reminder that as the Roman Catholic Church countered the Reformation, it made reforms of its own. For instance, altars were moved back so that the congregation could sit closer to the spectacular frescoes and stained glass. (These decorations were designed to impress commoners by illustrating the glory of heaven—and the Catholic Church needed that propaganda more than ever during the Counter-Reformation.) This confused patching marks where the altar stood prior to the Counter-Reformation.

Enjoy the richness that surrounds you. This cathedral put Orvieto on the map, and with lots of pilgrims came lots of wealth. Two future popes used the town—perched on its easy-to-defend hilltop—as a refuge when their enemies forced them to flee Rome. The brilliant stained glass is the painstakingly restored original, from the 14th century. The fine organ, high on the left, has more than 5,000 pipes. Look high up in the right transept at the alabaster rose window. Then turn and face down the nave, the way you came in. Note how the architect's trick—making the church look bigger from the rear—works in reverse from here. From this angle, the church appears stubbier than it actually is.

• *Turn around and face the front. A few steps to your left, near the pillar, is a beautiful white-marble statue.*

Pietà: The marble *pietà* (statue of Mary holding Jesus' just-crucified body) was carved in 1579 by local artist Ippolito Scalza. Clearly inspired by Michelangelo's *Pietà*, this exceptional work, with four figures, was sculpted from one piece of marble. Walk around it to notice the texture that Scalza achieved, and how the light plays on the sculpture from every angle.

• *To the right of the main altar is Orvieto's one must-see artistic sight, the...*

Chapel of San Brizio: This chapel features Luca Signorelli's brilliantly lit frescoes of the Day of Judgment and Life after Death (painted 1499-1504). Step into the chapel and you're surrounded by vivid scenes crammed with figures. Although the frescoes refer to themes of resurrection and salvation, they also reflect the turbulent political and religious atmosphere of late 15th-century Italy.

The chapel is decorated in one big and cohesive story. Start with the wall to your left as you enter, and do a quick counterclockwise spin to get oriented to the basic plot: Antichrist (a false prophet), end of the world (above the arch leading to the nave), Resurrection of the Bodies, hell, Judgment Day (Fra Angelico painted Jesus above the window), and finally heaven.

Now do a slower turn to take in the full story: In the **Sermon of the Antichrist** (left wall), a crowd gathers around a man preaching from a pedestal. It's the Antichrist, who comes posing as Jesus to mislead the faithful. This befuddled Antichrist forgets his lines mid-speech, but the Devil is on hand to whisper what to say next. His words sow wickedness through the world, including executions (upper right). The worried woman in red and white (foreground, left of pedestal) gets money from a man for something she's not proud of (perhaps receiving funds from a Jewish moneylender—notice the Stars of David on his purse).

Most likely, the Antichrist himself is a veiled reference to Savonarola (1452-1498), the charismatic Florentine monk who defied the pope, drove the Medici family from power, and riled the populace with apocalyptic sermons. Many Italians—including the painter Signorelli—viewed Savonarola as a tyrant and heretic, the Antichrist who was ushering in the Last Days.

In the upper left, notice the hardworking angel. He looks as if he's at batting practice, hitting followers of the Antichrist back to earth as they try to get through the pearly gates. In the bottom left is a self-portrait of the artist, **Luca Signorelli** (c. 1450-1523), well-dressed in black with long golden hair. Signorelli, from nearby Cortona, was at the peak of his powers, and this chapel was his masterpiece. He looks out proudly as if to say, "I did all this in just five years, on time and on budget," confirming his reputation as a speedy, businesslike painter. Next to him (also in black) is the artist Fra Angelico, who started the chapel decoration five decades earlier but completed only a small part of it.

Around the arch, opposite the windows, are signs of the **end of the world:** eclipse, tsunami, falling stars, earthquakes, violence in the streets, and a laser-wielding gray angel.

On the right wall (opposite the Antichrist) is the **Resurrection of the Bodies.** Trumpeting angels blow a wake-up call, and the dead climb dreamily out of the earth to be clothed with new bodies. On the same wall (below the action, at eye level) is a gripping *pietà*. Also by Signorelli, this *pietà* gives an insight into the artist's genius and personality. Look at the emotion in the faces of the two Marys and consider that Signorelli's son had just died. The Deposition scene (behind Jesus' leg) seems inspired by ancient

Greek scenes of a pre-Christian hero's death. In the confident spirit of the Renaissance, the artist incorporates a pagan scene to support a Christian story. This 3-D realism in a 2-D sketch shows the work of a talented master.

The altar wall (with the windows) features the **Last Judgment.** To the left of the altar (and continuing around the corner, filling half the left wall) are the **Elect in Heaven.** They spend eternity posing like bodybuilders while listening to celestial Muzak. To the right (and continuing around the corner on the right wall) are the **Damned in Hell,** in the scariest mosh pit ever. Devils torment sinners in graphic detail, while winged demons control the airspace overhead. In the center, one lusty demon turns to tell the frightened woman on his back exactly what he's got planned for their date. (According to legend, this was Signorelli's lover, who betrayed him...and ended up here.) Signorelli's ability to tell a story through human actions and gestures, rather than symbols, inspired his younger contemporary, Michelangelo, who meticulously studied the elder artist's nudes.

In this chapel, Christian theology sits physically and figuratively upon a foundation of classical logic. Below everything are Greek and Latin philosophers, plus Dante, struggling to reconcile Classic truth with Church doctrine. You can see the intellectual challenge on their faces as they ponder this puzzle. They're immersed in fanciful Grotesque (i.e., grotto-esque) decor. Dating from 1499, this is one of the first uses of the frilly, nubile, and even sexy "wallpaper pattern" so popular in the Renaissance. (It was inspired by the decorations found in Nero's Golden House in Rome, which had been discovered under street level just a few years earlier and was mistaken for an underground grotto.)

During the Renaissance, nakedness symbolized purity. When attitudes changed during the Counter-Reformation, the male figures in Signorelli's frescoes were given penis-covering sashes. During a 1982 restoration, most—but not all—of the sashes were removed. A little of that prudishness survives to this day, as those in heaven were left with their sashes modestly in place.

• *Our tour is finished. Leaving the church, turn left (passing a small parking lot and WC) to reach a park that affords a fine Umbrian view. Turn left twice, and you'll circle behind the church to reach the cathedral's art collections (part of MoDo, described next).*

Near the Duomo: MoDo and Other Museums
▲▲MoDo City Museum (Museo dell'Opera del Duomo)
This museum is a confusing ensemble of three different sights scattered around town: the cathedral art collection behind the cathedral; the Emilio Greco collection (next to the cathedral, in Palazzo Soliano); and, at the far end of town, the Church of Sant'Agostino,

ORVIETO & CIVITA

which has statues of the 12 apostles that were added to the Duomo in the Baroque Age (c. 1700) and removed in the late 1800s.

Cost and Hours: €4 MoDo ticket covers all MoDo sights (or get the €5 combo-ticket that includes the Duomo); April-Sept daily 9:30-19:00; March and Oct Wed-Mon 10:00-17:00, closed Tue; Nov-Feb Wed-Mon 10:00-13:00 & 14:00-17:00, closed Tue; last entry 30 minutes before closing, Piazza Duomo, tel. 0763-343-592, www.operadelduomo.it.

Cathedral Art Collections: Behind the Duomo, a complex of medieval palaces called Palazzi Papali shows off the city's best devotional art. It comes in two parts: the skippable collection of frescos on the ground floor, and a delightful collection up the metal staircase. Climb the stairs to buy your ticket. The highlight is just inside the upstairs entrance: a marble Mary and Child who sit beneath a bronze canopy, attended by exquisite angels. This proto-Renaissance ensemble, dating from around 1300, once filled the niche in the center of the cathedral's facade (where a replica sits today). In several art-filled rooms on this floor, you'll find Baroque paintings from the late 1500s that decorated the side chapels with a harsh Counter-Reformation message; a *Madonna and Child* from 1322 by the Sienese great Simone Martini, who worked in Orvieto; other saintly statues and fine inlaid woodwork from the original choir; a carved 14th-century Crucifixion that shows the dead Christ in gripping detail; and more church art surrounded by *sinopias* (preliminary drawings for the frescoes decorating the cathedral's Chapel of the Corporal, with a roughed-up surface so the wet plaster would stick).

Museo Emilio Greco: This fresh little collection shows off the work of Emilio Greco (1913-1995), a Sicilian artist who designed the modern doors of Orvieto's cathedral. His sketches and about 30 of his bronze statues are on display here, showing his absorption with gently twisting and turning nudes. Greco's sketchy outlines of women are simply beautiful. The artful installation of his work in this palazzo, with walkways and a spiral staircase up to the ceiling, is designed to let you view his sculptures from different angles.

National Archaeological Museum of Orvieto (Museo Archeologico Nazionale di Orvieto)

This small five-room collection, immediately behind the cathedral in the ground floor of Palazzi Papali (under MoDo), beautifully shows off a trove of well-preserved Etruscan bronzes, terra-cotta objects, and ceramics—many from the necropolis at the base of Orvieto, and some with painted colors surviving from 500 B.C. To see the treasure of this museum, ask an attendant for the Golini tombs (named after the man who discovered them in 1836). She'll escort you to the reconstructed, forth-century B.C. tombs, frescoed with scenes from an Etruscan banquet in the afterlife.

ORVIETO & CIVITA

Cost and Hours: €3, daily 8:30-19:30, tel. 0763-341-039.

Etruscan Museum (Museo Claudio Faina e Museo Civico)

This 19th-century, Neoclassical nobleman's palace stands on the main square facing the cathedral. Its elegantly frescoed rooms hold an impressive Etruscan collection. The ground floor features the "Museo Civico," with fragments of Etruscan sculpture. On the first floor is the "Collezione Conti Faina," with Etruscan jewelry and an extensive array of Roman coins (push the brass buttons and the coins rotate so you can see both sides). The top floor features the best of the Etruscan and proto-Etruscan (from the ninth century B.C.) vases and bronzes, lots of votives found buried in nearby tombs, and fine views of the Duomo.

Cost and Hours: €4.50; April-Sept daily 9:30-18:00; Oct-March Tue-Sun 10:00-17:00, closed Mon; English descriptions throughout, tel. 0763-341-511, www.museofaina.it.

Underground Orvieto

▲▲St. Patrick's Well (Pozzo di San Patrizio)

Modern engineers are impressed by this deep well—175 feet deep and 45 feet wide—designed in the 16th century with a double-helix pattern. The two spiral stairways allow an efficient one-way traffic flow: intriguing now, but critical then. Imagine if donkeys and people, balancing jugs of water, had to go up and down the same stairway. At the bottom is a bridge that people could walk on to scoop up water.

The well was built because a pope got nervous. After Rome was sacked in 1527 by renegade troops of the Holy Roman Empire, the pope fled to Orvieto. He feared that even this little town (with no water source on top) would be besieged. He commissioned a well, which was started in 1527 and finished 10 years later. It was a huge project. (As it turns out, the town was never besieged, but supporters believe that the well was worth the cost and labor because of its deterrence value—attackers would think twice about besieging a town with a reliable water source.) Even today, when a local is faced with a difficult task, people say, "It's like digging St. Patrick's Well." It's a total of 496 steps up and down—lots of exercise and not much to see other than some amazing 16th-century engineering.

Cost and Hours: €5, interesting €1 audioguide, daily May-Aug 9:00-19:45, March-April and Sept-Oct 9:00-18:45, Nov-Feb 10:00-16:45, the well is to your right as you exit the funicular, Viale

Sangallo, tel. 0763-343-768. Bring a sweater if you plan to descend to the chilly depths.

Well of the Cave (Pozzo della Cava)

While renovating its trattoria, an Orvieto family discovered a vast underground network of Etruscan-era caves, wells, and tunnels. The excavation started in 1984 and continues to this day. It's well-explained in English and makes for a fun subterranean wander.

Cost and Hours: €3, €2 if you have a St. Patrick's Well or funicular ticket, Tue-Sun 9:00-20:00, closed Mon, Via della Cava 28, tel. 0763-342-373, www.pozzodellacava.it.

Underground Orvieto Tours (Parco delle Grotte)

Guides weave archaeological history into a good look at about 100 yards of Etruscan and medieval caves. You'll see the remains of an old olive press, an impressive 130-foot-deep Etruscan well shaft, what's left of a primitive cement quarry, and an extensive dove-cote (pigeon coop) where the birds were reared for roasting (pigeon dishes are still featured on many Orvieto menus; look for—or avoid—*piccione*).

Cost and Hours: €6; 45-minute English tours depart at 11:15, 12:30, 16:15, and 17:30; more often with demand, book tour and depart from ticket office at Piazza Duomo 23 (next to main TI); confirm times at TI or by calling 0763-340-688, www.orvietounderground.it.

Etruscan Necropolis
(Necropoli Etrusca di Crocifisso del Tufo)

Below town, at the base of the cliff, is a remarkable "city of the dead" that dates back to the sixth to third century B.C. The tombs, which are laid out in a kind of street grid, are empty, and there's precious little to see here other than the basic stony construction. But it is both eerie and fascinating to wander the streets of an Etruscan cemetery.

Cost and Hours: €3, daily April-Sept 8:30-19:00, Oct-March 8:30-17:00.

View Walks

▲Hike Around the City on the Rupe

Orvieto's Rupe is a peaceful paved path that completely circles the town at the base of the cliff upon which it sits. With the help of the TI's *Anello delle Rupe* map, you'll see there are five access points from the town for the three-mile walk (allow about two hours round-trip). Once on the trail, it's fairly level and easy to follow. On one side you have the cliff, with the town high above. On the other side you have Umbrian views stretching into the distance. I'd leave Orvieto at Piazza Marconi and walk left (counterclockwise) three-quarters of the way around the town (there's a fine view down onto the Etruscan Necropolis mid-

way), and ride the escalator and elevator back up to the town from the big Campo della Fiera parking lot. If you're ever confused about the path, follow the *la Rupe* signs.

▲Shorter Romantic Rampart Stroll

Thanks to its dramatic hilltop setting, several fine little walks wind around the edges of Orvieto. My favorite after dark, when it's lamp-lit and romantic, is along the ramparts at the far west end of town. Start at the Church of Sant'Agostino. With your back to the church, go a block to the right to the end of town. Then head left along the ramparts, with cypress-dotted Umbria to your right, and follow Vicolo Volsinia to the Church of San Giovanni Evangelista, where you can re-enter the old town center near several recommended restaurants.

Near Orvieto

Wine-Tasting

Orvieto Classico wine is justly famous. Two inviting wineries sit just outside Orvieto on the scenic Canale route to Bagnoregio; if you're side-tripping to Civita, it's easy to stop at either or both for a tasting (but call ahead).

For a short tour of a winery with Etruscan cellars, visit **Tenuta Le Velette,** where English-speaking Corrado and Cecilia (cheh-CHEEL-yah) Bottai will welcome you if you've set up an appointment (€8-21 for tour and tasting, price varies depending on wines and number of people, Mon-Fri 8:30-12:00 & 14:00-17:00, Sat 8:30-12:00, closed Sun, also has accommodations, tel. 0763-29090, mobile 348-300-2002, www.levelette.it). From their sign (5-minute drive past Orvieto at top of switchbacks just before Canale, on road to Bagnoregio), cruise down a long tree-lined drive, then park at the striped gate (must call ahead; no drop-ins).

Custodi is another respected family-run winery that produces Orvieto Classico, grappa, and olive oil on their 140-acre estate. Helpful Chiara and Laura Custodi speak English. Reserve ahead for a tour of their cantina, an explanation of the winemaking process, and a tasting of four of their wines. An assortment of *salumi* and local cheeses to go with your wine-tasting is possible on request (€7/person for wines only, €16/person with light lunch, daily 8:30-12:30 & 15:30-18:30 except closed Sun afternoons, Viale Venere S.N.C. Loc. Canale; on the road from Orvieto to Civita, a half-mile after Le Velette, it's the first building before Canale; tel. 0763-29053, mobile 392-161-9334, www.cantinacustodi.com, info@cantinacustodi.com).

Sleeping in Orvieto

The prices I've listed are for high season—roughly May to early July and in September and October, as well as during the Umbria Jazz festival in the days before New Year's.

In the Town Center

$$$ Hotel Duomo is centrally located and modern, with splashy art and 17 rooms. Double-paned windows keep the sound of the church bells well-muffled (Sb-€80, Db-€120, Db suite-€140, Tb-€150, extra bed-€10, 10 percent discount with this book if you pay cash and book direct, air-con, elevator, free guest computer and Wi-Fi, private parking-€10, sunny terrace, a block from the Duomo at Vicolo di Maurizio 7, tel. 0763-341-887, www.orvietohotelduomo.com, info@orvietohotelduomo.com, Gianni and Maura Massaccesi don't speak English, daughter Elisa does). The Massaccesi family also owns a three-room B&B 50 yards from the hotel (Sb-€70, Db-€90, Tb-€110, breakfast and Wi-Fi at the main hotel).

$$$ Grand Hotel Italia feels businesslike, bringing predictable modern class to this small town. The 46 rooms are spacious and well-located in the heart of Orvieto (Sb-€80, Db-€140, extra bed-€30, air-con, elevator, stay-awhile lobby and terrace, free guest computer and Wi-Fi, parking-€10—reserve ahead, Via di Piazza del Popolo 13, tel. 0763-342-065, www.grandhotelitalia.it, hotelita@libero.it).

$$ Hotel Corso is friendly, with 18 frilly and flowery rooms—a few with balconies and views. Their sunlit little terrace is enjoyable, but the location—halfway between the center of town and the funicular—feels less convenient than others (Sb-€70, Db-€95, Tb-€120, 10 percent discount for my readers if you book direct, buffet breakfast-€6.50, ask for quieter room off street, air-con, elevator, free Wi-Fi, free public parking nearby and on main street, reserved parking-€7, up from funicular toward Duomo at Corso Cavour 343, tel. 0763-342-020, www.hotelcorso.net, info@hotelcorso.net, Carla).

$ Villa Mercede, a good value, is owned by a religious institution and offers 23 cheap, simple, mostly twin-bedded rooms, each

Sleep Code

(€1 = about $1.30, country code: 39)
S = Single, **D** = Double/Twin, **T** = Triple, **Q** = Quad, **b** = bathroom, **s** = shower only. Unless otherwise noted, credit cards are accepted, English is spoken, and breakfast is included (but usually optional). Many towns in Italy levy a hotel tax of about €2 per person, per night, which is generally not included in the rates I've quoted.

To help you sort easily through these listings, I've divided the accommodations into three categories based on the price for a standard double room with bath:

$$$ Higher Priced—Most rooms €100 or more.
$$ Moderately Priced—Most rooms between €70-100.
$ Lower Priced—Most rooms €70 or less.

Prices can change without notice; verify the hotel's current rates online or by email. For the best prices, always book direct.

with a big modern bathroom and many with glorious Umbrian views (Sb-€50, Db-€70, Tb-€90, elevator, free Wi-Fi, free parking, a half-block from Duomo at Via Soliana 2, reception upstairs, tel. 0763-341-766, www.villamercede.it, info@villamercede.it).

$ Istituto S.S. Salvatore rents nine spotless twin rooms and five singles in their convent, which comes with a peaceful terrace and garden, great views, and a 22:30 curfew. Though the nuns don't speak English, tech-savvy Sister Maria Stella has mastered Google Translate, and will happily use it to answer your questions (Sb-€38, Db-€58, €5 less per person Oct-March, cash only, no breakfast, elevator, free parking, no Internet access, just off Piazza del Popolo at Via del Popolo 1, tel. 0763-342-910, istitutosansalvatore@tiscali.it).

$ Affittacamere Valentina rents six clean, airy, well-appointed rooms, all with big beds and antique furniture. Her place is located in the heart of Orvieto, behind the palace on Piazza del Popolo (Db-€58/€65, Tb-€75/€85, studio with kitchen-€80/€90, lower rates are cash only and good with this book for stays of 2 or more nights; breakfast at nearby cafe-€5, air-con-€5, free Wi-Fi, parking-€10/day, Via Vivaria 7, tel. 0763-341-607, mobile 393-970-5868, www.bandbvalentina.com, valentina.z@tiscalinet.it). Valentina also rents three rooms across the square (D-€58, shared bath and kitchen, no air-con) and three offsite apartments (€170/night with 3-night minimum).

$ Hotel Posta is a dumpy, long-ago-elegant palazzo renting

20 quirky rooms with vintage furniture. The rooms without private bath are among the cheapest in town. It's clean, relatively well-maintained, and centrally located (S-€31, Sb-€37, D-€44, Db-€57, T-€60, Tb-€75, breakfast-€6, cash only, elevator, free Wi-Fi in common areas, Via Luca Signorelli 18, tel. 0763-341-909, www.orvietohotels.it, hotelposta@orvietohotels.it, Alessia).

$ La Magnolia B&B has lots of fancy terra-cotta tiles, a couple of rooms with frescoed ceilings, terraces, and other welcoming touches. Its seven unique rooms, some like mini-apartments with kitchens, are cheerfully decorated and on the town's main drag. The three units facing the busy street are air-conditioned and have good double-paned windows (Db-€65, plush Db apartment-€75, extra person-€15, family deals; book direct, pay cash, and stay at least 2 nights to get a 10 percent Rick Steves discount; no elevator, free Wi-Fi, use of washer-€3.50, Via Duomo 29, tel. 0763-342-808, mobile 349-462-0733, www.bblamagnolia.it, info@bblamagnolia.it, Serena and Loredana).

$ B&B Michelangeli offers two comfortable and well-appointed apartments hiding along a residential lane a few blocks from the tourist scene. It's run by eager-to-please Francesca, who speaks limited English but provides homey touches and free tea, coffee, and breakfast supplies. This is a good choice for families (Db-€70, kids-€10 extra, fully equipped kitchen, free Wi-Fi, washing machine, private parking-€5, Via dei Saracinelli 20—ring bell labeled *M. Michelangeli*, tel. 0763-393-862, mobile 347-089-0349, www.bbmichelangeli.com, f_michelangeli@alice.it).

Just Outside the Town Center: **$$ Casa Sèlita B&B,** a peaceful country house, offers easy access to Orvieto (best for drivers, but workable for adventurous train travelers). It's nestled in an orchard just below the town cliffs; to get to town, you'll climb a steep path through their fields to reach the big Campo della Fiera parking lot, with its handy escalator taking you the rest of the way up into Orvieto. Its five rooms with terraces are airy and fresh, with dark hardwood floors, fluffy down comforters, and modern baths. Enjoy the views from the relaxing garden. Conscientious Sèlita, her husband Ennio, and daughter Elena are gracious hosts (Sb-€55, Db-€80, Tb-€90, €5 less with stays of two or more nights, €5 more off-season for heat, these prices promised to my readers through 2014 if you book direct, cash preferred, fans, free Wi-Fi, free parking, Strada di Porta Romana 8, don't use GPS—sends you to the wrong location, mobile 339-225-4000 or 328-611-2052, tel. 0763-344-218, www.casaselita.com, info@casaselita.com).

Near Orvieto

All of these (except the last one) are within a 20-minute drive of Orvieto, in different directions, and require a car.

ORVIETO & CIVITA

$$$ La Rocca Orvieto, run by Emiliano and Sabrina, is a fancy spa-type "country resort," located 15 minutes north of Orvieto by car. They produce their own olive oil and wine and have nine rooms and 10 apartments—all with air-conditioning and Wi-Fi (Db-€90-150, 10 percent discount with this book—mention when you reserve, pool, panoramic view restaurant, wellness center with Jacuzzi and steam room, gym, mountain bikes, bocce court, hiking paths, tel. 0763-344-210 or 0763-393-437, mobile 348-640-0845, www.laroccaorvieto.com, info@laroccaorvieto.com).

At **$$$ Agriturismo Locanda Rosati,** you'll be greeted by friendly hosts Giampiero Rosati and niece Cristiana, who rent 10 tastefully decorated rooms in a pleasant, homey atmosphere (Db-€110-140, Tb-€140-160, full traditional dinners for €35 on request with this book, air-con, swimming pool, 5 miles from Orvieto on the road to Viterbo, tel. 0763-217-314, www.locandarosati.it, info@locandarosati.it).

$$$ Borgo Fontanile is a vacation home with a swimming pool, terrace, and kids' play area. Its five new apartments with rustic wood beams and terra-cotta tile floors sleep up to four people (€40-50/night per person, discounts for longer stays, €400-800/apartment per week, air-con, Vocabolo Fornace 159, Loc. Baschi, tel. 074-495-7342, www.borgofontanile.com, info@borgofontanile.com).

$$ Tenuta le Velette is a sprawling, family-run farmhouse. Cecilia and Corrado Bottai rent six fully furnished apartments and villas scattered over their expansive and scenic grounds. They range wildly in size—accommodating from 2 to 14 people—but they all nestle in perfect Umbrian rural peace and tranquility (Db apartment-€90-110, see website for details on various villas, 2-night minimum, 10 percent discount for weekly stay, free Wi-Fi, pool, bocce court, 5 minutes from Orvieto—drive toward Bagnoregio-Canale and follow *Tenuta le Velette* signs, tel. 0763-29090, mobile 348-300-2002, www.levelette.it, cecilialevelette@libero.it). They also offer wine-tastings.

$$ Agriturismo Cioccoleta ("Little Stone") has eight rooms with cozy country decor, each named after one of the grapes grown in the *agriturismo*'s vineyards. It's family-run and offers sweeping views of Orvieto and the pastoral countryside (Db-€75, Tb-€96, Qb-€110, 10 percent discount with this book—mention when you reserve, includes breakfast, free Wi-Fi, 3 miles north of Orvieto at Località Bardano 34 in Bardano, tel. 0763-316-011, mobile 349-860-9780, www.cioccoleta.it, info@cioccoleta.it, Angela Zucconi).

$$ Agriturismo Poggio della Volara, 12 miles southeast of Orvieto, has seven apartments (sleeping from two to five people) and seven rooms in two buildings overlooking a swimming pool (Db-€100, Tb-€120, smaller apartment-€100, larger apartment–€160, room rates include breakfast but costs €8 extra in apartments, air-con in all but four rooms, free Wi-Fi, tel. 0744-951-820, mobile 347-335-2523, www.poggiodellavolara.it, info@poggiodellavolara.it, Marco).

Farther Out, Northwest of Todi: **$$$ Agriturismo Fattoria di Vibio** produces olive oil and honey, sells organic products, and offers classes and spa services. In August, its 14 rooms rent at peak prices (and for one week during the month they require a minimum seven-night stay, with arrivals and departures on Saturdays). The rest of the year, no minimum stay is required, although rates drop dramatically for longer visits (Db–€200-300, includes breakfast and dinner). Its three cottages sleep from four to six people and rent only by the week (€1,260-2,100/week depending on amenities, see complicated rate table on website, farthest cottage is 20 miles northeast of Orvieto, tel. 075-874-9607, www.fattoriadivibio.com, info@fattoriadivibio.com).

Eating in Orvieto

Trattorias in the Center

La Palomba features game and truffle specialties in a wood-paneled dining room. Giampiero, Enrica, and the Cinti family enthusiastically take care of their regulars and visiting travelers, offering both a fine value and a classy conviviality. Truffles are shaved right at your table—try the *ombricelli al tartufo* (homemade pasta with truffles) or *spaghetti dall'Ascavo* (with truffles), then perhaps follow that with *piccione* (pigeon). As firm believers in the slow-food movement, they use ingredients that are mostly organic and locally sourced (€10 pastas, €9-15 *secondi,* 10 percent service charge, Thu-Tue 12:30-14:15 & 19:30-22:00, closed Wed and July, reservations smart, just off Piazza della Repubblica at Via Cipriano Manente 16, tel. 0763-343-395).

Trattoria Antico Bucchero, elegant under a big white vault, makes for a nice memory with its candlelit ambience and delicious food (€9 pastas, €12 *secondi,* no cover, daily 12:00-15:00 & 19:00-23:00—but closed Wed Nov-March, seating indoors and on a peaceful square in summer, air-con, a half-block south of Corso Cavour, between Torre del Moro and Piazza della Repubblica at Via de Cartari 4, tel. 0763-341-725; Piero and Silvana, plus sons Fabio and Pericle).

L'Antica Trattoria dell'Orso offers well-prepared Umbrian cuisine paired with fine wines in a homey, bohemian-chic, peaceful atmosphere. Ciro and chef Gabriele enjoy getting to know their diners, and will steer you toward the freshest seasonal plates of their famous pastas and passionately prepared vegetables. Gabriele—who loves to put together a "trust your chef" multicourse

ORVIETO & CIVITA

tasting *menu*—offers an amazing value for my readers: €30 for two people, including their fine house wine and water—my vote for the best dining value in town (€10-12 pastas, €12-16 *secondi*, Wed-Sat 12:00-14:00 & 19:30-22:00, Sun 12:00-14:00, closed Mon-Tue, just off Piazza della Repubblica at Via della Misericordia 18, tel. 0763-341-642).

Trattoria la Grotta prides itself on serving only the freshest food and finest wine. The decor is Signorelli-mod, and the ambience is quiet, with courteous service. Owner-chef Franco has been at it for 50 years, and promises diners a free coffee, grappa, *limoncello,* or Vin Santo with this book (€8 pastas, €14-18 *secondi*, Wed-Mon opens at 12:00 for lunch and at 19:00 for dinner, closed Tue, Via Luca Signorelli 5, tel. 0763-341-348).

Trattoria del Moro Aronne is a long-established family bistro run by Cristian and his mother Rolanda, who lovingly prepare homemade pasta and market-fresh meats and produce for their typical Umbrian specialties. Be sure to sample the *nidi*—folds of fresh pasta enveloping warm, gooey Pecorino cheese sweetened with honey. The crème brûlée is a winner for dessert. Three small and separate dining areas make the interior feel intimate. It's touristy and not particularly atmospheric, but this place is known locally as an excellent value (€7-10 pastas, €10-14 *secondi*, Wed-Mon 12:30-14:30 & 19:30-22:00, closed Tue, free Wi-Fi, Via San Leonardo 7, tel. 0763-342-763).

Trattoria da Carlo, hiding on its own little piazzetta between Via Corso Cavour and Piazza del Popolo, is a cozy spot with a charming interior and inviting tables outside. Animated and opinionated Carlo—a likeable loudmouth—holds court, chatting up his diners as much as he cooks, while his mama scuttles about taking orders, bussing dishes, and lovingly rolling her eyes at her son's big personality. The short, pricey menu changes constantly. Pasta with pork cheeks and fennel is a favorite here (€9 pastas, €12-16 *secondi*, daily 12:00-15:00 & 19:00-24:00, Vicolo del Popolo 1/9, tel. 0763-343-916).

Pizzeria & Restaurant Charlie is a local favorite. Its noisy dining hall and stony courtyard are popular with families and students for casual dinners of wood-fired €6-8 pizzas, big salads, homemade €7-9 pastas, or €12-15 grilled meat dishes. In a quiet courtyard guarded by a medieval tower, it's centrally located a block southwest of Piazza della Repubblica (Wed-Mon 12:30-14:30 & 19:00-23:00, closed Tue, dinner only Nov-Feb, Via Loggia dei Mercanti 14, tel. 0763-344-766).

Enoteca al Duomo, to the left of the Duomo with pleasant outdoor seating, is run by Roman transplants Emilano and Ilaria. They serve rustic *panini* (€6 to eat in, €4 to go), wines by the glass, and a full menu of local dishes in a wine-bar atmosphere (€10 pastas and meal-size salads, €10-19 *secondi*, daily 10:00-24:00, Piazza del Duomo 13, tel. 0763-344-607).

Fast and Cheap Eats

L'Oste del Re is a simple trattoria on Corso Cavour, with hearty sandwiches and pizza to go. They serve a two-course lunch-of-the-day (a pasta and a *secondo*) for about €15, and €7.50 pizza in the evenings (no cover, daily 11:00-15:30 & 19:00-22:30 but closed weekday evenings Oct-April, Corso Cavour 58, tel. 0763-343-846).

For lunch each day, **Caffé Montanucci,** along the main street, lays out an appetizing display of pastas (€7) and main courses (€10) behind the counter. Choose one (or mix—called a *bis*), find a seat in the modern interior, and they'll bring it out on a tray. You'll eat among newspaper-reading locals on lunch break (no cover, daily 7:00-24:00, Corso Cavour 21, tel. 0763-341-261).

Takeout Pizza: **Idea Pizza,** a few doors from Piazza Cahen, has the old town's biggest selection of pizza-by-weight (about €1.50/slice, also tables, Mon and Wed-Sat 10:00-14:00 & 17:00-21:00, Sun 17:00-21:00, closed Tue, Corso Cavour 326, tel. 0763 342-177).

Asian Food: **Peng Cheng** has an inexpensive menu of standard Chinese dishes (take out or indoor/outdoor seating, daily 11:00-15:00 & 18:00-21:30, close to Piazza Cahen at Corso Cavour 443, tel. 0763-343-355).

Groceries: Two smallish markets, both tucked away two minutes from the Duomo, have what you need to put together a functional picnic or stock your hotel room pantry: **Metà** (Mon-Sat 8:30-20:00, Sun 8:30-13:00, Corso Cavour 100, opposite Piazza Cesare Fracassini) and **Despar** (Mon-Sat 8:00-13:30 & 16:30-19:30, Sun 9:00-13:00, just past recommended Trattoria la Grotta at Via Luca Signorelli 23). A full-size supermarket is in the lower town, a few minutes' walk from the train station, near the laundry (see "Helpful Hints," earlier).

Gelato: For dessert, try the deservedly popular *gelateria* **Pasqualetti** (daily 11:30-21:00, open later June-Aug, closed Dec-Feb, next to left transept of church, Piazza del Duomo 14; another branch is at Corso Cavour 56, open daily 11:00-23:00, closes at 21:00 in winter).

Café Scene along Corso Cavour

Orvieto has a charming, traffic-free, pedestrian-friendly vibe. To enjoy it, be sure to spend a little time savoring *la dolce far niente* while sitting at a café. There are inviting places all over town. The first three listed below are along Corso Cavour, the main strolling drag, and offer the very best people-watching.

Café Clan Destino is the town hotspot, with a youthful

energy. It's well-located, with plenty of streetside seating and endless little bites served with your drink (Corso Cavour 42). **Café Barrique** is less crowded, less trendy, and quieter, with nice outdoor tables and good free snacks with your drink (Corso Cavour 111). **Caffé Montanucci,** where locals go to read their newspaper, is the town's venerable place for a coffee and pastry, but it has no on-street seating (Corso Cavour 21). **Bar Palace,** on Piazza del Popolo, is a sunny, relaxed perch facing a big square that's generally quiet (except on market day), with free Wi-Fi and quality coffee and pastries.

Cafés Facing the Cathedral: Several cafés on Piazza del Duomo invite you to linger over a drink with a view of Orvieto's amazing cathedral.

Orvieto Connections

From Orvieto by Train to: Rome (roughly hourly, 1-1.5 hours), **Florence** (hourly, 2 hours, use Firenze S.M.N. train station), **Siena** (12/day, 2.5 hours, change in Chiusi, all Florence-bound trains stop in Chiusi), **Assisi** (roughly hourly, 3 hours, 1 or 2 transfers), **Milan** (3/day direct, 5.5 hours; otherwise about hourly with a transfer in Florence, Bologna, or Rome, 4.75-5 hours). The train station's Buffet della Stazione is surprisingly good if you need a quick *focaccia* sandwich or pizza picnic for the train ride.

Tip for Drivers: If you're thinking of driving to Rome, consider stashing your car in Orvieto instead. You can easily park the car, safe and free, in the big lot below the Orvieto train station (for up to a week or more), and zip effortlessly into Rome by train (1.25 hours).

Getting to Civita di Bagnoregio

To reach Civita, you'll first head for the adjacent town of Bagnoregio. From there, it's a 30-minute walk or five-minute drive to Civita.

By Bus to Bagnoregio: The trip from Orvieto to Bagnoregio takes about 45 minutes (€2.20 one-way if bought in advance from bar or tobacco shop, €7 one-way if purchased from driver—this includes a fine for not buying your ticket in advance).

Here are likely departure times (but confirm) from Orvieto's Piazza Cahen on the blue Cotral bus, daily except Sunday (when this bus does not run at all): 6:20, *7:25, *7:50, 12:45, 15:45, and 18:20; slower buses depart at *13:55 and 17:40. Departures marked with an asterisk (*) run only during the school year (roughly Sept-June). It's nice to get up early, take the *7:50 bus, and see Civita in the cool morning calm. If you take the 12:45 bus, you can make the last (17:25) bus back, but your time in Civita may feel a little rushed.

Orvieto & Civita Area

To Florence

TRAIN STATION & FUNICULAR TO UPPER TOWN

A-1

S-79 bis

To Todi & Assisi

To Siena

Acquapendente

S-2 (VIA CASSIA)

Lake Corbara

ORVIETO EXIT

6

3

Orvieto
See detail map

S-74

S-448

4

Porano

2

1

Canale

5

7

Bolsena

Lubriano

Civita di Bagnoregio

Baschi

Bagnoregio

BRIDGE (FOR PEDESTRIANS & VESPAS)

Lake Bolsena

Tiber River

S-71

A-1

Capodimonte

Montefiascone

N

5 Kilometers

5 Miles

S-2 (VIA CASSIA)

To Viterbo & Rome

To Rome

ORVIETO & CIVITA

1 Tenuta le Velette Winery & Accommodations

2 Custodi Winery

3 La Rocca Orvieto

4 Agriturismo Locanda Rosati

5 Borgo Fontanile

6 Agriturismo Cioccoleta

7 Agriturismo Poggio della Volara

8 Agriturismo Fattoria di Vibio

Buy your ticket at the tobacco shop at Corso Cavour 306, a block up from the funicular (daily 8:00-13:00 & 16:00-20:00)—otherwise you'll pay the premium ticket price on board the bus. If you'll be returning to Orvieto by bus, it's simpler to get a return ticket now rather than in Bagnoregio.

Officially, the bus stop is at the far left end of Piazza Cahen (across the street from the bus section of the parking lot). The schedule is posted at the stop—look for the *A.co.tra.l. Capolinea* sign. Buses actually stop in the bus spaces in the parking lot (yellow lines). The bus you want says *Bagnoregio* in the window. You'll see lots of buses marked *Umbria Mobilità* stopping in front of the funicular; because Civita is in Lazio, it's served by a different bus company (Cotral).

Buses departing Piazza Cahen stop five minutes later at Orvieto's train station—to catch the bus there, wait to the left of the funicular station (as you're facing it); schedule and tickets are available in the tobacco shop/bar in the train station. For more information, call 06-7205-7205 or 800-174-471 (press 7 for English), or see www.cotralspa.it (click on "Orari" in the left menu, then on "Bagnoregio" in the alphabetical list—Italian only).

To reach Civita from Bagnoregio, follow the directions under "Arrival in Bagnoregio, near Civita," later.

By Car to Bagnoregio and Civita: Orvieto overlooks the autostrada (and has its own exit). From the Orvieto exit, the shortest way to Civita is to turn left (below Orvieto), and then simply follow the signs to *Lubriano* and *Bagnoregio*.

A more winding and scenic route takes about 10-15 minutes longer: From the freeway, pass under hill-capping Orvieto (on your right, signs to *Lago di Bolsena*, on Viale I Maggio), then take the first left (direction: Bagnoregio), winding up past great Orvieto views and the recommended Tenuta Le Velette and Custodi wineries (reservations required) en route to Canale, and through farms and fields of giant shredded wheat to Bagnoregio.

Either way, just before Bagnoregio, follow the signs left to *Lubriano*, head into that village, turn right as you enter town, and pull into the first little square by the yellow church (on the left) for a breathtaking view of Civita. You'll find an even better view farther inside the town, from the tiny square at the next church (San Giovanni Battista). Then return to the Bagnoregio road.

Drive through the town of Bagnoregio (following yellow *Civita* signs) and park in the lot at the base of the steep pedestrian bridge. You pay for parking at the ticket machine next to the bridge entrance (€2/first hour, €1/each additional hour, maximum €6.50/day, free 20:00-8:00, public WC at parking lot). Warning: The time limit on your parking ticket is strictly enforced. Finally, walk across the bridge to the traffic-free, 2,500-year-old canyon-swamped pinnacle town of Civita di Bagnoregio.

If the parking lot by the bridge is full, you can park at the belvedere overlook (above the lot) and take the stairs down to the bridge.

By Taxi or Shared Taxi: If you can share the cost, a **taxi** from Orvieto to Civita is perhaps the best deal of all. Giulio taxi service can take a group of up to four in a car (€80) or eight in a minibus (€100) to the base of the pedestrian bridge at Civita, wait two hours, and then bring you back to Orvieto.

Civita di Bagnoregio

Perched on a pinnacle in a grand canyon, the traffic-free village of Civita di Bagnoregio is Italy's ultimate hill town. In the last decade, the old, self-sufficient Civita (CHEE-vee-tah) has died—the last of its lifelong residents have passed on, and the only work here is in serving visitors. But relatives and newcomers are moving in and revitalizing the village, and it remains an amazing place to visit. (It's even become popular as a backdrop for movies, soap operas, and advertising campaigns.) Civita's only connection to the world and the town of Bagnoregio is a long pedestrian bridge.

Civita's history goes back to Etruscan and ancient Roman times. In the early Middle Ages, Bagnoregio was a suburb of Civita, which had a population of about 4,000. Later, Bagnoregio surpassed Civita in size—especially following a 1695 earthquake, after which many residents fled Civita to live in Bagnoregio, fearing their houses would be shaken off the edge into the valley below. You'll notice Bagnoregio is dominated by Renaissance-style buildings while, architecturally, Civita remains stuck in the Middle Ages.

While Bagnoregio lacks the pinnacle-town romance of Civita, it's actually a healthy, vibrant community (unlike Civita, the suburb now nicknamed "the dead city"). In Bagnoregio, get a haircut, sip a coffee on the square, and walk down to the old laundry (ask, *"Dov'è la lavanderia vecchia?"*).

Orientation to Civita

Arrival in Bagnoregio, near Civita

By Bus: If you're taking the bus from Orvieto, you'll get off at the bus stop in Bagnoregio. Look at the posted bus schedule and write down the return times to Orvieto, or check with the driver. If you have heavy bags, leave them with Mauro—see "Helpful Hints," later.

Once in Bagnoregio, you have to get to Civita, which sits at the opposite end of town, about a mile away from the bus stop. Whether you cover this mile by foot, bus, or car, you'll have another 10-minute walk from the base of Civita's bridge up to its main square.

Walking is the simplest way to get from the Bagnoregio bus stop to the base of Civita's bridge (20-30 minutes, slightly uphill at first, but downhill overall). The walk through Bagnoregio also offers a delightful look at a workaday Italian town. Take the road going uphill, Via Garibaldi (overlooking the big parking lot). Once on the road, take the first right, and then an immediate left, to cut

Civita di Bagnoregio

Note: Map not to scale; a walk across civita takes approx. 5 minutes—but don't rush it!

To Lubriano Town

Cliffs

Cliffs

OSTERIA AL FORNO DI AGNESE

ANTICO FORNO TRATTORIA & CIVITA B&B

CAMPANILE (BELL TOWER)

ANTICO FRANTOIO OLIVE PRESS & BRUSCHETTERIA

LOCANDA DELLA BUONA VENTURA

WC

OLD LAUNDRY

Piazza

CHURCH

ETRUSCAN COLUMNS

ALMA CIVITA

ARCH

MAIN

STRADA

FOOTBRIDGE

SNACK BAR

CANTINA DE ARIANNA

ANTICA CIVITA MUSEUM

To Bagnoregio

PALACE (PRIVATE)

WINE BAR DA PEPPONE & GEOLOGICAL MUSEUM

CAVES & CHAPEL CARVED IN ROCK

Cliffs

RUINS OF HOUSE OF ST. BONAVENTURE

Trail to Etruscan tunnel under Civita

ORVIETO & CIVITA

over onto the main drag, Via Roma. Follow this straight out to the belvedere for a superb viewpoint. From there, backtrack a few steps (staircase at end of viewpoint is a dead end) and take the stairs down to the road leading to the bridge.

There is also a **shuttle bus** to the base of the bridge to Civita, with a stop just 20 yards from where the bus from Orvieto drops you (in Piazzale Battaglini). However, by this stop you'll see large signs in English saying that you can board the bus only at another stop, which is halfway along the walking route to Civita (Piazza Sant'Agostino). Locals say the reason for this is to make visitors more likely to patronize the stores along the main street in Bagnoregio. Unless it's pouring rain, skip the shuttle bus, but do take advantage of the shuttle back *uphill* from the Civita bridge. On the return, the shuttle brings you all the way back to the Orvieto-bound bus stop. Note the return times on the schedule posted by the base of the bridge—if you forget, ask at the recommended Trattoria Antico Forno (usually 1-2/hour, but no buses 13:15-15:30, 5-minute ride, €0.70 one-way, €1 round-trip, pay driver, first bus runs at about 7:30, last at 18:15, no buses on Sun Oct-March).

By Car: Drive through Bagnoregio and park under the bridge at the base of Civita (for more driving tips, see "Orvieto Connections," earlier).

Helpful Hints

Market Day: A lively market fills the Bagnoregio bus-station parking lot each Monday.

Baggage Storage: While there's no official baggage-check service in Bagnoregio, I've arranged with Mauro Laurenti, who runs the **Bar/Enoteca/Caffè Gianfu** and **Cinema Alberto Sordi,** to let you leave your bags there (€1/bag, Fri-Wed 6:00-13:00 & 13:30-24:00, closed Thu, mobile 339-697-9340). As you get off the bus, go back 50 yards or so in the direction that the Orvieto bus just came from, and go right around corner.

Food near Bagnoregio Bus Stop: Across the street from Mauro's bar/cinema and baggage storage is **L'Arte del Pane,** with fresh pizza by the slice (Via Matteotti 5). On the other side of the old-town gate (Porta Albana), in the roundabout, is a small grocery store.

Orvieto Bus Tickets: To save money on bus fare to Orvieto, buy a ticket before boarding from the newsstand (with the awning marked *art.regalo edicola cartoleria*) near the Bagnoregio bus stop, across from the gas station (€2.20 one-way in advance; €7 from driver).

Self-Guided Walk

Welcome to Civita

Civita was once connected to Bagnoregio, before the saddle between the separate towns eroded away. Photographs around town show the old donkey path, the original bridge. It was bombed in World War II and replaced in 1966 with the new footbridge that you're climbing today.

• *Entering the town, you'll pass through Porta Santa Maria, a 12th-century Romanesque arch. This stone passageway was cut by the Etrus-*

cans 2,500 years ago, when this town was a stop on an ancient trading route. Inside the archway, you enter a garden of stones. Stand in the little square—the town's antechamber—facing the Bar La Piazzetta. To your right are the remains of a...

Renaissance Palace: The wooden door and windows (above the door) lead only to thin air. They were part of the facade of one of five palaces that once graced Civita. Much of the palace fell into the valley, riding a chunk of the ever-eroding rock pinnacle. Today, the door leads to a remaining section of the palace—complete with Civita's first hot tub, as it was once owned by the "Marchesa," a countess who married into Italy's biggest industrialist family.

• *A few steps uphill, farther into town (on your left, beyond the Bottega souvenir store), notice the two shed-like buildings.*

Old WC and Laundry: In the nearer building (covered with ivy), you'll see the town's old laundry, which dates from just after World War II, when water was finally piped into the town. Until a few years ago, this was a lively village gossip center. Now, locals park their mopeds here. Just behind that is another stone shed, which houses a poorly marked and less-than-pristine WC.

• *The main square is just a few steps farther along, but we'll take the scenic circular route to get there, detouring around to the right. Belly up to the...*

Canyon Viewpoint: Lean over the banister and listen to the sounds of the birds and the bees. Survey old family farms, noticing how evenly they're spaced. Historically, each one owned just enough land to stay in business. Turn left along the belvedere and walk a few steps to the site of the long-gone home of Civita's one famous son, St. Bonaventure, known as the "second founder of the Franciscans" (look for the small plaque on the wall).

• *From here, a lane leads past delightful old homes and gardens, and then to...*

Civita's Main Square: The town church faces Civita's main piazza. Grab a stone seat along the biggest building fronting the

square (or a drink at Peppone's bar) and observe the scene. They say that in a big city you can see a lot, but in a small town like this you can feel a lot. The generous bench is built into the long side of the square, reminding me of how, when I first discovered Civita back in the 1970s and 1980s, the town's old folks would gather here every night. The piazza has been integral to Italian culture since ancient Roman times. While Civita is humble today, imagine the town's former wealth, when mansions of the leading families faced this square, along with the former city hall (opposite the church, to your left). The town's history includes a devastating earthquake in 1695. Notice how stone walls were reinforced with thick bases, and how old stones and marble slabs were recycled and built into walls.

Here in the town square, you'll find Bar Da Peppone (open daily, local wines and microbrews, inviting fire in the winter) and two restaurants. There are wild donkey races on the first Sunday of June and the second Sunday of September. At Christmastime, a living nativity scene is enacted in this square, and if you're visiting at the end of July or beginning of August, you might catch a play here. The pillars that stand like giants' bar stools are ancient Etruscan. The church, with its *campanile* (bell tower), marks the spot where an Etruscan temple, and then a Roman temple, once stood. Across from Peppone's, on the side of the former city hall, is a small, square stone counter. Old-timers remember when this was a meat shop, and how one day a week the counter was stacked with fish for sale.

The humble **Geological Museum,** next to Peppone's, tells the story of how erosion is constantly shaping the surrounding "Bad Lands" valley, how landslides have shaped (and continue to threaten) Civita, and how the town plans to stabilize things (€3, June-Sept Tue-Sun 9:30-13:00 & 14:00-18:30, closed Mon, weekends only off-season, closed Jan-Feb, mobile 328-665-7205).

• *Now step inside...*

Civita's Church: A cathedral until 1699, the church houses records of about 60 bishops that date back to the seventh century (church open daily 10:00-13:00 & 15:00-17:00, often closed Jan-Feb). Inside you'll see Romanesque columns and arches with faint Renaissance frescoes peeking through Baroque-era whitewash. The central altar is built upon the relics of the Roman martyr St. Victoria, who once was the patron saint of the town. St. Marlonbrando served as a bishop here in the ninth century; an altar dedicated to him is on the right. The fine crucifix over this altar, carved out of pear wood in the 15th century, is from the school of Donatello. It's remarkably expressive and greatly venerated by locals. Jesus' gaze is almost haunting. Some say his appearance changes based on what angle you view him from: looking alive from the front, in agony from the left, and dead from the right. Regardless, his eyes follow you from side to side. On Good Friday, this crucifix goes out and is the focus of the midnight procession.

On the left side, midway up the nave above an altar, is an intimate fresco of the *Madonna of the Earthquake,* given this name because—in the great shake of 1695—the whitewash fell off and revealed this tender fresco of Mary and her child. (During the Baroque era, a white-and-bright interior was in vogue, and churches such as these—which were covered with precious and historic frescoes—were simply whitewashed over. Look around to see examples.) On the same wall—just toward the front from the *Madonna*—find the faded portrait of Santa Apollonia, the patron saint of your teeth; notice the scary-looking pincers.

• *From the square, you can follow...*

The Main Street: A short walk takes you from the church to the end of the town. Along the way, you'll pass a couple of little eateries (described later, under "Eating in Civita"), olive presses, gardens, a rustic town museum, and valley views. The rock below Civita is honeycombed with ancient tunnels, caverns (housing olive presses), cellars (for keeping wine at a constant temperature all year), and cisterns (for collecting rainwater, since there was no well in town). Many date from Etruscan times.

ORVIETO & CIVITA

Wherever you choose to eat (or just grab a *bruschetta* snack), be sure to take advantage of the opportunity to poke around—every place has a historic cellar. At the trendy **Alma Civita**, notice the damaged house facing the main street—broken since the 1695 earthquake and scarred to this day. Just beyond, the rustic **Antico Frantoio Bruschetteria** serves bruschetta in an amazing old space. Whether or not you buy food, venture into their back room to see an interesting collection of old olive presses (if you're not eating here, a €1 donation is requested). The huge olive press in the entry is about

1,500 years old. Until the 1960s, blindfolded donkeys trudged in the circle here, crushing olives and creating paste that filled the circular filters and was put into a second press. Notice the 2,500-year-old sarcophagus niche. The hole in the floor (with the glass top) was a garbage hole. In ancient times, residents would toss their jewels down when under attack; excavations uncovered a windfall of treasures.

In front is the well head of an ancient cistern—designed to collect rain water from neighboring rooftops—carved out of *tufo* and covered with clay to be waterproof.

• *Across the street and down a tiny lane, find...*

Antica Civita: This is the closest thing the town has to a history museum. The humble collection is the brainchild of Felice, the old farmer who's hung black-and-white photos, farm tools, olive presses, and local artifacts in a series of old caves. Climb down to the "warm blood machine" (another donkey-powered grinding wheel) and a viewpoint and to see rooms where a mill worker lived until the 1930s. Felice wants to give visitors a feeling for life in Civita when its traditional economy was strong (€1, daily 10:00-19:00, until 17:00 in winter, some English explanations).

• *Another few steps along the main street take you to...*

The End of Civita: Here the road is literally cut out of the stone, with a dramatic view of the Bad Lands opening up. Pop in to the cute "Garden of Poets" (immediately on the left just outside town, with the tiny local crafts shop) to savor the view. Then, look back up at the end of town and ponder the precarious future of Civita. There's a certain stillness here, far from the modern world and high above the valley.

Continue along the path a few steps toward the valley below the town, and you come to some shallow caves used as stables until a few years ago. The third cave, cut deeper into the rock, with a barred door, is the **Chapel of the Incarcerated** (Cappella del Carcere). In Etruscan times, the chapel—with a painted tile depicting the Madonna and child—may have been a tomb, and in medieval times, it was used as a jail (which collapsed in 1695).

Although it's closed to the public now, an Etruscan tunnel just beyond the Chapel of the Incarcerated cuts completely through the hill. Tall enough for a woman with a jug on her head to pass through, it may have served as a shortcut to the river below. It was widened in the 1930s so that farmers could get between their scattered fields more easily. Later, it served as a refuge for frightened villagers who huddled here during WWII bombing raids.

• *Hike back into town. Make a point to take some time to explore the peaceful back lanes before returning to the modern world.*

Sleeping in Civita or Bagnoregio

Civita has nine B&B rooms up for grabs. Bagnoregio has larger lodgings, and there are plenty of *agriturismi* nearby; otherwise, there's always Orvieto. Off-season, when Civita and Bagnoregio are deadly quiet—and cold—I'd side-trip in from Orvieto rather than spend the night here. Those staying overnight in Civita may be able to get a discount on parking at the base of the bridge—ask when you reserve.

In Civita
$$$ Locanda della Buona Ventura rents four overpriced rooms with tiny bathrooms, up narrow stairs, decorated in medieval rustic-chic, and overlooking Civita's piazza. Because you're not likely to see the owner, the shop across the square functions as the reception (Db-€120, or €100 in Oct-May, extra bed-€20, skimpy breakfast at nearby restaurant, no Internet access, tel. 0761-792-025, mobile 347-627-5628, www.locandabuonaventura.it, info@locandabuonaventura.it).

$$ Alma Civita is a classic old stone house that was recently renovated by a sister-and-brother team, Alessandra and Maurizio (hence the name: Al-Ma). These are Civita's two most comfortable, modern, and warmly run rooms (Db-€100, no Internet access, tel. 0761-792-415, mobile 347-449-8892, www.almacivita.com, prenotazione@almacivita.com). They also have a restaurant (see later).

$ Civita B&B, run by gregarious Franco Sala, has three little rooms above Trattoria Antico Forno, each overlooking Civita's main square. Two are doubles with private bath. The third is a triple (with one double and one kid-size bed), which has its own bathroom across the hall (S-€50, Sb-€55, D-€70, Db-€75, T-€95, continental breakfast, free Wi-Fi, Piazza del Duomo Vecchio, tel.

076-176-0016, mobile 347-611-5426, www.civitadibagnoregio.it, fsala@pelagus.it).

In Bagnoregio

$$ Romantica Pucci B&B is a haven for city-weary travelers. Its five spacious rooms are indeed romantic, with canopied beds and flowing veils (Db-€80, extra bed-€25, air-con, free guest computer and Wi-Fi, free parking, Piazza Cavour 1, tel. 0761-792-121, www.hotelromanticapucci.it, hotelromanticapucci@gmail.com). It's just above the public parking lot you see when you arrive in Bagnoregio. From the bus stop, take Via Garibaldi uphill above the parking lot, and then bear right at the tobacco shop onto Via Roma.

$ Hotel Divino Amore has 23 bright, modern rooms, four with perfect views of a miniature Civita. These view rooms, and the ones with air-conditioning, cost no extra—but are booked first (Sb-€50, Db-€70, Tb-€80, Qb-€90, air-con in seven rooms, no Internet access, closed Jan-Mar, Via Fidanza 25-27, tel. 076-178-0882, mobile 329-344-8950, www.hoteldivinoamore.com, info@hoteldivinoamore.com). From the bus stop, follow Via Garibaldi uphill above the parking lot for 200 yards.

Eating in Civita or Bagnoregio

In Civita

Osteria Al Forno di Agnese is a delightful spot where Manuela and her friends serve visitors simple yet delicious meals on a covered patio just off Civita's main square (nice €7 salads, €9 pastas—including gluten-free options, €7-12 *secondi*, good selection of local wines, opens daily at 12:00 for lunch, June-Sept also at 19:00 for dinner, closed Tue in winter and sometimes in bad weather, tel. 0761-792-571, mobile 340-1259-721).

Trattoria Antico Forno serves up rustic dishes, homemade pasta, and salads at affordable prices. Try their homemade pasta with truffles (€7 pastas, €7-12 *secondi*, €15 fixed-price meal, daily for lunch 12:30-15:30 and dinner 19:00-22:00, on main square, also rents rooms—see Civita B&B listing earlier, tel. 076-176-0016, Franco and his assistants Nina and Fiorella).

La Cantina de Arianna Trattoria Bruschetteria is a family affair, with a busy open fire specializing in grilled meat and wonderful bruschetta. It's run by Arianna, her sister Antonella, and their parents, Rossana and Antonio. After eating, wander down to their cellar, where you'll see traditional winemaking gear and provisions for rolling huge kegs up the stairs. Tap on the kegs in the bottom level to see which are full (daily 11:00-17:00, tel. 0761-793-270).

Alma Civita, a lunch-only place, feels like a fresh, new take on old Civita. It's owned by two of its longtime residents: Alessandra (an architect) and her brother Maurizio (who runs the restaurant). Choose from one of three different seating areas: outside on a stony lane, in the modern and trendy-feeling main-floor dining room, or in the equally modern but atmospheric cellar. Even deeper is an old Etruscan tomb that's now a wine cellar (€3-5 *bruschette* and *antipasti*, €7 pastas, €6-10 *secondi*, May-Oct Wed-Mon 10:30-18:00, closed Tue, Nov-April Fri-Sun only, tel. 0761-792-415).

Antico Frantoio Bruschetteria, the last place in town, is a rustic, super-atmospheric spot for a bite to eat. The specialty here: delicious bruschetta toasted over hot coals. Peruse the menu, choose your toppings (chopped tomato is super), and get a glass of wine for a fun, affordable snack or meal (roughly 10:00-18:00 in summer, off-season open weekends only 10:00-17:00, mobile 328-689-9375, Fabrizio).

At the Foot of the Bridge

Hostaria del Ponte is a more serious restaurant than anything in Civita itself. It offers creative and traditional cuisine with a great view terrace at the parking lot at the base of the bridge to Civita. Big space heaters make it comfortable to enjoy the wonderful view as you dine from their rooftop terrace, even in spring and fall (€9 pastas, €12-13 *secondi*, reservations often essential, Tue-Sun 12:30-14:30 & 19:30-21:30, closed Mon, Nov-April also closed Sun eve, tel. 076-179-3565, Lorena).

In Bagnoregio

The recommended **Romantica Pucci B&B** offers a small restaurant with tables in its private garden (€25-30 meals, closed Mon, see contact details earlier).

Bagnoregio Connections

From Bagnoregio to Orvieto: Public Cotral buses (45 minutes, €2.20 one-way if purchased in advance, €7 one-way from driver) connect Bagnoregio to Orvieto. Departures from Bagnoregio—Monday to Saturday only (no buses on Sunday or holidays)—are likely to be at the following times (but confirm): 5:30, *6:30, 6:50, 9:55, *10:10 or 10:25, 13:00, *13:35, 14:25, and 17:25. Departures marked with an asterisk (*) operate only during the school year (roughly Sept-June). For more information, call 06-7205-7205 or 800-174-471 (press 7 for English), or see www.cotralspa.it (click on "Orari" in the left-hand menu, then on "Bagnoregio" in the alphabetical list—Italian only). For info on coming from Orvieto, see "Orvieto Connections."

Remember to save money by buying your ticket in Bagnoregio

before boarding the bus—purchase one from the newsstand near the bus stop, across from the gas station. Better yet, if you're side-tripping from Orvieto, buy two tickets in Orvieto so you already have one when you're ready to come back.

From Bagnoregio to Points South: Cotral buses also run to **Viterbo,** which has a good train connection to Rome (buses go weekdays at 5:10, 6:30, 7:15, 7:40, 8:10, 10:00, 12:55, 13:45, and 14:50; less frequent Sat-Sun, 35 minutes, see phone number and website earlier).

ORVIETO & CIVITA

PRACTICALITIES

This section covers just the basics on traveling in Italy (for much more information, see *Rick Steves' Italy*). You can find free advice on specific topics at www.ricksteves.com/tips.

Money

Italy uses the euro currency: 1 euro (€) = about $1.30. To convert prices in euros to dollars, add about 30 percent: €20 = about $26, €50 = about $65. (Check www.oanda.com for the latest exchange rates.)

The standard way for travelers to get euros is to withdraw money from ATMs (which locals call a *bancomat*) using a debit or credit card, ideally with a Visa or MasterCard logo. Before departing, call your bank or credit-card company: Confirm that your card will work overseas, ask about international transaction fees, and alert them that you'll be making withdrawals in Europe. Also ask for the PIN number for your credit card in case it'll help you use Europe's "chip-and-PIN" payment machines (see below); allow time for your bank to mail your PIN to you. To keep your valuables safe while traveling, wear a money belt.

Dealing with "Chip and PIN": Much of Europe (including Italy) is adopting a "chip-and-PIN" system for credit cards, and some merchants rely on it exclusively. European chip-and-PIN cards are embedded with an electronic chip, in addition to the magnetic stripe used on our American-style cards. This means that your credit (and debit) card might not work at automated payment machines, such as those at train and subway stations, toll roads, parking garages, luggage lockers, and self-serve gas pumps. Memorizing your credit card's PIN lets you use it at some chip-and-PIN machines—just enter your PIN when prompted. If a payment machine won't take your card, look for a machine that takes cash or see if there's a cashier nearby who can process your transaction. The easiest solution is to pay for your purchases with cash you've withdrawn from an ATM using your debit card (Europe's ATMs still accept magnetic-stripe cards).

Phoning

Smart travelers use the telephone to reserve or reconfirm rooms, reserve restaurants, get directions, research transportation connections, confirm tour times, phone home, and lots more.

To call Italy from the US or Canada: Dial 011-39 and then the local number. (The 011 is our international access code, and 39 is Italy's country code.)

To call Italy from a European country: Dial 00-39 followed by the local number. (The 00 is Europe's international access code.)

To call within Italy: Just dial the local number.

To call from Italy to another country: Dial 00 followed by the country code (for example, 1 for the US or Canada), then the area code and number. If you're calling European countries whose phone numbers begin with 0, you'll usually have to omit that 0 when you dial.

Tips on Phoning: A mobile phone—whether an American one that works in Italy, or a European one you buy when you arrive—is handy, but can be pricey. If traveling with a smartphone, switch off data-roaming until you have free Wi-Fi. If you have a smartphone, you can use it to make free or inexpensive calls in Europe by using a calling app such as Skype or FaceTime when you're on Wi-Fi.

To make cheap international calls from any phone (even your hotel-room phone), you can buy an international phone card in Italy. These work with a scratch-to-reveal PIN code, allow you to call home to the US for pennies a minute, and also work for domestic calls.

Another option is buying an insertable phone card in Italy. These are usable only at pay phones, are reasonable for making calls within the country, and work for international calls as well (though not as cheaply as the international phone cards). Note that insertable phone cards—and most international phone cards—work only in the country where you buy them.

Calling from your hotel-room phone is usually expensive, unless you use an international phone card. For more on phoning, see www.ricksteves.com/phoning.

Making Hotel Reservations

To ensure the best value, I recommend reserving rooms in advance, particularly during peak season. Email the hotelier with the following key pieces of information: number and type of rooms;

PRACTICALITIES

From: rick@ricksteves.com
Sent: Today
To: info@hotelcentral.com
Subject: Reservation request for 19-22 July

Dear Hotel Central,

I would like to reserve a double room for 2 people for 3 nights, arriving 19 July and departing 22 July. If possible, I would like a quiet room with a bathroom inside the room.

Please let me know if you have a room available and the price.

Thank you!
Rick Steves

number of nights; date of arrival; date of departure; and any special requests. (For a sample form, see sidebar above.) Use the European style for writing dates: day/month/year. For example, for a two-night stay in July, you could request: "1 double room for 2 nights, arrive 16/07//14, depart 18/07/14." Hoteliers typically ask for your credit-card number as a deposit.

Given the economic downturn, hoteliers are often willing and eager to make a deal—try emailing several to ask their best price. In general, hotel prices can soften if you do any of the following: offer to pay cash, stay at least three nights, or mention this book. You can also try asking for a cheaper room or a discount, or offer to skip breakfast.

Eating

Italy offers a wide array of eateries. A *ristorante* is a formal restaurant, while a *trattoria* or *osteria* is usually more traditional and simpler (but can still be pricey). Italian "bars" are not taverns, but small cafés selling sandwiches, coffee, and other drinks. An *enoteca* is a wine bar with snacks and light meals. Take-away food from pizza shops and delis (such as a *rosticcería* or *tavola calda*) makes an easy picnic.

Italians eat dinner a bit later than we do; better restaurants start serving around 19:00. A full meal consists of an appetizer (antipasto), a first course (*primo piatto,* pasta, rice, or soup), and a second course (*secondo piatto,* expensive meat and fish/seafood dishes). Vegetables *(verdure)* may come with the *secondo,* but more often must be ordered separately as a side dish (*contorno*). Desserts (*dolci*) can be very tempting. The euros can add up in a hurry, but you don't have to order each course. My approach is to mix antipasti and *primi piatti* family-style with my dinner partners (skipping *secondi*). Or, for a basic value, look for a *menù del giorno,* a three- or four-course, fixed-price meal deal (avoid the cheapest ones, often called a *menù turistico*).

Good service is relaxed (slow to an American). You won't get the bill until you ask for it: *"Il conto?"* Most restaurants include a service charge in their prices (check the menu for *servizio incluso*—generally around 15 percent). To reward good service, add a euro or two for each person in your party. If you order at a counter rather than from waitstaff, there's no need to tip. Many (but not all) restaurants in Italy add a cover charge *(coperto)* of €1-3.50 per person to your bill.

At bars and cafés, getting a drink while standing at the bar *(banco)* is cheaper than drinking it at a table *(tavolo)* or sitting outside *(terrazza)*. This tiered pricing system is clearly posted on the wall. Sometimes you'll pay at a cash register, then take the receipt to another counter to claim your drink.

Transportation

By Train: In Italy, most travelers find it's cheapest simply to buy train tickets as they go. To see if a railpass could save you money, check www.ricksteves.com/rail. To research train schedules, visit Germany's excellent all-Europe website, www.bahn.com, or Italy's www.trenitalia.com. A private company called Italo is also running fast trains on major routes in Italy; see www.italotreno.it.

You can buy tickets at train stations (at the ticket window or at automated machines with English instructions) or from travel agencies. Before boarding the train, you must validate your train documents by stamping them in the machine near the platform (usually marked *convalida biglietti* or *vidimazione)*. Strikes *(sciopero)* are common and generally announced in advance (but a few sporadic trains still run—ask around).

By Car: It's cheaper to arrange most car rentals from the US. For tips on your insurance options, see www.ricksteves.com/cdw, and for route planning, consult www.viamichelin.com. Theft insurance is mandatory in Italy ($15-20/day). Bring your driver's license. You're also technically required to have an International Driving Permit (sold at your local AAA office for $15 plus the cost of two passport-type photos; see www.aaa.com).

Italy's freeway *(autostrada)* system is slick and speedy, but you'll pay about a dollar for every 10 minutes of use. Be warned that car traffic is restricted in many city centers—don't drive or park in any area that has a sign reading *Zona Traffico Limitato* *(ZTL,* often shown above a red circle)...or you might be mailed a ticket later.

Local road etiquette is similar to that in the US. Ask your car-rental company about the rules of the road, or check the US State Department website (www.travel.state.gov, click on "International Travel," then specify your country of choice and click "Traffic Safety and Road Conditions").

A car is a worthless headache in cities—park it safely (get tips from your hotel). As break-ins are common, be sure all of your valuables are out of sight and locked in the trunk, or even better, with you or in your hotel room.

Helpful Hints

Emergency Help: For English-speaking **police** help, dial 113. To summon an **ambulance**, call 118. For passport problems, call the **US Embassy** (in Rome, 24-hour line—tel. 06-46741) or **US Consulates** (Milan—tel. 02-290-351, Florence—tel. 055-266-951, Naples—tel. 081-583-8111); or the **Canadian Embassy** (in Rome, tel. 06-854-441). For other concerns, get advice from your hotelier.

Theft or Loss: Italy has particularly hardworking pickpockets—wear a money belt. Assume beggars are pickpockets and any scuffle is simply a distraction by a team of thieves. If you stop for any commotion or show, put your hands in your pockets before someone else does.

To replace a passport, you'll need to go in person to an embassy or consulate (see above). Cancel and replace your credit and debit cards by calling these 24-hour US numbers collect: Visa—tel. 303/967-1096, MasterCard—tel. 636/722-7111, American Express—tel. 336/393-1111. File a police report either on the spot or within a day or two; you'll need it to submit an insurance claim for lost or stolen railpasses or travel gear, and it can help with replacing your passport or credit and debit cards. Precautionary measures can minimize the effects of loss—back up your digital photos and other files frequently. For more information, see www.ricksteves.com/help.

Time: Italy uses the 24-hour clock. It's the same through 12:00 noon, then keep going: 13:00, 14:00, and so on. Italy, like most of continental Europe, is six/nine hours ahead of the East/West Coasts of the US.

Business Hours: Many businesses have now adopted the government's recommended 8:00 to 14:00 workday (although in tourist areas, shops are open longer). Still, expect small towns and villages to be more or less shut tight during the midafternoon. Stores are also usually closed on Sunday, and often on Monday.

Sights: Opening and closing hours of sights can change unexpectedly; confirm the latest times with the local tourist information office or its website. Some major churches enforce a modest dress code (no bare shoulders or shorts) for everyone, even children.

Holidays and Festivals: Italy celebrates many holidays, which can close sights and attract crowds (book hotel rooms ahead). For information on holidays and festivals, check Italy's website: www. italia.it. For a simple list showing major—though not all—events, see www.ricksteves.com/festivals.

Numbers and Stumblers: What Americans call the second floor of a building is the first floor in Europe. Europeans write dates as day/month/year, so Christmas is 25/12/14. Commas are decimal points and vice versa—a dollar and a half is 1,50, and there are 5.280 feet in a mile. Italy uses the metric system: A kilogram is 2.2 pounds; a liter is about a quart; and a kilometer is six-tenths of a mile.

Resources from Rick Steves

This Snapshot guide is excerpted from my latest edition of *Rick Steves' Italy*, which is one of more than 30 titles in my series of guidebooks on European travel. I also produce a public television series, *Rick Steves' Europe*, and a public radio show, *Travel with Rick Steves*. My website, www.ricksteves.com, offers free travel information, a Graffiti Wall for travelers' comments, guidebook updates, my travel blog, an online travel store, and information on European railpasses and our tours of Europe. If you're bringing a mobile device on your trip, you can download free information from Rick Steves Audio Europe, featuring podcasts of my radio shows, free audio tours of major sights in Europe, and travel interviews about Italy (via www.ricksteves.com/audioeurope, iTunes, Google Play, or the Rick Steves Audio Europe free smartphone app). You can follow me on Facebook and Twitter.

Additional Resources

Tourist Information: www.italia.it
Passports and Red Tape: www.travel.state.gov
Travel Insurance Tips: www.ricksteves.com/insurance
Packing List: www.ricksteves.com/packlist
Cheap Flights: www.kayak.com
Airplane Carry-on Restrictions: www.tsa.gov/travelers
Updates for This Book: www.ricksteves.com/update

How Was Your Trip?

If you'd like to share your tips, concerns, and discoveries after using this book, please fill out the survey at www.ricksteves.com/feedback. Thanks in advance—it helps a lot.

Italian Survival Phrases

English	Italian	Pronunciation
Good day.	*Buon giorno.*	bwohn **jor**-noh
Do you speak English?	*Parla inglese?*	**par**-lah een-**glay**-zay
Yes. / No.	*Sì. / No.*	see / noh
I (don't) understand.	*(Non) capisco.*	(nohn) kah-**pees**-koh
Please.	*Per favore.*	pehr fah-**voh**-ray
Thank you.	*Grazie.*	**graht**-seeay
You're welcome.	*Prego.*	**pray**-go
I'm sorry.	*Mi dispiace.*	mee dee-speeah-chay
Excuse me.	*Mi scusi.*	mee **skoo**-zee
(No) problem.	*(Non) c'è un problema.*	(nohn) cheh oon proh-**blay**-mah
Good.	*Va bene.*	vah **behn**-ay
Goodbye.	*Arrivederci.*	ah-ree-vay-**dehr**-chee
one / two	*uno / due*	**oo**-noh / **doo**-ay
three / four	*tre / quattro*	tray / **kwah**-troh
five / six	*cinque / sei*	**cheeng**-kway / **seh**ee
seven / eight	*sette / otto*	**seht**-tay / **ot**-toh
nine / ten	*nove / dieci*	**nov**-ay / **deeay**-chee
How much is it?	*Quanto costa?*	**kwahn**-toh **kos**-tah
Write it?	*Me lo scrive?*	may loh **skree**-vay
Is it free?	*È gratis?*	eh **grah**-tees
Is it included?	*È incluso?*	eh een-**kloo**-zoh
Where can I buy / find...?	*Dove posso comprare / trovare...?*	**doh**-vay **pos**-soh kohm-**prah**-ray / troh-**vah**-ray
I'd like / We'd like...	*Vorrei / Vorremmo...*	vor-**reh**ee / vor-**ray**-moh
...a room.	*...una camera.*	**oo**-nah **kah**-meh-rah
...a ticket to ____.	*...un biglietto per ____.*	oon beel-**yeht**-toh pehr
Is it possible?	*È possibile?*	eh poh-**see**-bee-lay
Where is...?	*Dov'è...?*	**doh**-veh
...the train station	*...la stazione*	lah staht-**seeoh**-nay
...the bus station	*...la stazione degli autobus*	lah staht-**seeoh**-nay **dayl**-yee **ow**-toh-boos
...tourist information	*...informazioni per turisti*	een-for-maht-see**oh**-nee pehr too-**ree**-stee
...the toilet	*...la toilette*	lah twah-**leht**-tay
men	*uomini, signori*	**woh**-mee-nee, seen-**yoh**-ree
women	*donne, signore*	**don**-nay, seen-**yoh**-ray
left / right	*sinistra / destra*	see-**nee**-strah / **dehs**-trah
straight	*sempre diritto*	**sehm**-pray dee-**ree**-toh
When do you open / close?	*A che ora aprite / chiudete?*	ah kay **oh**-rah ah-**pree**-tay / keeoo-**day**-tay
At what time?	*A che ora?*	ah kay **oh**-rah
Just a moment.	*Un momento.*	oon moh-**mayn**-toh
now / soon / later	*adesso / presto / tardi*	ah-**dehs**-soh / **prehs**-toh / **tar**-dee
today / tomorrow	*oggi / domani*	**oh**-jee / doh-**mah**-nee

In an Italian-speaking Restaurant

English	Italian	Pronunciation
I'd like...	Vorrei...	vor-**rehee**
We'd like...	Vorremmo...	vor-**ray**-moh
...to reserve...	...prenotare...	pray-noh-**tah**-ray
...a table for one / two.	...un tavolo per uno / due.	oon **tah**-voh-loh pehr **oo**-noh / **doo**-ay
Non-smoking.	Non fumare.	nohn foo-**mah**-ray
Is this seat free?	È libero questo posto?	eh **lee**-bay-roh **kwehs**-toh **poh**-stoh
The menu (in English), please.	Il menù (in inglese), per favore.	eel may-**noo** (een een-**glay**-zay) pehr fah-**voh**-ray
service (not) included	servizio (non) incluso	sehr-**veet**-seeoh (nohn) een-**kloo**-zoh
cover charge	pane e coperto	**pah**-nay ay koh-**pehr**-toh
to go	da portar via	dah **por**-tar **vee**-ah
with / without	con / senza	kohn / **sehn**-sah
and / or	e / o	ay / oh
menu (of the day)	menù (del giorno)	may-**noo** (dayl **jor**-noh)
specialty of the house	specialità della casa	spay-chah-lee-**tah dehl**-lah **kah**-zah
first course (pasta, soup)	primo piatto	**pree**-moh peeah-toh
main course (meat, fish)	secondo piatto	say-**kohn**-doh peeah-toh
side dishes	contorni	kohn-**tor**-nee
bread	pane	**pah**-nay
cheese	formaggio	for-**mah**-joh
sandwich	panino	pah-**nee**-noh
soup	minestra, zuppa	mee-**nehs**-trah, **tsoo**-pah
salad	insalata	een-sah-**lah**-tah
meat	carne	**kar**-nay
chicken	pollo	**poh**-loh
fish	pesce	**peh**-shay
seafood	frutti di mare	**froo**-tee dee **mah**-ray
fruit / vegetables	frutta / legumi	**froo**-tah / lay-**goo**-mee
dessert	dolci	**dohl**-chee
tap water	acqua del rubinetto	**ah**-kwah dayl roo-bee-**nay**-toh
mineral water	acqua minerale	**ah**-kwah mee-nay-**rah**-lay
milk	latte	**lah**-tay
(orange) juice	succo (d'arancia)	**soo**-koh (dah-**rahn**-chah)
coffee / tea	caffè / tè	kah-**feh** / teh
wine	vino	**vee**-noh
red / white	rosso / bianco	**roh**-soh / beeahn-koh
glass / bottle	bicchiere / bottiglia	bee-keeay-ray / boh-**teel**-yah
beer	birra	**bee**-rah
Cheers!	Cin cin!	cheen cheen
More. / Another.	Ancora un po.' / Un altro.	ahn-**koh**-rah oon poh / oon **ahl**-troh
The same.	Lo stesso.	loh **stehs**-soh
The bill, please.	Il conto, per favore.	eel **kohn**-toh pehr fah-**voh**-ray
tip	mancia	**mahn**-chah
Delicious!	Delizioso!	day-leet-seeoh-zoh

For more user-friendly Italian phrases, check out *Rick Steves' Italian Phrase Book & Dictionary* or *Rick Steves' French, Italian, and German Phrase Book*.

INDEX

INDEX

Audio Europe™

Rick's Free Travel App

Get your FREE **Rick Steves Audio Europe**™ app to enjoy...

- Dozens of self-guided tours of Europe's top museums, sights and historic walks

- Hundreds of tracks filled with cultural insights and sightseeing tips from Rick's radio interviews

- All organized into handy geographic playlists

- For iPhone, iPad, iPod Touch, Android

With Rick whispering in your ear, Europe gets even better.

Find out more at ricksteves.com

Join a Rick Steves tour

**Enjoy Europe's warmest welcome...
with the flexibility and
friendship of a small group
getting to know Rick's
favorite places and people.
It all starts with our free
tour catalog and DVD.**

**Great guides, small
groups, no grumps.**

▸ Explore Europe

Browse thousands of articles, video clips, photos and radio interviews, plus find a wealth of money-saving tips for planning your dream trip. You'll find up-to-date information on Europe's best destinations, packing smart, getting around, finding rooms, staying healthy, avoiding scams and more.

▸ Travel News

Subscribe to our free Travel News e-newsletter, and get monthly updates from Rick on what's happening in Europe!

▸ Travel Forums

Learn, ask, share—our online community of savvy travelers is a great resource for first-time travelers to Europe, as well as seasoned pros.

Rick Steves' Europe Through the Back Door,

Avalon Travel
a member of the Perseus Books Group
1700 Fourth Street
Berkeley, CA 94710

Printed in Canada by Friesens
First printing January 2014

ISBN 978-1-61238-686-7

For the latest on Rick's lectures, guidebooks, tours, public radio show, and public television series, contact Europe Through the Back Door, Box 2009, Edmonds, WA 98020, tel. 425/771-8303, fax 425/771-0833, www.ricksteves.com, rick@ricksteves.com.

Europe Through the Back Door

Managing Editor: Risa Laib
Editorial & Production Manager: Jennifer Madison Davis
Editors: Glenn Eriksen, Tom Griffin, Cameron Hewitt, Suzanne Kotz, Cathy Lu, Carrie Shepherd, Gretchen Strauch
Editorial Assistant: Jessica Shaw
Editorial Intern: Alex Jacobs
Researchers: Ben Cameron, Cameron Hewitt, Helen Inman, Suzanne Kotz, Marijan Kriskovic, Cary Walker, Ian Watson
Maps & Graphics: David C. Hoerlein, Lauren Mills, Dawn Tessman Visser, Laura VanDeventer

Avalon Travel

Senior Editor and Series Manager: Madhu Prasher
Editor: Jamie Andrade
Associate Editor: Annette Kohl
Assistant Editor: Maggie Ryan
Copy Editor: Jennifer Malnick
Proofreader: Suzie Nasol
Indexer: Stephen Callahan
Cover Design: Kimberly Glyder Design
Maps & Graphics: Kat Bennett, Mike Morgenfeld

Photo page 1: Volterra © darios/123rf.com
Front Cover Photo: Montepulciano © Jenifoto406/Dreamstime.com
Additional Photography: Dominic Bonuccelli, Ben Cameron, Jennifer Hauseman, Cameron Hewitt, David C. Hoerlein, Anne Jenkins, Gene Openshaw, Michael Potter, Robyn Stencil, Rick Steves, Bruce VanDeventer, Laura VanDeventer, Les Wahlstrom, Ian Watson, Wikimedia Commons

ABOUT THE AUTHOR

RICK STEVES

Since 1973, Rick Steves has spent 100 days every year exploring Europe. Along with writing and researching a bestselling series of guidebooks, Rick produces a public television series *(Rick Steves' Europe)*, a public radio show *(Travel with Rick Steves)*, and an app and podcast *(Rick Steves Audio Europe)*; writes a nationally syndicated newspaper column; organizes guided tours that take over ten thousand travelers to Europe annually; and offers an information-packed website (www.ricksteves.com). With the help of his hardworking staff of 80 at Europe Through the Back Door—in Edmonds, Washington, just north of Seattle—Rick's mission is to make European travel fun, affordable, and culturally enlightening for Americans.

Connect with Rick:

 facebook.com/RickSteves   twitter: @RickSteves

Soave —
Locanda Lo Scudo
Via Covergnino, 9, Soave

San Lea — Cortona

Hotel Duomo —
Orvieta

Venie — Galleria

Want More Italy?
Maximize the experience wit
Rick Steves as your guide

Guidebooks
Venice, Florence, and Rome guide
make side-trips smooth and afford

Phrase Books
Rely on Rick's
Italian Phrase Book
and Dictionary

Rick's DVDs
Preview where you're
going with 15 shows
on Italy

Free! Rick's
Audio Europe™ App
Get free audio tours for Italy's
top sights

Small-Group Tours
Rick offers a dozen great itinerarie
through Italy

For all the details, visit ricksteves.cor